Sarah Fennel began ██████████████, as a hobby that com██████████████ goods with her pass██████████████ millions of readers ███ ██ ████ ████ ████ ████████ recipes for nostalgic desserts with a modern twist: Strawberry Shortcake Cake, Oatmeal Cream Cookies, and White Chocolate Brownies.

In *Sweet Tooth*, Sarah introduces brand-new recipes—like Matilda's Chocolate Cake and Orange Pull-Apart Bread—and offers a few classic fan favorites, such as her famous Best Chocolate Chip Cookies in the World, shared, liked, and commented on by millions of fans. Whether you're a new or experienced baker, the tips and insights throughout the book will make your cakes fluffier and crusts flakier while building your confidence along the way. With an essential baker's pantry and a guide to never overbaking again, Sarah sets you up for success with each recipe, from Small-Batch Blueberry Muffins and make-ahead Tiramisu Icebox Cake to an impressive Baklava Cheesecake for a crowd.

Useful, entertaining, and with "I can't believe it was so simple!" instructions, *Sweet Tooth* is for bakers of all levels. The only requirement? A deep, unwavering love for dessert.

SWEET TOOTH

SWEET TOOTH

100 DESSERTS TO SAVE ROOM FOR

Sarah Fennel

RECIPES CO-WRITTEN BY SOFI LLANSO

Food photographs by Sarah Fennel
Lifestyle photographs by Bettina Bogar
Illustrations by Meghan Kreger

Clarkson Potter/Publishers
New York

To Mom, thank you for showing me
how sweet life can be.

And to Sofi, this is your book, too.

Contents

Intro
9

Weeknight Treats
43

Elevated Nostalgia
75

Inventive Sweets
111

Brunch Bakes
145

Holiday Baking
221

Almost Too Pretty to Eat
179

Dessert for One
253

INTRO

Some things in life are unnecessary to our survival. Often, these are the best things. Baked goods, for example. I don't need them to survive, but I can't survive without them. And maybe, because you opened this book, you can't either.

Whether you bake brownies for a movie night with friends or Sunday dinner with your family, everybody leaves happy. Baking is an act of love, plain and simple. The process of folding the batter, cleaning the bowl (with your finger, obviously), and experiencing that luxurious brownie perfume as they bake—also extremely enjoyable. And yet a lot of people fear baking, because there's science involved, and that oven's hot! In a dream world, we'd all have a person on call as we bake, giving us tips on how to measure flour correctly, test when a cake's done, and microwave butter without exploding it.

Let me be that person.

In *Sweet Tooth*, my goal is to encourage you to bake more, and bake often. Oh, and help you steer clear of *most* of the mistakes I made. (I mean, we're human.) The secret, I learned, is: just start.

When I began baking in college, using a binder of printed recipes in 24-point font my mom had made for me, I'm pretty sure I was using baking powder and baking soda interchangeably (oops). I baked like a bull in a china shop, getting flour all over my dorm kitchen and burning my fingertips removing cookies from sheet pans. But after a few years, I got good enough at baking that I decided to start a blog, *Broma Bakery*, to document my favorite recipes.

I picked the name almost at random, "Broma" because a site with plain HTML text and a magenta background told me it was Latin for "that which is eaten." (Nope. It's definitely Spanish, and it might be ancient Greek, but the jury's out on that one.) Mostly, I wanted to satisfy my sweet tooth and practice photography, another side passion, while I worked on majoring in something more responsible—anthropology. But no disrespect to Darwin, it became pretty apparent pretty quickly that I wanted to make my blog a way of living. Because as much as humans have evolved, we still can't resist a warm chocolate chip cookie.

As the blog (and my baking skills) grew, it became my full-time job, and I feel absurdly lucky to say that. Now I have an invaluable second-in-command, Sofi Llanso, who helps me develop and test recipes, and so much more. Our mission is to consistently deliver desserts that offer home bakers maximum deliciousness. The recipes are predominantly rooted in Americana classics (fudgy brownies, fruit pies, and frosted sheet cakes), but are often updated and/or refined for today's palates. What I'm saying is, don't worry, they're not too sweet, and yes, you really do still want an Oatmeal Cream Cookie (page 105).

When I bake, I'm trying to reconnect to a time, place, and even to people. The homemade Coffee, Caramel, Cookies and Cream Ice Cream (page 191) reminds me of scooping endless cones for customers (and myself) at my first job. The Maple-Glazed Apple Blondies (page 240) bring me back to New England falls, apple picking with my mom and sister. When I make a whole tray of fudgy Crackle-Top Brownies (page 63), I no longer have to break one brownie into tiny pieces to share with my entire cafeteria table, because this time, there's enough to go around. It's crazy and beautiful to me that sweets can make us feel this warm, wonderful contentment deep in our souls. Is it . . . love? Anthropologists should study *that*.

To me, baking is and should be an everyday thing. That's why I keep my processes uncomplicated; I want everyone invited to the party. No fancy bread machine, lame knife (don't even ask), or cheesecloth is required. This cookbook includes easy and crowd-pleasing treats in every chapter, as well as a few higher-skill recipes for anyone who wants to strengthen their pastry muscles. Like any hobby, you'll get better the more you do it, which is a win-win, because it means there will always—I hope!—be something sweet on your counter.

Whether you're baking for comfort, to spread happiness, to feel full-blown nostalgia, or to make a single damn cookie whenever you feel like it, *Sweet Tooth* has recipes for you. After all, we don't bake out of necessity. We bake for the love of dessert. It's joyful, rewarding, and just plain fun.

This book celebrates dessert for dessert's sake. And there's *always* room for it.

99% of Your Baking Problems, Solved

Here's the deal: I've seen a lot *of baking fails.* I get DMs every day from people asking me what went south with their cake (they used the wrong pan), emails wondering why their cookies turned out puffy (they overpacked their flour), and comments on my website interrogating me as to why their brownies taste like bricks (because coconut flour is not the same as all-purpose flour). I've basically become an encyclopedia of baking errors.

About 99% of the time, your baking problems are avoidable. Because when you've done all this work, you deserve a delicious little treat at the end of it, not a brick. But first, we have to chat through a few things. I promise this information will change your baking life.

WHAT TO BAKE IN

My baking philosophy is that you should be able to make a fleet of cookies, cakes, and ice cream without having to pull out five different pans, two cutting boards, and twelve bowls. That said, the right tools can make a huge difference in the success of your baked goods. For example, if you mix with a whisk when a recipe calls for a spatula, there will be consequences (tougher batter, likely). And if you bake one batch of cookies on a light-colored metal sheet pan and a second batch on a dark-colored pan (which conducts more heat), you risk overbaking the second batch. Oof. So trust me, baking is not just about the ingredients—tools matter!

Things *Every* Baker Should Have

STAND MIXER

Whether it's for mixing cookie dough, whipping buttercream, or kneading dough for sticky buns, I can't live without my KitchenAid Artisan 5-Quart Tilt-Head Stand Mixer. Its size is perfect for small batches of cookies and large cake batters alike, with a powerful motor to boot. If it isn't in your budget, an electric hand mixer is a great alternative.

MIXING BOWLS

Essential! I pull out my set of glass Duralex mixing bowls every time I bake; they allow me to pre-portion ingredients, make small batches with ease, and microwave chocolate (which is crucial when you love brownies as much as I do).

WHISK

Every recipe in this book requires either a whisk or a silicone spatula at some point. So I'm saying . . . you need both. Standard "balloon" whisks help to aerate batter, better incorporate dry ingredients, and mix more thoroughly than a spoon or fork.

SILICONE SPATULA

A flexible, heatproof silicone or rubber spatula folds ingredients more gently than a whisk, not to mention helps scrape batters out of bowls . . . though fingers are good at that, too.

MEASURING CUPS AND SPOONS

Though dry and liquid cup measurers are both volume measurements, dry measuring cups allow you to get a much more precise measurement by leveling off your flour/sugar/etc. with the back of a butter knife, while liquid cup measures have pour-spout containers and measurements up the side specifically for liquids. So have a set of both. And measuring spoons? Can't bake without 'em!

SAUCEPANS

You need three saucepans, Goldilocks: small, medium, and large. I've found All-Clad's stainless-steel saucepans to be the top of the line for both cooking and baking. They conduct heat evenly and their light color makes it easy to see when butter is properly browned.

COOKIE SCOOPS

Every. Single. Cookie in this book is portioned with a cookie scoop, and for good reason: without it, your cookies will be inconsistent shapes and bake for different amounts of time. Buy a pack, because you'll use 1-ounce, 1½-ounce, and 3-ounce scoops.

METAL SPATULA

In college, I refused to buy a metal spatula and instead picked cookies off sheet pans with my fingers, and I think those years are why I've lost a lot of the feeling in my fingertips. Metal spatulas are thinner than plastic or silicone spatulas, so they seamlessly remove cookies from sheet pans. Save your fingertips. Get a metal spatula.

COOLING RACKS

Not only do cooling racks provide a heatproof surface to set things on, but they allow heat to escape through the bottom, which helps to ensure your desserts don't overbake as they cool.

OVEN THERMOMETERS

An oven thermometer that hangs in your oven is crucial to double-check the temperature (news flash: an oven's display is often inaccurate!). Some bakers (myself included) keep their thermometer in the oven at all times, just to be sure.

Equipment That Takes Your Baking to the *Next Level*

PIPING BAGS AND PIPING TIPS

With piping bags and tips, you can pipe poufs of whipped cream, create even kisses of sandwich cookie filling, and produce pleasantly rounded macarons. If you don't have any bags or tips, you can always transfer your filling into a large resealable plastic bag and cut off a corner to create a makeshift "tip" to pipe through.

ROLLING PIN

A French-style rolling pin is a smooth, cylindrical pin with tapered edges to roll out dough evenly (though any rolling pin will get the job done). If you don't have a rolling pin, here's a little secret: a wine bottle works in a pinch.

KITCHEN TORCH

An inexpensive kitchen torch is used in just four recipes in the book, all of which are absolute bangers. If you're thinking of getting one, just do it.

MICROPLANE

Perfect for zesting citrus, grating ginger, and creating teensy shavings of chocolate. Totally not necessary, but totally nice to have.

SIFTER

I reach for my sifter (a.k.a. a fine-mesh sieve) constantly to dust confectioners' sugar over muffins, crumb cakes, and tarts. If you don't have one, you can also sprinkle things with your hands (it kind of makes you feel like a fairy).

DIGITAL KITCHEN SCALE

In this book you'll use a digital kitchen scale for the Lemon Meringue Pie Macarons (page 119). And there it's 100% necessary. And if you ever halve recipes or want perfectly portioned cake layers, a scale is nice to have on hand.

OFFSET SPATULA

I used to frost everything with a butter knife. My cakes were . . . *rustic*. But an offset spatula, which is like $10, makes a world of difference. Everything you frost will be prettier, and you'll feel more confident, too.

CAKE SPINNER

If cakes are your thing, you should consider investing in a cake spinner (mine's from Amazon). It's basically a lazy Susan for cake decorating and makes frosting cakes so much easier, cleaner, and more even.

FOOD PROCESSOR

Once I made pie crust in the food processor, I never went back. It pulses everything together in a matter of seconds, evenly distributing the butter for flaky crust city. Cuisinart's 14-cup food processor is my fave.

PASTRY BRUSH

I use a pastry brush to apply an egg wash to a pie or galette crust, which makes it glisten and golden (in savory cooking, too, it's handy for glazing things on the grill).

Stand Mixer Etiquette

Your stand mixer is a thing of beauty and reverence—also heavy. So heavy. And expensive. So expensive! A few little rules will help you use it like a pro.

1. NEVER FULL-SEND THE MIXER.

Unless you'd like to turn your kitchen into a Jackson Pollock painting, always start your stand mixer on low and gradually increase the speed to whatever speed the recipe says. Always.

2. MAKE A HABIT OF SCRAPING DOWN THE SIDES AND BOTTOM OF THE BOWL.

Stand mixers do a wonderful job at incorporating ingredients, but they do need a little help from time to time to get all the stuff from the bottom mixed in. A good rule of thumb is that anytime you add new ingredients, it's a good idea to mix about halfway, stop the mixer, scrape down the sides and bottom of the bowl with a silicone spatula, and finish your mixing.

3. WHISKS AND PADDLES ARE NOT INTERCHANGEABLE.

If a recipe calls for you to use the whisk attachment, use the whisk attachment (and vice versa for the paddle attachment). In general, the whisk attachment will aerate your batter, better incorporate dry ingredients together, and mix your batter more thoroughly. The paddle attachment will mix your batter more gently, while incorporating less air.

4. DON'T OVERMIX YOUR BATTER.

Generally, when you're making a batter (and *especially* once you add in flour), you want to mix as little as possible. The longer you mix, the more glutens (or protein structures) form in your dough, which leads to a tougher, denser baked good. You want more gluten when you're making yeasted breads, but for most of the recipes here, we're mixing batters only until the dry ingredients are just incorporated.

Baking Pan HQ

8 × 8-INCH SQUARE BAKING PAN, 9 × 9-INCH SQUARE BAKING PAN, 9 × 13-INCH RECTANGULAR BAKING PAN

Meet my MVP baking vessels. If you want to get technical, look for pans made of aluminized steel, which combines the sturdy, dent-resistant properties of steel with the conductivity of aluminum. Nordic Ware makes some great ones, as does USA Pan.

HALF SHEET PANS

Two half sheet pans will typically hold a whole batch of cookies. Opt for a light-colored aluminum sheet pan (Nordic Ware is my go-to) with a lip around the edge so your cookies don't go sliding onto the floor (definitely *not* saying this from experience).

8- AND 9-INCH ROUND CAKE PANS

I love 8-inch round metal cake pans for tall and luxurious layer cakes and 9-inch round cake pans for large and celebratory single-layer cakes. I prefer aluminized steel cake pans from USA Pan.

12-CUP MUFFIN TIN

A standard 12-cup muffin tin is necessary for making muffins, cupcakes, or my personal favorite, Small-Batch Blondies (page 278). For a light golden brown bake, go for a light-colored aluminum muffin pan.

9-INCH PIE PAN

Mmm, pie. I prefer a 9-inch ceramic pie pan because it's well insulated, leading to a crispy pie crust and gooey/juicy interior (not glass, which retains too much heat and might overbake the crust).

1-POUND (8½ × 4½-INCH) LOAF PAN

A loaf pan is your trusty sidekick for creating sky-high Double Chocolate Banana Bread (page 44) and perfectly risen Orange Pull-Apart Bread (page 174). Take note: the larger your loaf pan, the more squat your loaves will be, so opt for this "smaller" size if you can. In my kitchen, USA Pan strikes again.

BUNDT PAN

Only one recipe in this book calls for a Bundt pan (the Zebra Bundt Cake on page 170), but I love to have a Bundt pan on hand. Nordic Ware is my favorite Bundt brand.

6-OUNCE RAMEKINS

Ceramic ramekins are not only essential for Une Crème Brûlée (page 272) but are also handy for portioning out smaller ingredients in baking and cooking.

9-INCH TART PAN

A tart pan has a fluted edge and a removable bottom so you can carefully take out your finished tart to show off to your friends. As much as I wish you could substitute it for a 9-inch round cake pan, it's next to impossible to remove without cracking your tart.

9-INCH SPRINGFORM PAN

Springform pans have a removable bottom and tall, vertical sides for cheesecakes to puff up against. I prefer a pure aluminum pan because it doesn't brown your cheesecake as much as an aluminized-steel one might.

9-INCH CAST-IRON SKILLET

Cast-iron skillet = a crispy crust on your Mixed Berry Skillet Crisp (page 64). Cast iron retains heat well, so your batters and crumbles will get crispier around the edges than usual. Yum.

Parchment Paper Is My Best Friend

Let's get one thing straight: you should line all your baking pans with parchment paper. It's more fool-proof than greasing your pan, plus it's a way easier cleanup. Parchment baking sheets (find them on Amazon or in some baking supply/grocery stores) come in a flat package (not a tight spiral), so there's no awkward ripping off the sheet from its spool and trying to get it to sit perfectly in your pan when all it wants to do is curl back up into a spiral—the worst! So get yourself some. And thank me later.

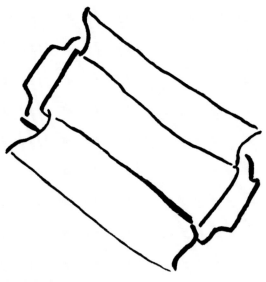

SQUARE AND RECTANGULAR PANS

Get out two large parchment paper sheets. Line one sheet up to one side of the pan. Cut the sheet to the width of the side, then place the sheet in the bottom of the pan and use your fingers to crease the corners. Repeat with the second sheet of parchment, placing it up to the second side of the pan, cutting to the width of the side, placing the sheet in the bottom of the pan, and using your fingers to crease the corners.

LOAF PANS

Get out two large parchment paper sheets. Line one sheet up to one side of the pan. Cut the sheet to the width of the side, then place the sheet in the bottom of the pan and use your fingers to crease the corners. Repeat with the second sheet of parchment, placing it up to the second side of the pan, cutting to the width of the side, placing the sheet in the bottom of the pan, and using your fingers to crease the corners.

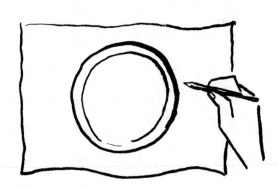

BAKING SHEETS

Get out a large parchment paper sheet. Line the sheet up to the long-side edge of the pan. Cut the sheet to the exact width of the side, then place it into the bottom of the pan. If necessary, cut the short side of the sheet, too.

ROUND PANS

Get out a large parchment paper sheet. Place the sheet on a work surface, then place the round pan over the sheet. Use a pencil to outline the edge of the pan onto the parchment paper. Cut the sheet into the outlined circle, then place the circle in the bottom of your pan.

WHAT TO BAKE WITH

Baking on an impulse is the most fun way to bake (she typed, pulling a batch of blondies from the oven), and a well-stocked pantry will set you up for baking whenever the mood strikes (often, I hope). And while I'm not going to run you through every ingredient in this book, I do want to share what you should look for as you shop for some of the most-used ingredients.

What's on My Shelves

OLD-FASHIONED OATS

When my recipes call for oats, I mean old-fashioned oats, which are steamed and flattened oat groats (the whole oat grain minus the husk) that absorb liquid well and bake up beautifully. Instant or quick-cook oats are not a good substitute in baking; they break down faster, leading to more mealy and mushy baked goods.

ALMOND FLOUR

Make sure you get finely ground or superfine almond *flour,* and not almond *meal,* which is made from ground unpeeled almonds. Almond flour is made from ground blanched and peeled almonds, leading to a lighter color and finer texture. My favorite is Bob's Red Mill.

GRANULATED SUGAR

Granulated sugar, also called white sugar or "regular" sugar, is either cane or beet sugar with all its naturally occurring molasses removed (through a process called refining). Granulated sugar is different from natural cane sugar, which has not been refined and contains more moisture, almost like brown sugar, creating different baked results. When a recipe in this book calls for granlated sugar, it's referring to *refined* granulated sugar. In the sugar department, I'm a Domino girl.

ALL-PURPOSE FLOUR

All-purpose flour is basically "regular" flour, a.k.a. the default flour for most baking recipes. What makes it different from other types of flour? The flour's protein content. Generally, the less protein in your flour, the more delicate the crumb will be, while more protein makes sturdier and denser baked goods. All-purpose flour, which contains between 9% and 12% protein content, sits right in the middle of the protein flour scale, which is why it's a versatile choice for nearly everything. For this book's recipes, you can use bleached or unbleached all-purpose flour interchangeably, though my go-to bags are the Unbleached All-Purpose Flour from King Arthur Baking Company and the Unbleached White All-Purpose Flour from Bob's Red Mill.

CAKE FLOUR

Cake flour has a lower protein content than all-purpose flour, roughly 7% to 9%. This lower percentage gives baked goods a softer, fluffier, and more delicate texture. (Psst: If you don't have cake flour, you can substitute 1 cup of cake flour for 1 cup minus 2 tablespoons all-purpose flour mixed in with 2 tablespoons cornstarch.)

LIGHT BROWN SUGAR

Both light and dark brown sugar are made from a combination of granulated sugar and molasses—with slightly more molasses added to dark brown sugar. The molasses imparts moisture and a slight warmth in taste, giving your baked goods an added chew and depth of flavor. I call for only light brown sugar because it provides the ideal balance of moisture without imparting too much caramel flavor. If all you have is dark brown sugar, just know that your baked goods will end up darker, more moist, less crispy, and with an even deeper molasses flavor.

CONFECTIONERS' SUGAR

Confectioners' sugar is made by pulverizing granulated sugar down into a fine powder, mixed with a teensy bit of cornstarch to prevent clumping. Whereas powdered sugar is usually pure sugar, pulverized. For this book, you can use confectioners' sugar and powdered sugar interchangeably.

VANILLA EXTRACT

Vanilla is more than just a flavor. It enhances the subtle flavors of milk, sugar, and butter, and adds its own warmth and caramelly depth to your baked goods. If it's in your budget, opt for pure vanilla extract, which is a combination of steeped vanilla beans in alcohol and water. My favorites are Nielsen-Massey and Rodelle. Imitation vanilla extract, made from synthetic vanillin, has a slightly more artificial taste, but it will work.

BAKING SODA

Baking soda (scientific name, sodium bicarbonate) is a leavener, meaning that when it comes into contact with an acidic ingredient (like lemon juice, buttermilk, or yogurt), it creates gas (carbon dioxide), which makes your baked goods rise. The big to-do with baking soda is to make sure to swap it out every 6 months so it doesn't get stale and lose its leavening properties.

BAKING POWDER

Baking powder is made of pure baking soda, plus a weak acidic agent like cream of tartar and a buffering agent like cornstarch. Basically, baking powder creates a totally different rise in your baked goods, which, if you're feeling scientific, you can read more about on websites like Serious Eats (J. Kenji López-Alt, thank you for your service). Like baking soda, swap it out every 6 months.

SALT

Unless otherwise specified, salt means good old-fashioned table salt. Its small granules melt well into baked goods, producing an even mixture. In this book, any brand will work, though I use Morton. If you have only fine-grain kosher salt, that works, too.

SPICES

A lot of recipes in this book call for dried spices such as cinnamon, nutmeg, and ginger. In general, you get what you pay for with dried spices; the lower the price, the lower the quality, flavor, and freshness. My preferred brands are Simply Organic, Morton & Bassett, and Burlap & Barrel.

COCOA POWDER

Let's get one thing straight: when a baking recipe calls for cocoa powder, it's calling for *unsweetened* cocoa powder. There are two main types of unsweetened cocoa powder: natural and Dutch-processed. Natural cocoa powder contains the natural acids present in the cocoa bean and can make baked goods taste slightly more acidic, while Dutch-processed cocoa powder is treated with an alkalizing agent that neutralizes the acidity of the cocoa powder, creating a smoother and more balanced cocoa flavor. The recipes in this book call for and were tested with Dutch-processed cocoa powder. My favorite brand is Rodelle.

CHOCOLATE CHIPS

I stock my pantry with both semisweet and bittersweet chocolate chips. You can use them interchangeably, though I use semisweet in recipes that aren't cloyingly sweet and bittersweet when I want to cut the sweetness of a recipe a tad. You can buy regular-size chips, larger "baking" chips, or chocolate disks . . . whatever your heart desires. My favorite brands are Ghirardelli, Guittard, or, if I feel like splurging, Valrhona or Callebaut.

CHOCOLATE BARS

When it comes to melting chocolate, chocolate bars are always superior to chocolate chips. Chocolate chips contain stabilizers that help them keep their shape, while chocolate bars don't, so they melt more freely. I love a good 60% to 75% bittersweet chocolate bar from Ghirardelli, Guittard, or on fancy days, Valrhona or Callebaut.

WHITE CHOCOLATE

White chocolate is made from cocoa butter (a compound that is light in color and flavor), but it contains no cocoa solids (a compound that is darker in color and flavor), hence its color. It's very sensitive to heat, so get the highest quality you can find to decrease chances of a clumpy disaster. I like Ghirardelli and Callebaut brands.

FRUIT JAMS AND PRESERVES

Did you know jelly, jam, and preserves are all (legally!) different things? Jelly contains the least amount of fruit and is made with only fruit juice. Jam is made with crushed fruit pieces for a spreadable consistency. And preserves are made with crushed fruit plus actual pieces of fruit. I bake with preserves the most (always Bonne Maman), though jams work interchangeably in this book.

What's in My Fridge

BUTTER

Butter not only makes a baked good tender, flaky, and moist, but it can bring a rich, round flavor when you invest in the good stuff. I always suggest unsalted butter because it allows you to control the amount of salt in your recipe. My favorites are Vermont Creamery, Vital Farms, and Kerrygold.

EGGS

Large eggs. Not medium or extra-large. Large. The others will have less/more volume and throw off the proportions of the recipe, and possibly the final texture. I buy brands like Vital Farms with the "Certified Humane" designation on them because it's the highest standard for chicken welfare.

MILK

For most recipes in this book, when milk is specified there is a note that "any kind of dairy milk will work," because most of the time it's there for moisture more than anything. With that said, there are a few recipes that call for a specific milk due to the way it bakes, so when it's specified, use that type!

HEAVY CREAM

Heavy cream (or heavy whipping cream) is different from light cream, so when a recipe calls for cream, we're referring to heavy cream. Please don't try to make whipped cream with light cream—it's a losing battle.

YOGURT

Full-fat sour cream imparts a luxurious crumb in loaves, cakes, and muffins, and it makes cheesecakes extra velvety and smooth. That said, I always have Greek yogurt in my fridge, so if that's all you got, I get you! Unless otherwise specified, for most of the recipes in this book, you can use either interchangeably.

CREAM CHEESE

Full-fat cream cheese is the way and the truth. Nonfat or low-fat are not the same (they are usually cut with water and added filler ingredients, and they'll throw off our recipe, plus the dessert won't taste as creamy).

FRESH AND FROZEN FRUIT

Fresh fruit keeps its structure, frozen fruit falls apart more easily. Why? Freezing breaks down the fruit's cell walls, so come baking time, it'll defrost softer and bake up mushier. So if you want bites of bursting blueberries in your muffins, use fresh, but for fruits that'll get jammy in a recipe (as in the Mixed Berry Skillet Crisp, page 64) frozen is the way to go.

BUTTERMILK

The main purpose of buttermilk in baking is to add acidity, which interacts with things like baking soda to help your baked goods rise and make a moist, tender crumb. This is good. We like this. But most of the time when I buy store-bought buttermilk for a baking recipe, I use a cup or so, then the rest sits in the very back of my fridge, forgotten. So instead, I'll usually make a homemade "buttermilk" that works just as well.

1. Add 1 tablespoon freshly squeezed lemon juice, distilled white vinegar, or cider vinegar to a 1-cup liquid measure.

2. Pour in milk (both dairy and nondairy milk work here) until it reaches 1 cup of liquid.

3. Stir and allow the mixture to sit for 5 minutes. After 5 minutes, the mixture should curdle a little. This is correct! You can now use your "buttermilk."

HOW TO BE A BETTER BAKER

It's one thing to have the right equipment and ingredients for a recipe. It's another to have that almost sixth sense that tells you exactly when to take cookies out of the oven for peak chewiness. And since I'm someone who has baked, oh, roughly 10,000 baked goods over the course of my life, my baking sixth sense is pretty strong. But don't worry; you don't need to bake a bajillion batches of brownies to achieve that sixth sense, too. You just need the next few pages of this book. :)

Measure Like a Scientist

Baking is a science, and being off by even tiny amounts can lead to big changes in your baked goods. And while using a digital scale is the most accurate way to measure ingredients, it seems like an American pastime to bake with measuring cups. So here's how to be as precise as possible when using them.

FLOUR

Flour gets compacted in shipping and processing, so before measuring it out, open up the flour bag and use a fork to "fluff" up the flour for a few seconds. Then, use a large spoon to scoop it into a measuring cup until it's overflowing. Last, hold the measuring cup over your bag of flour and run the back side of a butter knife along the top of the cup to level off your measurement.

MELTED BUTTER

Unless otherwise specified, if a recipe calls for X tablespoons/cups of melted butter, it means that number of tablespoons/cups before it is melted, not after. People ask me this all the time.

BROWN SUGAR

A proper cup of brown sugar is meant to be compacted. So if you scoop a cup of brown sugar without packing it down, you're going to get much less brown sugar than you intended. Instead, scoop your brown sugar into a measuring cup and push down on it with your fingers like a kid making a sandcastle. Then level the cup with the back of a butter knife.

COCOA POWDER, OATS, ALMOND FLOUR, AND CONFECTIONERS' SUGAR

These ingredients follow the same rule as flour: they can get compacted in packaging, so make sure to fluff, scoop, and level them, too!

BAKING CONVERSION CHART

With that said, if you're a grams baker, good on you! Below you'll find a handy volume to weight conversion chart you can use to help you bake through this book, too.

FLOUR

1 Tbsp	8 grams
1/4 cup	32 grams
1/3 cup	43 grams
1/2 cup	64 grams
2/3 cup	86 grams
3/4 cup	96 grams
1 cup	128 grams

BUTTER

1 Tbsp	14 grams
1/4 cup	56 grams
1/3 cup	75.5 grams
1/2 cup	113 grams
2/3 cup	151 grams
3/4 cup	168 grams
1 cup	226 grams

GRANULATED SUGAR

1 Tbsp	13 grams
1/4 cup	52 grams
1/3 cup	70 grams
1/2 cup	104 grams
2/3 cup	140 grams
3/4 cup	156 grams
1 cup	208 grams

LIGHT BROWN SUGAR

1 Tbsp	13 grams
1/4 cup	53 grams
1/3 cup	71 grams
1/2 cup	106 grams
2/3 cup	142 grams
3/4 cup	165 grams
1 cup	212 grams

CONFECTIONERS' SUGAR

1 Tbsp	7 grams
1/4 cup	28 grams
1/3 cup	38 grams
1/2 cup	56 grams
2/3 cup	76 grams
3/4 cup	84 grams
1 cup	112 grams

DUTCH-PROCESSED COCOA POWDER

1 Tbsp	7 grams
1/4 cup	28 grams
1/3 cup	38 grams
1/2 cup	56 grams
2/3 cup	76 grams
3/4 cup	84 grams
1 cup	112 grams

ALMOND FLOUR

1 Tbsp	6 grams
1/4 cup	24 grams
1/3 cup	32 grams
1/2 cup	48 grams
2/3 cup	64 grams
3/4 cup	72 grams
1 cup	96 grams

MILK, HEAVY CREAM, SOUR CREAM/YOGURT*

1 Tbsp	15 grams
1/4 cup	60 grams
1/3 cup	80 grams
1/2 cup	120 grams
2/3 cup	160 grams
3/4 cup	180 grams
1 cup	240 grams

BAKING POWDER

1/4 tsp	1.25 grams
1/2 tsp	2.5 grams
1 tsp	5 grams
2 tsp	12 grams
1 Tbsp	18 grams

BAKING SODA

1/4 tsp	1.5 grams
1/2 tsp	3 grams
1 tsp	6 grams
2 tsp	12 grams
1 Tbsp	18 grams

SALT

1/4 tsp	2 grams
1/2 tsp	4 grams
1 tsp	8 grams
2 tsp	16 grams
1 Tbsp	24 grams

OIL

1 Tbsp	13 grams
1/4 cup	52 grams
1/3 cup	70 grams
1/2 cup	105 grams
2/3 cup	140 grams
3/4 cup	157 grams
1 cup	210 grams

These have nominal weight differences, but not enough to have a noticeable effect on the final baked good.

Never Overbake Again

A true tragedy in baking is when you overbake your dessert. All that hard work and wasted ingredients . . . for what?! A dry and crumbly cake/cookie/brownie/pie?!?! *Yuck.* And unfortunately, because so many ovens run hot and cold, no matter what bake or cook time a recipe says, your timing is probably going to be different from the recipe developer's. But have no fear; let me show you how to tell *exactly* when to take your dessert out of the oven.

1. ALWAYS SET A TIMER FOR THE LOWEST END OF THE BAKE TIME LISTED IN A RECIPE.

For example, if a recipe says "bake for 45 to 50 minutes," set your timer for 45 minutes and check for doneness then. If you *really* hate dry cakes? Set it for 40 minutes.

2. DON'T COUNT ON COOK TIME ALONE! YOUR OVEN COULD RUN HOTTER OR COLDER THAN MINE.

So in addition to buying that oven thermometer I suggested on page 16, pay attention to cues and clues for when your dessert is perfectly baked. Here are the cues for the most common treats in this book.

COOKIES

You can tell when a cookie is done when it has puffed up slightly in the center, is set and firm around the edges, and when the middle is soft and spongy. In general, cookies *should look underbaked* when they come out of the oven, because they'll continue to bake and firm up as they cool on the hot sheet pan.

CHEESECAKES, MOUSSES, AND CUSTARDS

Cheesecakes, mousses, and custards should be puffed up slightly in the center, and when you gently jiggle them, the edges should be set, but they should be a little wobbly (like JELL-O) in the very middle.

CAKES AND CAKE-LIKE THINGS

Cakes are done once they've risen, the top-center springs back to the touch, and a butter knife inserted into the center of the cake comes out mostly clean (a crumb or two attached is okay). I've found butter knives to be superior to cake testers, because you can see the crumbs better. And speaking of crumbs, contrary to what you may have heard, a few moist crumbs indicate your cake is still moist. No crumbs on your knife *could* mean your cake is overcooked.

BROWNIES AND BARS

Brownies and bars should be baked until the surface has puffed up, the edges are set and somewhat firm, and a butter knife inserted into the center comes out mostly clean (a crumb or two attached is okay).

PIES

The telltale signs for a fruit pie are that the fruits have burst and the inside (if you can see it) looks jammy and thick (sometimes it will bubble up and gel around the crust edges), and the crust is golden brown all over. The telltale signs for a custard or pumpkin pie are that the filling has puffed up but is still somewhat wobbly in the very middle when you gently shake it, and the crust is golden brown all over.

Make-Ahead Strategies

Whether you're making a three-layer cake for a dinner party or cinnamon rolls for Sunday brunch, you don't need to wake up at the crack of dawn to have your dessert done in time. Here are the strategies that let me—and you!—sleep in.

COOKIES

Almost all of the cookies in this book can be frozen as dough balls before being baked.* Roll up your balls of dough and place them so they're not touching on a sheet pan. Cover them and place them in the fridge to firm up for about 1 hour. Then, transfer the chilled dough balls into large, freezer-safe resealable plastic bags, keeping the dough balls about 2 inches apart. Seal each bag almost all the way, keeping about ½ inch of the zipper or seal open, then place your mouth or a straw up to the opening and suck out all the air (I call this the human vacuum seal). Quickly seal the bag and place it in the freezer for up to 2 months (or longer . . . I'll let you experiment with that one). When you're ready to bake, remove the dough balls from the freezer and allow them to come to room temperature before baking; if you bake them frozen, they won't spread properly.

*For any cookie that is rolled in something, best to make it on the day-of.

CAKES

Layer cakes can be a bit of a process, so I almost always make my layers ahead and freeze them. Then all I have to do is unfreeze and frost them when the cake day arrives. Bake and cool the layers completely on cooling racks, then wrap each layer in plastic wrap. Put those layers into a large, freezer-safe resealable plastic bag and freeze for up to 2 months. When you're ready to serve, remove them from the freezer and allow them to thaw out for 30 minutes before frosting.

BROWNIES AND BARS

Almost all baked brownies and bars can be frozen for up to 2 months. Allow them to fully cool, cut them up, and place them (it's okay if they touch) in large, freezer-safe resealable plastic bags. Seal each bag, keeping about ½ inch of the zipper or seal open, then place your mouth or a straw up to the opening and suck out all the air. Quickly seal the bag and freeze. When you're ready to serve, remove them from the freezer and allow them to come to room temperature before serving (I usually do this overnight in the fridge, or for 4 hours on the counter). Do note that the crackly top on your brownie might be slightly moistened by this process, but the brownies will taste just as good.

MUFFINS AND SCONES

Muffins and scones freeze surprisingly well. Bake them off, allow them to fully cool, and place them (it's okay if they touch) in large, freezer-safe resealable plastic bags. Seal each bag almost all the way, keeping about ½ inch of the zipper or seal open, then place your mouth or a straw up to the opening and suck out all the air. Quickly seal the bag and freeze it for up to 2 months. When you're ready to serve, remove the muffins or scones from the freezer and allow them to come to room temperature before serving. You can also pop them back into a 350°F oven for 3 to 5 minutes to warm them up.

THINGS I WOULD NOT MAKE AHEAD

1. **CRISPS / CRUMBLES** (they turn to mush)

2. **WAFFLES / PANCAKES** (more mush)

3. **PIES / GALETTES / TARTS** (that flaky magic is lost)

4. **DONUTS** (duh)

5. **CROISSANTS** (wow, you're making home-made croissants?)

6. **PAVLOVAS** (delicate enough as it is)

Storage Strategies

Generally, baked goods will always be the best day-of, but as someone who wants to snack on a batch of brownies all week, keeping things fresh is important. Use your best judgment: if a recipe has dairy in a frosting or topping, it should go into the fridge. And if you can't remember how long those cookies have been in the jar, a dunk in milk might be necessary. Other storage tips follow.

MUFFINS AND SCONES

Wrap tightly in plastic wrap or aluminum foil and keep on the counter for up to 2 days, or in the fridge for up to 5 days.

MOUSSES AND CUSTARDS

Cover tightly in plastic wrap or aluminum foil and keep in the fridge for up to 5 days.

ICE CREAM

Store in a sealed container and keep in the freezer for up to 3 weeks.

COOKIES, BROWNIES, AND BARS

Seal in an airtight container or wrap tightly in aluminum foil and keep on the counter for up to 3 days, or in the fridge for up to 5 days.

CAKES

Cover tightly in plastic wrap, aluminum foil, or a cake carrier and keep in the fridge for up to 5 days.

LOAF CAKES AND QUICK BREADS

Wrap tightly in plastic wrap or aluminum foil and keep on the counter for up to 3 days, or in the fridge for up to 5 days.

YEASTED BREADS

Wrap tightly in plastic wrap or aluminum foil and keep on the counter for up to 2 days, or in the fridge for up to 3 days.

CHEESECAKES

Cover tightly in plastic wrap or aluminum foil and keep in the fridge for up to 5 days.

PIES AND TARTS

Wrap tightly in plastic wrap or aluminum foil and keep in the fridge for up to 5 days.

10 Lessons to Live and Bake By

As a self-taught baker, I've had my fair share of baking lessons (and So. Many. Fails.) over the years. Here are ten of the most helpful things I've learned—so you don't have to.

1. A microwave oven is not an oven.

2. Extra butter on your hands is a surprisingly good moisturizer.

3. As soon as you substitute an ingredient that is not called out in a recipe, you can't blame the recipe if it doesn't work out.

4. Salt enhances sweet. Don't skip it.

5. It's okay to have a blondie made with almond flour, coconut oil, and coconut sugar. But it's equally okay to have a blondie made with wheat flour, butter, and granulated sugar.

6. Nobody cares if your cake isn't picture-perfect—they just want cake.

7. Every batch of cookies should be taste-tested by the cook.

8. Vanilla extract should be measured with the heart.

9. The biggest secret in the dessert world is underbaking.

10. There is no greater bribe than a homemade cherry pie.

WEEK-NIGHT TREATS

If you're like me (which you probably are if you have this book), you know that dinner isn't finished until you've had dessert. There's always, always room. But especially on weekdays, I don't usually have the time or energy to whip up something fancy-schmancy. Enter these weeknight treats, designed for quick, spur-of-the-moment baking. They all come together in less than an hour, and are made in one bowl, so you can have warm Chewy Peanut Butter–Chocolate Chip Cookies in your belly before the clock strikes bedtime. Because every day should end on a sweet note.

Double Chocolate Banana Bread

MAKES ONE 8½-INCH LOAF

PREP TIME 15 MINUTES
COOK TIME 45 MINUTES
TOTAL TIME 1 HOUR

½ cup (1 stick) unsalted butter, melted

1 cup granulated sugar

1½ cups mashed overripe bananas (about 3 large), plus 1 banana for topping (optional)

2 large eggs, at room temperature

2 teaspoons vanilla extract

½ cup full-fat sour cream (plain Greek yogurt also works)

½ cup Dutch-processed cocoa powder

1 cup all-purpose flour

¾ teaspoon baking soda

½ teaspoon salt

1 cup semisweet or bittersweet chocolate chips, plus more for topping (optional)

PRO TIP
Whenever you have extra overripe bananas lying around, peel them, pop them into a freezer-safe bag, and freeze them. When you want to bake with them, just let them come to room temperature. Baking-ready bananas on demand.

Banana bread may seem like a brunch thing, but we all know it's cake, right? It also happens to make the perfect throw-together weeknight treat, because you probably have some questionable bananas lying around and an emergency stash of chocolate chips (if not, get on that). In addition to the chips, this banana bread is extra chocolaty from cocoa powder and super moist thanks to bananas and sour cream. Mix it up in one bowl, and I'm telling you, it's a cake that's pretty hard to mess up. It's even better the next morning for breakfast, or as a lunch dessert, tea cake, neighborly gift . . . or all of the above.

1 Preheat the oven to 350°F. Line a 1-pound loaf pan with parchment paper on all sides (see page 23).

2 In a large bowl, whisk the melted butter, granulated sugar, and bananas until completely combined. Add the eggs, vanilla extract, and sour cream (or yogurt) and whisk until evenly mixed.

3 Add the cocoa powder, flour, baking soda, and salt, and use a silicone spatula to fold the dry ingredients into the wet until combined and no streaks of flour remain. Fold the chocolate chips into the batter, mixing until well incorporated.

4 Use the silicone spatula to transfer the batter to the prepared pan and spread it evenly to the edges. Cut another banana in half lengthwise (if using) and place it on top of the batter, then sprinkle the top with more chocolate chips. Bake until the bread has domed, the center springs back to a light touch, and a butter knife inserted into the center comes out mostly clean (a crumb or two attached is okay), about 45 minutes.

5 Place the pan on a cooling rack and let the bread cool slightly in the pan. Use the parchment paper to lift the bread from the pan, then transfer the bread to a cutting board, slice, and serve.

Chewy Peanut Butter–Chocolate Chip Cookies

MAKES 16 COOKIES

PREP TIME 15 MINUTES
COOK TIME 14 MINUTES
TOTAL TIME 29 MINUTES

¼ cup (½ stick) unsalted butter, at room temperature

¾ cup creamy peanut butter (such as Jif, Skippy, or Peter Pan—*not* natural peanut butter)

1 cup packed light brown sugar

¼ cup granulated sugar

1 large egg plus 1 large egg yolk, at room temperature

2 teaspoons vanilla extract

¾ cup all-purpose flour

½ teaspoon baking soda

½ teaspoon salt

1 cup semisweet or bittersweet chocolate chips

While I'm a ginormous peanut butter fan, I won't lie: most peanut butter cookies let me down. They can be dry, crumbly, and so dense that I need to chug a whole glass of milk to get the cookie down. So I said to myself, *Sarah, a better peanut butter cookie is out there . . . now you need to figure out how to make it.* Less flour and an extra egg yolk did the trick. The result is a soft, chewy peanut butter cookie that's so tender you'll forget about that glass of milk (though it would be a nice touch). Sprinkle in some chocolate chips and you've got a weeknight treat that will satisfy all your chewy, salty, peanut-y, and chocolaty cravings in one.

1 Preheat the oven to 350°F. Line two sheet pans with parchment paper.

2 In a stand mixer fitted with the paddle attachment, beat together the butter, peanut butter, brown sugar, and granulated sugar on low speed until combined. Gradually increase the speed to medium-high and beat until light and fluffy, about 2 minutes.

3 Add the egg, extra egg yolk, and vanilla extract. Beat on medium-high until the mixture is fluffy and lightens in color, about 2 minutes, scraping down the bowl as needed.

4 Stop the mixer, then add the flour, baking soda, and salt and beat on low speed until just combined and no streaks of flour remain. Remove the bowl from the stand mixer and use a silicone spatula to fold the chocolate chips into the batter, mixing until the chips are evenly incorporated.

5 Use a 1½-ounce cookie scoop to portion out equal amounts of dough (a large spoon also works; the ball should be about 3 tablespoons). Roll the dough in your hands to smooth the edges, then place 2 inches apart on the prepared sheet pans (you may need to bake in batches).

6 Bake until the cookies have puffed up and are set and firm around the edges but still somewhat soft in the middle, 12 to 14 minutes. Remove the sheet pans from the oven and allow the cookies to cool slightly on the sheet pans before serving.

Jam Jam Bars

MAKES 12 RECTANGULAR BARS

PREP TIME 15 MINUTES
COOK TIME 25 MINUTES
TOTAL TIME 40 MINUTES

½ cup (1 stick) unsalted butter,
 at room temperature

½ cup granulated sugar

¼ cup packed light brown sugar

1 large egg, at room temperature

2 teaspoons vanilla extract

2 cups all-purpose flour

½ teaspoon baking soda

½ teaspoon salt

½ cup fruit jam or preserves
 of choice

Confectioners' sugar, for topping
 (optional)

PRO TIP *I love
Bonne Maman
preserves in this
recipe. Bonne
Maman is higher in
fruit content than
some other brands.
My favorite flavors
are raspberry,
blueberry, and
apricot.*

Like a lot of kids in the 1990s, I went through a years-long, dedicated strawberry Toaster Strudel phase. The combination of sweet strawberry jam and rich, buttery pastry never got old (until I discovered s'mores Pop-Tarts, but that's another story). Plus, squiggling the glaze on top was like being in your own personal art class before school. And while these Jam Jam Bars aren't Toaster Strudels, they do have that same gloriously uncomplicated combination of jam and butter.

1 Preheat the oven to 350°F. Line an 8 × 8-inch square baking pan with parchment paper on all sides (see page 23).

2 In a stand mixer fitted with the paddle attachment, add the butter, granulated sugar, and brown sugar and beat on low speed until combined. Gradually increase the speed to medium-high and beat until light and fluffy, about 2 minutes. Use a silicone spatula to scrape down the sides and bottom of the bowl, then add the egg and vanilla extract. Beat on medium-high speed until the mixture is smooth and combined, about 30 seconds.

3 Add the flour, baking soda, and salt. Mix on low speed until combined and no streaks of flour remain. Scrape down the sides and bottom of the bowl as needed.

4 Using your fingers, press about two-thirds of the dough into the bottom of the prepared pan. Spoon the jam on top of the dough, spreading it to the edges. Use your hands to squeeze the remaining dough into your palms, then break it apart into big and small clusters, sprinkling them all over the jam layer like a fruit crisp (some pockets of exposed jam are okay!). Bake until the top crumbles of the bars are light golden brown, 20 to 25 minutes.

5 Place the pan on a cooling rack and allow the bars to cool completely in the pan. Use the parchment paper to lift the bars from the pan, then transfer the bars to a cutting board. Cut the bars in half, then cut each half into sixths, creating 12 rectangular bars. Dust the top with confectioners' sugar (if using), and serve.

Weeknight Chocolate Snacking Cake

PREP TIME 15 MINUTES
COOK TIME 35 MINUTES
TOTAL TIME 50 MINUTES

1 cup all-purpose flour

1 cup packed light brown sugar

½ cup Dutch-processed cocoa powder

1 teaspoon baking soda

½ teaspoon baking powder

½ teaspoon salt

½ cup vegetable oil

½ cup buttermilk, at room temperature (get my homemade version on page 28)

1 large egg, at room temperature

1 teaspoon vanilla extract

¼ cup strongly brewed coffee, hot

Confectioners' sugar, for topping (optional)

PRO TIP *This cake is so moist that it truly doesn't need frosting, but if you're really craving some, try halving the recipe for the chocolate frosting from the Yellow Sheet Cake with Chocolate Frosting on page 85.*

Any given weeknight when I was growing up, my mom would come home from her full-time office job and whip up a chocolate layer cake (now you know why I am the way I am). Cakes didn't need an occasion in our household, and I hope they don't need one in yours, either. That said, making a frosted layer cake on a Tuesday after work isn't *everyone's* idea of a good time. That's why this one-bowl chocolate snacking cake is so fudgy that (gasp!) it doesn't even need frosting. Top with a dusting of confectioners' sugar—or not, you do you.

1 Preheat the oven to 350°F. Line the bottom of an 8-inch round cake pan with parchment paper (see page 23) and grease the sides with nonstick cooking spray.

2 In a large bowl, whisk the flour, brown sugar, cocoa powder, baking soda, baking powder, and salt to combine.

3 Make a well in the center of the bowl and to it add the vegetable oil, buttermilk, egg, and vanilla extract. Starting from the center of the bowl, whisk outward, pulling the dry ingredients into the middle. Whisk until no lumps remain—the batter will be thick. Pour in the hot coffee, whisking until the batter is smooth.

4 Use a silicone spatula to transfer the batter to the prepared pan, smoothing it out to an even layer. Bake until the center of the cake resists light pressure and a butter knife inserted into the center comes out mostly clean (a crumb or two attached is okay), 30 to 35 minutes.

5 Place the cake pan on a cooling rack and allow the cake to cool slightly in the pan. To remove the cake from the pan, drag a butter knife around the edges of the cake, flip the cake out onto a plate, peel away the parchment paper, then re-invert the cake, right-side up, onto a serving plate. Dust the top with confectioners' sugar (if using), slice, and serve.

Oatmeal Chocolate Chip Cookies

MAKES 15 COOKIES

PREP TIME 20 MINUTES
COOK TIME 11 MINUTES
TOTAL TIME 31 MINUTES

¾ cup (1½ sticks) unsalted butter, melted

1 cup packed light brown sugar

1 large egg plus 1 large egg yolk, at room temperature

2 teaspoons vanilla extract

1½ cups all-purpose flour

¼ teaspoon baking soda

½ teaspoon salt

1 cup old-fashioned oats

1 cup semisweet or bittersweet chocolate chips

Flaky sea salt, for sprinkling (optional)

Not that anyone is asking, but if you wanted to know my perfect oatmeal chocolate chip cookie (also called oatmeal CCCs in my house), it would look something like this: crispy on the outside with a super-chewy center, studded with oats but still supremely moist, loaded with chocolate chips, and most important: *not* puffy (the secret is using only a teensy bit of baking soda). And as luck would have it, I've made that exact cookie right here. For you.

1 Preheat the oven to 350°F. Line two sheet pans with parchment paper.

2 In a large bowl, use a silicone spatula to combine the melted butter and brown sugar. Add the egg, extra egg yolk, and vanilla extract and mix well.

3 Add the flour, baking soda, and salt and fold until just combined and no streaks of flour remain. Add the oats and fold until combined. Stir in the chocolate chips until evenly distributed. Do not overmix. Allow the dough to rest for 5 minutes so the flour can absorb some of the wet ingredients.

4 Use a 1½-ounce cookie scoop to portion out equal amounts of dough (a large spoon also works; the ball should be about 3 tablespoons). Roll the dough in your hands to smooth the edges, then place 2 inches apart on the prepared sheet pans.

5 Bake until the cookies have puffed up and are light golden brown around the edges but still somewhat soft in the middle, 10 to 11 minutes. Remove the sheet pans from the oven, sprinkle the cookies with sea salt (if using), and allow the cookies to cool slightly on the sheet pans before serving.

Red Wine Brownies

MAKES 9 BROWNIES

PREP TIME 20 MINUTES
COOK TIME 35 MINUTES
TOTAL TIME 55 MINUTES

½ cup (1 stick) unsalted butter,
  cut into tablespoons

1½ cups granulated sugar

4 ounces bittersweet chocolate,
  coarsely chopped

2 large eggs

1 teaspoon vanilla extract

¼ cup red wine

¾ cup Dutch-processed cocoa
  powder

¼ cup all-purpose flour

½ teaspoon salt

Picture this: you opened up a bottle of wine, cooked yourself a nice dinner, and now you want a little somethin' sweet. Correction—something chocolaty-sweet. But you also have leftover wine, and that definitely can't go to waste. Clearly, the logical next step is to make Red Wine Brownies. They have a subtle depth from a splash of wine (it won't taste boozy; it's only ¼ cup) and a decadent, dense texture. Plus, people always say that wine and chocolate pair perfectly together, so . . . why not?

1 Preheat the oven to 350°F. Line an 8 × 8-inch square baking pan with parchment paper on all sides (see page 23).

2 In a large microwave-safe bowl, combine the butter and granulated sugar. Microwave until the butter is fully melted and the mixture is hot to the touch, about 1 minute, then remove and stir using a whisk. Add the chopped chocolate to the bowl and microwave for 30 seconds more. Remove the bowl—the chocolate should be completely melted. If it isn't, microwave for another 15 seconds. Whisk again.

3 Add the eggs (straight from the fridge) and vanilla extract and whisk vigorously until the mixture becomes glossy, about 30 seconds. (Don't worry about cooling the chocolate mixture before adding your eggs; whisk them in immediately and you're good.) Whisk in the wine until combined.

4 Add the cocoa powder, flour, and salt and whisk slowly until evenly incorporated. Use a silicone spatula to scrape the batter into the prepared baking pan, spreading evenly to the edges and smoothing out the top. Bake until the surface is shiny, the edges are set, and a butter knife inserted into the center comes out mostly clean (a crumb or two attached is okay), 30 to 35 minutes.

5 Place the pan on a cooling rack and allow the brownies to cool completely in the pan. Use the parchment paper to lift the brownies from the pan, then transfer the brownies to a cutting board, cut into 9 squares, and serve.

PRO TIP *Any red wine will work in these brownies, but I recommend a juicier wine like merlot so the flavor shines through.*

Unbirthday Cake Cookies

MAKES 10 COOKIES

PREP TIME 15 MINUTES
COOK TIME 13 MINUTES
TOTAL TIME 28 MINUTES

½ cup (1 stick) unsalted butter, at room temperature

½ cup packed light brown sugar

2 tablespoons granulated sugar

1 large egg, at room temperature

1 teaspoon vanilla extract

¼ teaspoon almond extract

1¼ cups all-purpose flour

½ teaspoon baking soda

½ teaspoon salt

½ cup white chocolate chips

¼ cup rainbow sprinkles

These cookies have two points of inspiration. One, the flavor "birthday cake" typically refers to a dessert with a vanilla base, plus rainbow sprinkles (and before you start wondering if rainbow sprinkles are a flavor, they certainly are . . . just don't ask me to explain it). And two, "The Unbirthday Song" from the movie *Alice in Wonderland*. So these cookies have all those wonderful birthday cake flavors, but I've found they taste best when it's not your birthday, and I bet that means today. Right now.

1 Preheat the oven to 350°F. Line two sheet pans with parchment paper.

2 In a stand mixer fitted with the paddle attachment, combine the butter, brown sugar, and granulated sugar and beat on medium-high speed until light and fluffy, about 2 minutes.

3 Use a silicone spatula to scrape down the sides and bottom of the bowl, then add the egg, vanilla extract, and almond extract. Beat on medium-high speed until the mixture is smooth and combined, about 1 minute, scraping down the bowl as needed.

4 Add the flour, baking soda, and salt to the bowl and beat on low until just combined and no streaks of flour remain. Remove the bowl from the stand mixer and use a silicone spatula to fold in the white chocolate chips and rainbow sprinkles, mixing until both are evenly incorporated.

5 Use a 1½-ounce cookie scoop to portion out equal amounts of dough (a large spoon also works; the ball should be about 3 tablespoons). Roll the dough in your hands to smooth the edges, then place 2 inches apart on the prepared sheet pans.

6 Bake until the cookies have puffed up and are set and firm around the edges but still somewhat soft in the middle, 11 to 13 minutes. Remove the sheet pans from the oven and allow the cookies to rest on the sheet pans for 5 minutes, then use a metal spatula to transfer the cookies to a cooling rack to cool completely.

Nutella-Swirled Chocolate Chip Blondies

MAKES 9 BLONDIES

PREP TIME 15 MINUTES
COOK TIME 30 MINUTES
TOTAL TIME 45 MINUTES

½ cup (1 stick) unsalted butter, melted

1 cup packed light brown sugar

1 large egg plus 1 large egg yolk, at room temperature

1 tablespoon vanilla extract

1 cup all-purpose flour

¼ teaspoon baking powder

½ teaspoon salt

1 cup semisweet or bittersweet chocolate chips

½ cup Nutella

There are months where I totally forget about Nutella; then I see that quintessential brown jar with red lettering at the store, put two to five jars in my grocery cart, and spend the next few weeks putting Nutella into everything (ask me about the time I made a Havarti grilled cheese with Nutella and raspberry jam—surprisingly good!). One of my favorite ways to use the chocolaty hazelnut spread, though, is by swirling ribbons of it through chewy chocolate chip blondies.

1 Preheat the oven to 350°F. Line an 8 × 8-inch square baking pan with parchment paper on all sides (see page 23).

2 In a large bowl, whisk the melted butter and brown sugar until combined. Whisk in the egg, extra egg yolk, and vanilla extract until combined.

3 Add the flour, baking powder, and salt. Use a silicone spatula to fold until combined and no streaks of flour remain. Gently fold in the chocolate chips, mixing only until combined.

4 Use the silicone spatula to scrape the batter into the prepared pan, spreading evenly to the edges and smoothing out the top. Drop spoonfuls of Nutella on top of the batter (6 to 8 spoonfuls from the ½ cup measurement). Use a butter knife to drag and swirl the Nutella through the blondie batter.

5 Bake until the edges are set and the blondies are golden brown, 25 to 30 minutes. The middle may still look underbaked, but the blondies will continue to cook as they cool in the pan.

6 Place the pan on a cooling rack and allow the blondies to cool completely in the pan. Use the parchment paper to lift the blondies from the pan, then transfer the blondies to a cutting board, cut into 9 squares, and serve.

PRO TIP *Want to jazz up these babies even more? Sub half the Nutella for a spreadable peanut butter for double the fun.*

Blueberry Almond Cake

MAKES ONE 9-INCH CAKE

PREP TIME 20 MINUTES
COOK TIME 40 MINUTES
TOTAL TIME 1 HOUR

½ cup (1 stick) unsalted butter, at room temperature

1 cup granulated sugar

2 large eggs, at room temperature

3 tablespoons milk (any dairy or nondairy milk works)

1 teaspoon almond extract

1 teaspoon vanilla extract

1½ cups all-purpose flour

½ cup superfine almond flour

1 teaspoon baking powder

¾ teaspoon salt

1 cup fresh or frozen blueberries

½ cup sliced almonds

Confectioners' sugar, for topping (optional)

PRO TIP
Wondering whether you should use fresh or frozen berries in a recipe? Fresh berries hold their shape more, while frozen tend to burst and "stain." Both are lovely for different reasons!

For some people, dessert cravings subside when warm weather arrives. Not me. My cravings just change from chocolate to not chocolate. This simple blueberry cake is one of my standby summer-evening hits; it takes an hour from start to finish and lets the blueberries shine. Almond flour adds a delicate nutty flavor and keeps the cake soft for days. If you have whipped cream to dollop on top, great, but ice cream works, too.

1 Preheat the oven to 350°F. Line the bottom of a 9-inch round cake pan with parchment paper (see page 23) and grease the sides with nonstick cooking spray.

2 In a stand mixer fitted with the paddle attachment, combine the butter and granulated sugar and beat on medium-high speed until light and fluffy, about 2 minutes.

3 Add the eggs, milk, almond extract, and vanilla extract and mix on low speed until smooth. Scrape down the sides and bottom of the bowl, then add the all-purpose flour, almond flour, baking powder, and salt. Beat on low speed until just combined and no streaks of flour remain. The batter will be thick.

4 Remove the bowl from the stand mixer and use the silicone spatula to gently fold in the blueberries, being careful not to crush them. Transfer the batter to the prepared cake pan, smoothing out the top so you have an even layer. Sprinkle the sliced almonds on top. Bake until the cake is lightly golden brown on top and a butter knife inserted into the center of the cake comes out mostly clean (a crumb or two attached is okay), 35 to 40 minutes.

5 Place the cake pan on a cooling rack and allow the cake to cool completely in the pan. To remove from the pan, drag a butter knife around the edge of the cake, then carefully flip the cake out onto a plate, peel away the parchment paper, and re-invert the cake, right-side up, onto a serving plate. Dust the top with confectioners' sugar (if using), slice, and serve.

Crackle-Top Brownies

MAKES 9 BROWNIES

PREP TIME 20 MINUTES
COOK TIME 30 MINUTES
TOTAL TIME 50 MINUTES

¾ cup (1½ sticks) unsalted butter

¾ cup Dutch-processed cocoa powder

1 teaspoon vanilla extract

1¾ cups packed light brown sugar

3 large eggs, at room temperature

¾ cup all-purpose flour

½ teaspoon salt

½ cup semisweet or bittersweet chocolate chips

Brownies are my love language. So much so that I've literally sold sweatshirts that say BROWNIES in collegiate letters on the front. And I'm not ashamed to admit that I'm a huge boxed brownie fan. They're chewy, fudgy, and not too dense—so this homemade version *has* to rival the box, down to that crackly, meringue-like top. Of course, I am not proposing you make meringue, especially on a weeknight. Instead, whip brown sugar into eggs to create a shiny, crackly top as the brownies bake. I rarely let these brownies cool, instead scooping them warm from the pan onto my plate, messy and magnificent.

1 Preheat the oven to 350°F. Line an 8 × 8-inch square baking pan with parchment paper on all sides (see page 23).

2 In a small saucepan over medium-low heat, add the butter and cook, occasionally stirring with a whisk, until the butter melts completely. Remove the saucepan from the heat. Add the cocoa powder and vanilla extract and whisk until no lumps of cocoa remain. Set aside.

3 In a stand mixer fitted with the whisk attachment, combine the brown sugar and eggs and whisk until the mixture turns light and pale in color, and when you smoosh a little batter between your fingertips, you can no longer feel any granules of sugar, about 3 minutes. With the mixer on low speed, slowly pour the butter and cocoa mixture into the egg mixture and mix until just incorporated.

4 Remove the bowl from the stand mixer and use a silicone spatula to fold in the flour and salt until no streaks of flour remain, being careful not to overmix the batter. Fold in the chocolate chips.

5 Pour the batter into the prepared baking pan, spreading it evenly to the edges. Bake until the surface is shiny, the edges are set, and a butter knife inserted into the center comes out mostly clean (a crumb or two attached is okay), 25 to 30 minutes.

6 Place the pan on a cooling rack and allow the brownies to cool completely in the pan. Use the parchment paper to lift the brownies from the pan, then transfer the brownies to a cutting board, cut into squares, and serve.

Mixed Berry Skillet Crisp

MAKES ONE 9-INCH CRISP

PREP TIME 15 MINUTES
COOK TIME 45 MINUTES
TOTAL TIME 1 HOUR

FOR THE BERRIES

7 cups fresh or frozen mixed berries, such as blueberries, raspberries, blackberries, and strawberries

⅓ cup granulated sugar

¼ cup all-purpose flour

1 tablespoon freshly squeezed lemon juice (from about 1 lemon)

Pinch of salt

FOR THE CRISP TOPPING

⅔ cup all-purpose flour

⅔ cup old-fashioned oats

½ cup granulated sugar

½ cup packed light brown sugar

¼ teaspoon ground cinnamon

¼ teaspoon salt

½ cup (1 stick) unsalted butter, melted

Vanilla ice cream, for serving (optional, but is it really?)

PRO TIP *If you don't have a skillet, you can bake this in pretty much any medium baking pan you have (such as a 9 × 9-inch square pan or an 8 × 12-inch oval pan). The bake time remains the same.*

This crisp doesn't require a laundry list of ingredients; you literally toss everything into a bowl, then dump everything into a skillet. Baking a fruit crisp always makes me feel like a heroine in a Nancy Meyers movie, especially if I've also just whipped up a roast chicken dinner and there's an open bottle of red wine on the table (and if I've really timed it right, the crisp bakes for an hour while we eat, then I serve it warm). And thanks to cast iron's ability to retain heat so well, the berries get extra jammy and almost caramelized in the skillet. The scoops of ice cream on top? Legally required.

1 Preheat the oven to 375°F. Generously grease the bottom and sides of a 9-inch round cast-iron skillet with nonstick cooking spray.

2 *First, prepare the berries.* In a large bowl, combine the berries, granulated sugar, flour, lemon juice, and salt. Use a silicone spatula to toss together, then pour the mixture into the prepared skillet (especially if you're using frozen berries, it may seem as if you have too much flour, but this is correct; pour it all into the skillet).

3 *Next, make the crisp topping.* In that now-empty mixing bowl (no need to clean it), use the silicone spatula to roughly stir together the flour, oats, granulated sugar, brown sugar, cinnamon, and salt. Pour in the melted butter and mix until combined. Use your hands to squeeze the crumble into your palms, then break it apart into big and small clusters, sprinkling them all over the berries in the skillet.

4 Cover the skillet loosely with aluminum foil, then bake the crisp for 15 minutes. Remove the foil and continue to bake, uncovered, until the topping is golden brown and the fruit is bubbling around the edges, 25 to 30 minutes more. Place the skillet on a cooling rack and allow the crisp to cool slightly before serving with a few scoops of vanilla ice cream (if using).

Dark Chocolate, Date, and Oatmeal Bars

MAKES 9 BARS

PREP TIME 15 MINUTES
COOK TIME 25 MINUTES
TOTAL TIME 40 MINUTES

½ cup (1 stick) unsalted butter,
  at room temperature

½ cup granulated sugar

¼ cup packed light brown sugar

1 large egg, at room temperature

2 teaspoons vanilla extract

1 cup all-purpose flour

1 cup old-fashioned oats

½ teaspoon baking soda

¼ teaspoon baking powder

½ teaspoon salt

¼ teaspoon ground cinnamon

6 ounces bittersweet or dark
  chocolate, coarsely chopped

7 Medjool dates, pitted and
  coarsely chopped (about ½ cup)

There was something about that just-right porridge Goldilocks was seeking that always made me crave it as a kid (the rest of the bedtime story's morals were lost on me). I still consider oatmeal supremely comforting—made at home, though, not stolen from some bears' house I broke into. In these cozy oatmeal bars, dark chocolate chunks and sweet dates bring a little extra grown-up *oomph*.

1 Preheat the oven to 350°F. Line an 8 × 8-inch square baking pan with parchment paper on all sides (see page 23).

2 In a stand mixer fitted with the paddle attachment, combine the butter, granulated sugar, and brown sugar and beat on medium-high speed until light and fluffy, about 2 minutes.

3 Use a silicone spatula to scrape down the sides and bottom of the bowl, then add the egg and vanilla extract. Beat on medium-high speed until the mixture is smooth and combined, about 30 seconds, scraping down the bowl as needed.

4 Add the flour, oats, baking soda, baking powder, salt, and cinnamon and beat on low speed until just combined and no streaks of flour remain. Remove the bowl from the stand mixer and use the silicone spatula to fold in the chocolate and dates, mixing until both are evenly incorporated.

5 Transfer the dough to the prepared pan, spreading it evenly to the edges. Bake until the top is golden brown and the edges are set, 20 to 25 minutes.

6 Place the pan on a cooling rack and allow the bars to cool completely in the pan. Use the parchment paper to lift the bars from the pan, then transfer the bars to a cutting board, cut into 9 squares, and serve.

PRO TIP *If dates aren't your thing, swap in ½ cup chopped dried figs or dried cherries.*

Strawberries and Cream Crispy Treats

MAKES 12 BARS

PREP TIME 15 MINUTES
(PLUS 20 MINUTES CHILL TIME)
TOTAL TIME 35 MINUTES

6 cups Rice Krispies cereal

6 tablespoons (¾ stick) unsalted butter

12 ounces large marshmallows (about 6½ cups)

2 teaspoons vanilla extract

¼ teaspoon salt

1½ cups freeze-dried strawberries, lightly crushed into pieces (I get mine from Trader Joe's)

1 cup white chocolate chips

I have this thing where recipe ideas come to me when I'm trying to fall asleep. I lie there horizontally, start to doze off, and then *bam*! My head is filled with celebratory layer cakes, unique cookie combinations, and browned butter everything (might I recommend this instead of those sheep you're counting?). These Strawberries and Cream Crispy Treats with freeze-dried strawberries and white chocolate chips are one of those sleepy-time ideas. If they sound like something from a dream, it's because, in a way, they are.

1 Line a 9 × 9-inch square baking pan with parchment paper on all sides (see page 23) and grease the parchment with nonstick cooking spray.

2 In an extra-large bowl, add the Rice Krispies cereal. Set aside.

3 In a medium saucepan over medium-low heat, add the butter and cook, stirring occasionally with a silicone spatula, until the butter melts completely. Add the marshmallows, vanilla extract, and salt and cook, stirring occasionally, until the marshmallows melt completely. Remove from the heat.

4 Pour the marshmallow mixture into the bowl with the Rice Krispies and use the silicone spatula to fold everything together until evenly combined. Fold in the strawberries and white chocolate chips, reserving a few tablespoons of each to garnish the top.

5 Transfer the mixture into the prepared pan. Rinse off your spatula, then use it (still a little bit wet, this helps!) to pat the mixture into an even layer. Top with the reserved freeze-dried strawberries and white chocolate chips, pushing them down into the bars. Place in the fridge to set for 20 minutes, then remove and cut into 12 bars.

Lemon–Olive Oil Cake

MAKES ONE 9-INCH CAKE

PREP TIME 20 MINUTES
COOK TIME 40 MINUTES
TOTAL TIME 1 HOUR

¾ cup extra-virgin olive oil,
plus 1 to 2 teaspoons for
greasing the pan

1¼ cups granulated sugar

2 large eggs, at room
temperature

1 tablespoon freshly grated
lemon zest (from about 1 lemon)

¼ cup freshly squeezed lemon
juice (from 1 to 2 lemons)

½ cup milk (any dairy or nondairy
milk works)

1 teaspoon vanilla extract

1 teaspoon lemon extract

1⅓ cups all-purpose flour

½ cup superfine almond flour

½ teaspoon baking powder

½ teaspoon baking soda

½ teaspoon salt

Confectioners' sugar, for topping
(optional)

Lemon + olive oil isn't the first combination you'd think makes a great cake, but hear me out. Olive oil in cake is the golden ticket to a velvety crumb. By using it instead of butter, you end up with a cake that melts in your mouth (think about how butter is solid at room temperature, making more structured cakes, while oil remains liquid, creating more moist cakes). Then it's a trio of lemony delights: lemon zest, lemon juice, and lemon extract. They complement the green notes from the olive oil and blanket any savoriness, leaving a rich, sophisticated cake that's not too sweet. Serve with fresh fruit, depending on the season, or a spoonful of your fanciest jam.

1 Preheat the oven to 350°F. Line the bottom of a 9-inch round cake pan with parchment paper (see page 23) and generously grease the sides with olive oil.

2 In a stand mixer fitted with the whisk attachment, combine the granulated sugar, eggs, and lemon zest and beat on medium-high speed until fluffy and pale in color, about 2 minutes.

3 Turn the mixer to medium-low speed, then slowly stream in the olive oil until fully incorporated. Turn off the mixer; pour in the lemon juice, milk, vanilla extract, and lemon extract; and mix on medium-low until combined.

4 Add the all-purpose flour, almond flour, baking powder, baking soda, and salt. Mix on medium-low speed until combined and no streaks of flour remain. Use a silicone spatula to scrape down the sides and bottom of the bowl as needed. Do not overmix.

5 Pour the batter into the prepared cake pan, spreading it to the edges. Bake until the cake is golden brown and a butter knife inserted into the center of the cake comes out mostly clean (a crumb or two attached is okay), 35 to 40 minutes.

6 Place the cake pan on a cooling rack and allow the cake to cool completely in the pan. To remove the cake from the pan, drag a butter knife around the edges of the cake, flip the cake out onto a plate, peel away the parchment paper, then re-invert the cake, right-side up, onto a serving plate. Dust the top with confectioners' sugar (if using), slice, and serve.

PRO TIP *When they're in season, Meyer lemons—a sweet, floral winter lemon with slightly less acidity—are wonderful in this cake.*

Peanut Butter–Mocha Crunch Bars

MAKES 8 LARGE OR
16 SMALL BARS

PREP TIME 15 MINUTES
(PLUS 45 MINUTES CHILL TIME)
TOTAL TIME 1 HOUR

1½ cups semisweet or
   bittersweet chocolate chips

½ cup creamy peanut butter
   (such as Jif, Skippy, or Peter
   Pan—*not* natural peanut butter)

2 tablespoons instant espresso
   powder

1½ cups puffed rice cereal

As a kid, I remember endless opportunities to eat candy bars, whether as after-school snacks from the corner store or from bowls mounded with snack-size versions at birthday parties. That was the life. My adulthood doesn't have nearly enough candy bar opportunities, and I'm starting to wonder if the adult candy bar is actually a protein bar (how depressing). This homemade candy bar recipe requires only four ingredients and almost zero work: microwave some stuff, toss in some other stuff, and spread it in a pan. The end result is that winning combination of peanut butter and melted chocolate, with crunch for texture and coffee for complexity.

1 Line a 1-pound loaf pan with parchment paper on all sides (see page 23).

2 In a large microwave-safe bowl, combine the chocolate chips, peanut butter, and espresso powder. Microwave in 30-second increments, using a silicone spatula to stir between each, until the mixture is fully melted.

3 Remove from the microwave and use the silicone spatula to gently fold in the puffed rice until evenly combined. Transfer the mixture to the prepared pan, spreading evenly to the edges. Place in the fridge until the bars are set, 40 to 45 minutes.

4 Use the parchment to lift the bars from the loaf pan, then peel away the parchment. Transfer the bars to a cutting board, cut crosswise into 8 large bars (or cut those in half for smaller bites), and serve.

ELEVATED NOSTAL-GIA

I know I'm not the only person whose love of dessert is wrapped up in memories of childhood. But now when I eat the childhood treats I used to crave, they don't taste the same. Maybe it's because that one-note, intense sweetness doesn't hit the way it used to, or maybe it's because I can now taste the preservatives. But this chapter's classic childhood treats have a depth of flavor (and short ingredient list) you won't find in packaged sweets, making them even better than the originals. And instead of saving your babysitting money for these treats and unwrapping them at the cafeteria table, all you need is the grown-up willpower to wait for them to cool on the counter.

The Best Chocolate Chip Cookies in the World

MAKES 15 COOKIES

PREP TIME 30 MINUTES
(PLUS 1 HOUR AND 20 MINUTES
COOL/CHILL/REST TIME)
COOK TIME 13 MINUTES
TOTAL TIME 2 HOURS 3 MINUTES

¾ cup (1½ sticks) unsalted butter

1 cup packed light brown sugar

¼ cup granulated sugar

1 large egg plus 1 large egg yolk,
   at room temperature

1 tablespoon vanilla extract

1¾ cups all-purpose flour

¾ teaspoon baking soda

¾ teaspoon salt

8 ounces semisweet or
   bittersweet chocolate, coarsely
   chopped, or 1½ cups semisweet
   or bittersweet chocolate chips

Flaky sea salt, for sprinkling
   (optional)

These may look like ordinary chocolate chip cookies, but they're anything but. They were developed by Sofi Llanso (my second in command) before she started working for me. When she suggested we put them on the blog in 2020, I said, "Are you sure?!" because I knew how special they were to her. She said yes, the world should experience them. Flash forward to today, and they are the most popular recipe on our site with more than 4 million page views. Nine times out of ten when I ask my readers what their favorite Broma recipe is, it's these cookies. And for me, these cookies hold an *extra* special meaning: they signify how special Sofi is, both to me and to the world. I simply couldn't publish this cookbook without them.

1 In a small saucepan, add the butter and cook over medium-low heat. Use a silicone spatula to stir and scrape the butter from the bottom and sides of the pan every 10 to 15 seconds. At first, the butter will melt and foam, then over time the foam bubbles will get smaller and the butter will begin to emit a warm, nutty aroma. Continue to cook the butter, occasionally stirring and scraping with your spatula, until the butter begins to take on color and you see small, floating brown bits (these are the milk solids in your butter separating and toasting), 5 to 7 minutes. Once the butter is golden brown, remove it from the heat and allow it to cool in the saucepan for 10 minutes.

2 In a large bowl, combine the brown butter, brown sugar, and granulated sugar. Use the silicone spatula to mix together. Add the egg, extra egg yolk, and vanilla extract and mix well.

3 Add the flour, baking soda, and salt and use the silicone spatula to fold until no streaks of flour remain, being careful not to overmix your batter. The dough should be soft but not sticky, so when you touch it with your finger, it gives just a little.

4 Fold in the chocolate until evenly distributed. Do not overmix. Cover the bowl and place it in the fridge to chill for at least 1 hour and up to overnight.

5 Preheat the oven to 350°F. Line two sheet pans with parchment paper. Remove the dough from the fridge and allow it to soften at room temperature until it's scoopable, about 20 minutes.

6 Use a 1½-ounce cookie scoop to portion out equal amounts of dough (a large spoon also works; the ball should be about 3 tablespoons). Roll the dough in your hands to smooth the edges, then place 2 inches apart on the prepared sheet pans.

7 Bake until the cookies have puffed up and are light golden brown around the edges but still somewhat soft in the middle, 12 to 13 minutes. Remove the sheet pans from the oven, sprinkle the cookies with sea salt (if using), and allow the cookies to cool slightly on the sheet pans before serving.

Matilda's Chocolate Cake

MAKES ONE 3-LAYER 8-INCH CAKE

PREP TIME 45 MINUTES
(PLUS 30 MINUTES COOL TIME)
COOK TIME 25 MINUTES
TOTAL TIME 1 HOUR 40 MINUTES

FOR THE CAKE

4 tablespoons flaxseed meal

¾ cup water

3 cups gluten-free baking flour
(I suggest Bob's Red Mill Gluten
Free 1 to 1 Baking Flour)

2⅔ cups granulated sugar

1 cup Dutch-processed cocoa
powder

1 tablespoon baking powder

2¼ teaspoons baking soda

1½ teaspoons salt

1½ cups milk (any dairy or
nondairy milk works)

1 cup vegetable oil

1 tablespoon vanilla extract

¾ cup strongly brewed coffee,
hot

FOR THE FROSTING

1½ cups (3 sticks) unsalted
butter, at room temperature

1½ cups Dutch-processed cocoa
powder

⅓ cup whole milk, warmed
slightly

¼ cup heavy cream, warmed
slightly

3 tablespoons corn syrup

1 teaspoon vanilla extract

4½ cups confectioners' sugar

¾ teaspoon salt

Inspired by the famous scene in the movie (and book) *Matilda*, in which Bruce Bogtrotter has to eat an entire chocolate cake in front of his school, this cake will make you want to do the same. What makes it so special? First, gluten-free flour, which creates an otherworldly, moist, and fudgy crumb that regular flour can't compete with. Second, flaxseed meal in place of eggs, which acts as a binder as eggs do, but makes the cake even more moist. FYI: I've made this cake countless times with all-purpose flour and regular eggs to see if those ingredients could replicate the same texture—they never do. Trust me on this.

1 *First, make the cake.* Preheat the oven to 350°F. Line the bottom of three 8-inch round cake pans with parchment paper (see page 23) and grease the sides with nonstick cooking spray.

2 In a small bowl, combine the flaxseed meal and water and mix together using a fork. Allow the mixture to sit until it has thickened and congealed, about 5 minutes.

3 In a large bowl, whisk together the flour, granulated sugar, cocoa powder, baking powder, baking soda, and salt. In a separate bowl, whisk together the milk, vegetable oil, vanilla extract, and thickened flax mixture. Pour the wet ingredients into the dry and whisk until no lumps remain. Pour in the coffee, whisking until just combined.

4 Divide the batter evenly between the prepared pans. Bake until the cakes are risen, the tops spring back to the touch, and a butter knife inserted into the centers of the cakes comes out mostly clean (a crumb or two attached is okay), 20 to 25 minutes.

5 Place the cake pans on a cooling rack and allow the cakes to cool slightly. To remove the cakes from the pans, drag a butter knife around the edges of each cake, then carefully flip each cake out onto a plate, peel away the bottom sheet of parchment paper, and re-invert the cake, right-side up, onto a cooling rack to cool completely, about 30 minutes.

6 *Once the cakes have cooled, make the frosting.* In a stand mixer fitted with the paddle attachment, add the butter and cocoa powder and beat on low speed until combined, about 20 seconds. Add the warm milk, cream, corn syrup, and vanilla extract, and beat on low speed until combined, scraping down the sides and bottom of the bowl as needed. Add the confectioners' sugar and salt and beat on low speed until the frosting is fully combined and no streaks of sugar remain, about 20 seconds. Do not overmix.

7 Place the first cake layer, right-side up, onto a cake stand or plate. Spread a large dollop of frosting on top, using an offset spatula to spread a thick layer evenly to the edges. Repeat with the second and third cake layers. Use the remaining frosting to frost the top and sides of the cake. Use the back of a large spoon to create swirls around the cake. Marvel at the beauty—then dive in!

CAKE VARIATIONS

VEGAN VERSION Substitute vegan butter and nondairy milk for the butter and dairy milk in equal quantities

REGULAR EGG VERSION Substitute 3 large eggs for the flaxseed meal and water

REGULAR FLOUR VERSION Substitute all-purpose flour for the gluten-free flour in equal quantity

PRO TIP *These cookies can be easily holiday-ified with different color frostings and sprinkles: red, white, and blue for Memorial Day; black, green, orange, and/or purple for Halloween; blue and white for Hanukkah; or green and red for Christmas.*

Grocery Store Frosted Sugar Cookies

MAKES 16 COOKIES

PREP TIME 30 MINUTES (PLUS 30 MINUTES COOL TIME)
COOK TIME 14 MINUTES
TOTAL TIME 1 HOUR 14 MINUTES

FOR THE COOKIES

5 tablespoons unsalted butter, at room temperature

3 tablespoons vegetable oil

¾ cup granulated sugar

¾ cup confectioners' sugar

1 large egg, at room temperature

2 teaspoons vanilla extract

⅛ teaspoon almond extract

1 tablespoon milk (any dairy or nondairy milk works)

2 cups cake flour

½ teaspoon baking powder

¼ teaspoon baking soda

½ teaspoon salt

FOR THE FROSTING

½ cup (1 stick) unsalted butter, at room temperature

3 cups confectioners' sugar

2 tablespoons milk (any dairy or nondairy milk works)

1 teaspoon vanilla extract

⅛ teaspoon almond extract

¼ teaspoon salt

Food coloring of choice

Rainbow sprinkles, for topping

You might know these cookies as Lofthouse cookies or "those grocery store cookies that are super soft, with a hockey puck of frosting and tons of sprinkles." During my childhood, Lofthouse cookies were as reliable at school functions and birthday parties as grass stains on my overalls. Eating them was like biting into a cushion of happiness. It took me several rounds to pinpoint the softness (low-protein cake flour and the right balance of granulated sugar to confectioners' sugar is key). The result is purely transportive joy.

1 *First, make the cookies.* Preheat the oven to 325°F. Line two sheet pans with parchment paper.

2 In a stand mixer fitted with the whisk attachment, add the butter and vegetable oil and whisk together on low speed until combined (so the oil doesn't fly everywhere). Gradually increase the speed to medium-high and whisk until smooth and homogenous, about 2 minutes.

3 Keep the mixer going as you slowly pour in the granulated sugar until combined. Turn off the mixer, add the confectioners' sugar, and beat on low speed, gradually increasing the speed to medium, until combined.

4 Add the egg, vanilla extract, almond extract, and milk. Beat on medium-high until the mixture is smooth, about 1 minute, scraping down the bowl as needed.

5 Add the cake flour, baking powder, baking soda, and salt to the bowl and beat on low speed until just combined and no streaks of flour remain.

6 Use a 1-ounce cookie scoop to portion out equal amounts of dough (a large spoon also works; the ball should be about 2 tablespoons). Roll the dough in your hands to smooth the edges, then place 2 inches apart on the prepared sheet pans and flatten the top of the balls gently with your palm.

7 Bake until the cookies have puffed up and are set and firm around the edges but still somewhat soft in the middle, 13 to 14 minutes. Remove the sheet pans from the oven and allow the cookies to rest on the sheet pans for 5 minutes, then use a metal spatula to transfer the cookies to a cooling rack to cool completely, about 25 minutes more.

8 *Once the cookies have cooled, make the frosting.* In a stand mixer fitted with the paddle attachment, combine the butter, confectioners' sugar, milk, vanilla extract, almond extract, and salt. Beat on medium speed, scraping down the sides and bottom of the bowl with the silicone spatula as needed, until the frosting is fluffy, about 1 minute. Add food coloring of your choice a few drops at a time until the desired color is reached.

9 Use an offset spatula to frost the cookies with about 2 tablespoons of frosting, spreading it into an even layer. Top with sprinkles and sink those teeth in!

Peanut Butter and Jelly–Swirled Blondies

MAKES 9 SQUARE OR 18 TRIANGLE BLONDIES

PREP TIME 15 MINUTES
COOK TIME 30 MINUTES
TOTAL TIME 45 MINUTES

½ cup (1 stick) unsalted butter, melted

1 cup packed light brown sugar

1 large egg plus 1 large egg yolk, at room temperature

1 tablespoon vanilla extract

1 cup all-purpose flour

¼ teaspoon baking powder

½ teaspoon salt

¼ cup creamy peanut butter (such as Jif, Skippy, or Peter Pan—*not* natural peanut butter)

¼ cup fruit jam or preserves of choice

An iconic flavor duo swirled into chewy blondies. Stick with the peanut butter brand and jam preference that you insisted on throughout elementary school (creamy Jif and Smucker's red raspberry for me, thanks), or change it up with whatever nut butter and fancy jam you've grown to prefer as a sophisticated adult. Or maybe you haven't changed at all, in which case, carry on. Just don't dare cut the crusts off these blondies—that's the best part.

1 Preheat the oven to 350°F. Line an 8 × 8-inch square baking pan with parchment paper on all sides (see page 23).

2 In a large bowl, whisk the melted butter and brown sugar until combined. Whisk in the egg, extra egg yolk, and vanilla extract.

3 Add the flour, baking powder, and salt. Use a silicone spatula to fold until combined and no streaks of flour remain.

4 Transfer the batter to the prepared pan, using the silicone spatula to spread it evenly to the edges and smooth out the top. Drop spoonfuls of peanut butter and jam on top of the batter (6 to 8 spoonfuls of each from the ¼ cup measurements). Use a butter knife to drag and swirl the peanut butter and jam through the batter.

5 Bake until the edges are set, the blondies are golden brown, and a butter knife inserted into the center (avoid the swirls) comes out clean, 25 to 30 minutes.

6 Place the pan on a cooling rack and allow the blondies to cool completely in the pan. Use the parchment paper to lift the blondies from the pan, then transfer the blondies to a cutting board, cut into 9 squares (or cut those squares into triangles for smaller triangular blondies), and serve.

Yellow Sheet Cake with Chocolate Frosting

MAKES ONE 9 × 13-INCH CAKE

PREP TIME 30 MINUTES (PLUS 30 MINUTES COOL TIME)
COOK TIME 40 MINUTES
TOTAL TIME 1 HOUR 40 MINUTES

FOR THE CAKE

½ cup (1 stick) unsalted butter, at room temperature

½ cup vegetable oil

1½ cups granulated sugar

4 large eggs plus 2 large egg yolks, at room temperature

1 tablespoon vanilla extract

2⅔ cups all-purpose flour

2½ teaspoons baking powder

¾ teaspoon salt

1⅓ cups buttermilk (get my homemade version on page 28)

FOR THE FROSTING

1 cup (2 sticks) unsalted butter, at room temperature

¾ cup Dutch-processed cocoa powder

3 cups confectioners' sugar

2 tablespoons milk (any dairy milk works)

2 tablespoons heavy cream

1 tablespoon light corn syrup (honey also works)

1 teaspoon vanilla extract

¼ teaspoon salt

¼ cup chocolate sprinkles (optional)

I'm a chocolate cake girlie through and through, especially on a birthday, but I make an occasional exception for this supremely moist yellow sheet cake. This chocolate-frosted cake (got to get chocolate in there somehow!) is as simple as they come: there's no layering, offset spatula, or cake spinner required. Yet it never fails to bring the party. A mixture of butter and vegetable oil gives the cake its bouncy but moist structure, while the chocolate frosting has that shimmering sheen that makes you want to dive right in. The sprinkles, while optional, give this cake a celebratory razzle-dazzle. And who skips sprinkles?

1 *First, make the cake.* Preheat the oven to 350°F. Line a 9 × 13-inch rectangular baking pan with parchment paper on all sides (see page 23).

2 In a stand mixer fitted with the whisk attachment, add the butter and vegetable oil and beat on low speed until combined, so the oil doesn't fly everywhere. Gradually increase the speed to medium-high and beat until smooth, about 2 minutes.

3 With the mixer running, slowly pour in the granulated sugar and continue to beat on medium-high speed until the mixture is light, fluffy, and turns a very pale yellow color, about 2 minutes.

4 Add the eggs, extra egg yolks, and vanilla extract and beat on medium-high until the mixture is light and fluffy, about 2 minutes. Use a silicone spatula to scrape down the sides and bottom of the bowl as needed.

5 In a separate bowl, whisk together the flour, baking powder, and salt. With the mixer on low speed, alternate adding the dry ingredients and the buttermilk in 3 additions (you'll add half the dry, then all of the wet, then the other half of the dry). It's okay if the batter still has a few lumps in it—you don't want to overmix.

6 Transfer the cake batter into your prepared pan, using the silicone spatula to spread it into an even layer. Bake until the cake has risen, the top springs back to the touch, and a butter knife inserted into the center comes out mostly clean (a crumb or two attached is okay), 35 to 40 minutes. Place the baking pan on a cooling rack and allow the cake to cool completely, about 30 minutes.

7 *Once the cake has cooled, make the frosting.* In a stand mixer fitted with the paddle attachment, combine the butter and cocoa powder and beat on low speed until fully incorporated, about 30 seconds. Add the confectioners' sugar, milk, cream, corn syrup, vanilla extract, and salt. Beat on medium speed, scraping down the sides and bottom of the bowl with the silicone spatula as needed, until the frosting is fluffy and has lightened in color slightly, about 30 seconds.

8 Spread the frosting over the cake, using the back of a large spoon to create swirls. Top with chocolate sprinkles (I hope), then cut into squares and enjoy.

Giant Brown Sugar Not-a-Pop-Tart

MAKES 1 GIANT POP-TART

PREP TIME 35 MINUTES (PLUS
1 HOUR CHILL/REST TIME)
COOK TIME 25 MINUTES
TOTAL TIME 2 HOURS

FOR THE PIE DOUGH

2½ cups all-purpose flour, plus
more for rolling out the dough

1 tablespoon granulated sugar

1 teaspoon salt

1 cup (2 sticks) unsalted butter,
cold and cut into cubes

3 to 4 tablespoons ice water or
chilled vodka (water is standard
in a pie crust, but vodka will
make your crust extra flaky!)

1 large egg, for egg wash

FOR THE BROWN SUGAR FILLING

¾ cup packed light brown sugar

2 tablespoons ground cinnamon

1 tablespoon all-purpose flour

¼ teaspoon salt

3 tablespoons unsalted butter,
melted

FOR THE GLAZE

2 cups confectioners' sugar

3 tablespoons milk (any dairy or
nondairy milk works)

1 teaspoon vanilla extract

1 teaspoon ground cinnamon

Pinch of salt

Years ago, I was painstakingly carving out precise rectangles of home-made Pop-Tarts (my back hunched over the counter, cursing every uneven slice) when I had an epiphany: *There's a much easier way to do this.* Since then, I opt to make one giant Pop-Tart, which cuts the prep time in half and makes the whole thing feel more festive. It's like a slice of pie but thinner, with emphasis on the flaky crust and just enough filling to balance it. To make life even easier, use store-bought pie dough and skip to Step 4. Cut the big tart into (imprecise, *phew*) squares before serving, and let that warm, cinnamon-butter perfume waft through your entire home . . . and into your soul.

1 *First, make the pie dough.* In a food processor, add the flour, granulated sugar, and salt and pulse to combine. Add the butter and pulse until the mixture resembles wet sand and no chunks of butter remain, about 20 seconds.

2 Add 3 tablespoons of the ice water, then pulse until the dough begins to form a ball around the blade, about 20 seconds. If your dough doesn't come together, add another tablespoon of water and pulse again.

3 Turn the dough out onto a clean work surface and divide it into 2 equal pieces. Flatten each piece into a 1-inch-thick oval disk, then wrap in plastic wrap. Place in the fridge for at least 30 minutes and up to 2 days.

4 *Next, make the filling.* In a medium bowl, combine the brown sugar, cinnamon, flour, salt, and melted butter. Use a fork to mix everything together until it forms a paste. Set aside.

5 Preheat the oven to 375°F. Line a sheet pan with parchment paper.

6 Remove both disks of dough from the fridge and set on the counter to soften for 5 minutes. Place a large rectangle of plastic wrap on a clean work surface and dust it with flour (the plastic wrap will help you lift the dough once it's rolled out). Unwrap one disk of dough and place it on the surface. Dust with more flour and use a rolling pin to roll out the dough into a roughly 9 × 13-inch rectangle, dusting the top with more flour as needed. Use a ruler and a sharp knife to cut the dough into an exact 8 × 12-inch rectangle. Lift the plastic wrap off of your work surface (the dough will still be on the plastic wrap) and carefully flip the dough onto your prepared sheet pan. Peel off the plastic wrap.

7 In a small bowl, whisk together the egg with 2 tablespoons water. Use a pastry brush to brush the outer inch of dough. Spread the cinnamon sugar filling over the dough, using the egg-brushed edges as a border (don't add filling over the egg wash).

8 Roll out the second disk of dough on a new sheet of plastic wrap into a roughly 9 × 13-inch rectangle (the same way you rolled out the first), then cut it into an 8 × 12-inch rectangle. Carefully place the second piece of dough over the first and remove the plastic wrap. Use your fingers to slightly press the edges of the 2 pieces together. Use a large fork to make indents around the border of the Pop-Tart, then lightly poke across the surface of the Pop-Tart 3 or

4 times with the fork to allow air to escape as it bakes. If at this point the edges of your dough look uneven, use a sharp knife to trim and clean the edges.

9 Brush the entire top of the Pop-Tart with the remaining egg wash. Bake until the Pop-Tart is light golden brown all over, 20 to 25 minutes. Remove the sheet pan from the oven and allow the Pop-Tart to cool slightly on the sheet pan.

10 *Last, make the glaze.* In a medium bowl, whisk together the confectioners' sugar, milk, vanilla extract, cinnamon, and salt until smooth and homogenous. Spoon the glaze evenly over the Pop-Tart (the Pop-Tart should be warm but not hot), then cool until the glaze is set, about 30 minutes. Use a sharp, thin knife to cut 8 equal pieces straight from the pan. Enjoy!

Cosmic Cookies

PREP TIME 30 MINUTES (PLUS
1 HOUR COOL TIME)
COOK TIME 12 MINUTES
TOTAL TIME 1 HOUR 42 MINUTES

FOR THE COOKIES

½ cup (1 stick) unsalted butter,
at room temperature

1 cup packed light brown sugar

1 large egg, at room temperature

2 teaspoons vanilla extract

1¼ cups all-purpose flour

⅓ cup Dutch-processed cocoa
powder

½ teaspoon baking soda

½ teaspoon salt

FOR THE GANACHE

⅓ cup heavy cream

1 cup semisweet or bittersweet
chocolate chips

Rainbow candy-coated chocolate
chips (or M&M's in a pinch!)

I hate to admit this, but I used to trade my mom's homemade brownies for store-bought Little Debbie Cosmic Brownies in my school cafeteria (sorry, Mom). Those chewy brownies topped with chocolate frosting and rainbow-colored chocolate pieces were the AmEx Black Card of cafeteria currency, and Mom didn't have the marketing department to compete. Now imagine those Cosmic Brownies as a super-fudgy chocolate cookie slathered in a glossy ganache and topped with those signature rainbow-coated chocolate pieces. It's got that hit of delicious nostalgia, and it's still easy to pop into your lunch box. But please don't trade it for a bag of Gushers.

1 *First, make the cookies.* Preheat the oven to 350°F. Line two sheet pans with parchment paper.

2 In a stand mixer fitted with the paddle attachment, add the butter and brown sugar and beat on medium-high speed until light and fluffy, about 2 minutes.

3 Use a silicone spatula to scrape down the sides and bottom of the bowl, then add the egg and vanilla extract. Beat on medium-high until the mixture is fluffy and pale in color, about 2 minutes.

4 Stop the mixer and scrape down the bowl, then add the flour, cocoa powder, baking soda, and salt and beat on low speed until just combined and no streaks of flour remain.

5 Use a 1½-ounce cookie scoop to portion out equal amounts of dough (a large spoon also works; the ball should be about 3 tablespoons). Roll the dough in your hands to smooth the edges, then place 2 inches apart on the prepared sheet pans.

6 Bake until the cookies have puffed up and are set and firm around the edges but still somewhat soft in the middle, 11 to 12 minutes. Remove the sheet pans from the oven and allow the cookies to rest on the sheet pans for 5 minutes, then use a metal spatula to transfer the cookies to a cooling rack to cool completely, about 25 minutes more.

7 *Once the cookies have cooled, make the ganache.* In a medium microwave-safe bowl, add the cream. Microwave until the cream is hot to the touch but not boiling, 30 to 45 seconds. Add in the chocolate chips and let sit for 1 minute, then use a spoon to stir the mixture together until smooth and glossy.

8 Use a small offset spatula or a spoon to frost each cookie with about 1 tablespoon of the ganache, spreading it in an even circle around the top of the cookie. Sprinkle with the rainbow candy-coated chocolate chips, then place the cookies back on the cooling rack for the ganache to set, about 30 minutes.

Rebe's Carrot Cake with Cream Cheese Frosting

MAKES ONE 2-LAYER 8-INCH CAKE

PREP TIME 30 MINUTES
(PLUS 1 HOUR COOL TIME)
COOK TIME 30 MINUTES
TOTAL TIME 2 HOURS

FOR THE CAKE

2 cups finely shredded carrots

4 large eggs, at room temperature

1 cup granulated sugar

¾ cup vegetable oil

1 (8-ounce) can crushed pineapple, drained (about ¾ cup)

1 cup sweetened shredded coconut

½ cup raisins (if you can't get down with raisins, you can omit)

2 teaspoons vanilla extract

2 cups all-purpose flour

2 teaspoons ground cinnamon

1½ teaspoons baking powder

1 teaspoon baking soda

¾ teaspoon salt

FOR THE CREAM CHEESE FROSTING

1 cup (2 sticks) unsalted butter, at room temperature

8 ounces cream cheese, at room temperature

5 cups confectioners' sugar

2 teaspoons vanilla extract

½ teaspoon salt

¼ cup coarsely chopped walnuts, for topping (optional)

Picture a tiny button-nosed five-year-old asking for carrot cake for her birthday. Congrats, now you've met my sister, Rebe. Every year on her birthday she'd request our mom's loaded carrot cake, made with a combination of shredded carrots, canned pineapple, sweetened shredded coconut, cinnamon, and raisins (always raisins, never nuts). Using vegetable oil instead of butter in the batter means an out-of-this-world moistness, and a cream cheese frosting tops it off with a bright tang. Though I've tinkered with my mom's recipe slightly over the years, the warm and tropical flavors remain the same.

1 *First, make the cake.* Preheat the oven to 350°F. Line the bottom of two 8-inch round cake pans with parchment paper (see page 23) and grease the sides with nonstick cooking spray.

2 In a medium bowl, whisk together the shredded carrots, eggs, granulated sugar, vegetable oil, pineapple, coconut, raisins, and vanilla extract.

3 In a separate large bowl, whisk together the flour, cinnamon, baking powder, baking soda, and salt. Make a well in the center of the bowl and pour in the wet ingredients. Starting from the center of the bowl, whisk outward, pulling the dry ingredients into the middle. Whisk until no streaks of flour remain.

4 Divide the batter evenly between the prepared pans. Bake until the cakes are golden brown, the tops spring back to the touch, and a butter knife inserted into the centers of the cakes comes out mostly clean (a crumb or two attached is okay), 25 to 30 minutes.

5 Place the cake pans on a cooling rack and allow the cakes to cool slightly. To remove the cakes from the pans, drag a butter knife around the edges of each cake, then carefully flip each cake out onto a plate, peel away the parchment paper, and re-invert each cake, right-side up, onto a cooling rack to cool completely, about 1 hour.

6 *Once the cakes have cooled, make the frosting.* In a stand mixer fitted with the paddle attachment, add the butter and cream cheese and beat on medium speed until well combined. Add the confectioners' sugar, vanilla extract, and salt. Beat on medium speed, scraping down the sides and bottom of the bowl with a silicone spatula as needed, until the frosting is fluffy, about 2 minutes.

7 Place the first cake layer, right-side up, on a plate or cake stand. Spread a large dollop of frosting on top, using an offset spatula to spread a thick layer evenly to the edges. Repeat with the second cake layer and frosting, then frost the sides of the cake with the remaining frosting. Top the cake with walnuts, if using. Cut into slices and serve.

Chocolate Sandwich Cookies

MAKES 22 SANDWICH COOKIES

PREP TIME 30 MINUTES (PLUS 1 HOUR 35 MINUTES CHILL/REST/COOL TIME)
COOK TIME 10 MINUTES
TOTAL TIME 2 HOURS 15 MINUTES

FOR THE COOKIES

1¼ cups all-purpose flour

⅓ cup Dutch-processed cocoa powder, plus more for rolling out the dough

⅓ cup granulated sugar

⅓ cup packed light brown sugar

10 tablespoons (1¼ sticks) unsalted butter, cold and cut into small cubes

1 teaspoon vanilla extract

½ teaspoon salt

FOR THE FILLING

¼ cup (½ stick) unsalted butter or shortening, at room temperature

1 cup confectioners' sugar

1½ teaspoons milk (any dairy or nondairy milk works)

1 teaspoon vanilla extract

Pinch of salt

PRO TIP *When making these cookies, both butter and shortening will work. The butter will make the cookie taste more homemade, but the shortening will taste (and bite) more like a real Oreo!*

If your first reaction to the idea of a homemade Oreo is: *Sounds hard. Why would I take on an already perfect food?* Hold on, stay with me. You—I mean *we*—can do this. We're making a super-simple dark chocolate cookie that replicates that crispy-bitter-buttery-crunch, then a frosting that whips up quickly in the stand mixer. Sandwiching the two together is a fun little activity, and once you have one bite, all that work will be forgotten. And if you choose not to share, you'll get to have the whole batch to yourself, ideally in front of the TV with an open container of peanut butter (or maybe that's just a me thing?).

1 *First, make the cookies.* In a stand mixer fitted with the paddle attachment, combine the flour, cocoa powder, granulated sugar, brown sugar, butter, vanilla extract, and salt. Beat on low speed until the mixture starts to clump together and form a dough, about 3 minutes. (The dough will be crumbly at first, but it will come together as you mix it.)

2 Turn the dough out onto a clean work surface. Use your hands to pat the dough into a flat, oval disk that's about 1-inch thick. Wrap tightly in plastic wrap and place in the fridge for 1 hour or up to 2 days to firm up.

3 Preheat the oven to 325°F. Line two sheet pans with parchment paper.

4 Lightly dust a clean work surface with cocoa powder, unwrap the dough, and place the dough on the surface. Allow the dough to rest on the counter to soften for 5 minutes, then sprinkle more cocoa over the top. Use a rolling pin to roll the dough into a ⅛-inch-thick circle, dusting the top and underside with more cocoa powder as needed to prevent sticking.

5 Use a 1-inch round cookie cutter to cut out circles of dough, then use an offset spatula to transfer them to the prepared sheet pans, spacing them 1 inch apart.

6 Bake until the cookies are fully set and firm around the edges, about 10 minutes. Remove the sheet pans from the oven and allow the cookies to rest on the sheet pans for 5 minutes, then use a metal spatula to transfer the cookies to a cooling rack to cool completely, about 25 minutes more.

7 *Once the cookies have cooled, make the filling.* In a stand mixer fitted with the paddle attachment, combine the butter, confectioners' sugar, milk, vanilla extract, and salt. Beat on low speed to combine, then gradually increase the speed to high and beat until the filling is creamy and combined, about 45 seconds. Do not overbeat the filling; you want it to be dense like an Oreo's cream filling and not too fluffy/airy. Transfer the filling to a piping bag fitted with a small round tip. Pipe about 1 teaspoon of filling onto the underside of a cookie and place a second cookie on top to sandwich. Repeat with the remaining cookies.

Jammy Cherry Pie

MAKES ONE 9-INCH PIE

PREP TIME 1 HOUR (PLUS 3 HOURS 30 MINUTES CHILL/REST TIME)
COOK TIME 50 MINUTES
TOTAL TIME 5 HOURS 20 MINUTES

FOR THE PIE DOUGH

2½ cups all-purpose flour, plus more for rolling out the dough

1 tablespoon granulated sugar

1 teaspoon salt

1 cup (2 sticks) unsalted butter, cold and cut into cubes

3 to 4 tablespoons ice water or chilled vodka (Water is standard in pie crust, but vodka will make your crust extra flaky!)

1 large egg, for egg wash

FOR THE FILLING

2 pounds fresh or frozen sour cherries, stemmed and pitted (about 5 cups)

⅓ cup granulated sugar

2 tablespoons cornstarch, divided

¼ teaspoon salt

2 teaspoons vanilla extract

½ teaspoon ground cinnamon

Cherry pie is that quintessential Americana dessert that's so good it's always getting stolen off windowsills in cartoons. You deserve a recipe that lives up to the hype. What makes this pie so special is a combination of fresh and cooked sour cherries, which are pleasantly acidic and juicy. By cooking down half the cherries, then mixing them with the fresh ones, you end up with both a lusciously jammy texture *and* whole cherries that burst in your mouth as you bite into them. But maybe let it cool on a rack—not a windowsill.

1 *First, make the pie dough.* In a food processor, add the flour, granulated sugar, and salt and pulse to combine. Add the butter and pulse until the mixture resembles wet sand and no chunks of butter remain, about 20 seconds.

2 Add 3 tablespoons of the ice water, then pulse until a dough begins to form a ball around the blade, about 20 seconds. If your dough doesn't come together, add another tablespoon of water and pulse again.

3 Turn the dough out onto a clean work surface and divide it into 2 equal pieces. Flatten each piece into a 1-inch-thick oval disk, then wrap in plastic wrap. Refrigerate for at least 30 minutes and up to 2 days.

4 *Next, make the cherry filling.* In a medium saucepan over medium heat, combine half of the cherries with the granulated sugar, 1 tablespoon of the cornstarch, and the salt. Bring the mixture to a simmer, then reduce the heat to low and cook the cherries down, stirring constantly, until the cherries are broken down and a jammy consistency, about 8 minutes. Remove from the heat and stir in the vanilla extract, cinnamon, the remaining half of the cherries, and the remaining 1 tablespoon cornstarch. Set aside to cool slightly while you roll out your pie dough.

5 Remove both pie disks from the fridge and set on the counter to soften for 5 minutes. Lightly dust a clean work surface with flour, unwrap one disk, and place it on the surface. Dust with more flour and use a rolling pin to roll out the dough into a roughly 12-inch circle, dusting the top and underside with more flour as needed. Carefully roll up the dough around your rolling pin like a scroll, then drape it into a 9-inch pie pan. Press the dough into the bottom and sides of the pie pan, then use scissors to trim around the edges of the dough, leaving a ½-inch overhang.

6 Pour the cherry filling into the pie pan, then set aside while you roll out your second disk. Dust your work surface with more flour and use a rolling pin to roll out the disk into a roughly 12-inch circle, dusting the top and underside with more flour as needed.

(Continued on page 97)

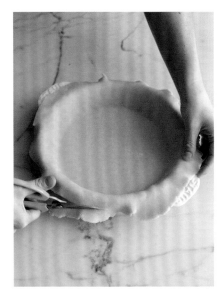

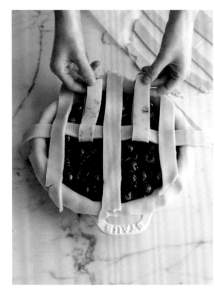
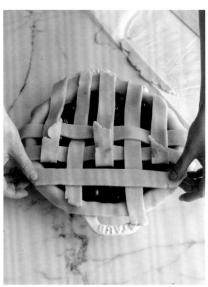

(Continued from page 95)

7 Cut the dough circle into ¾-inch-wide strips. Place half of the strips parallel to one another along the top of the pie, leaving about ½ inch between each strip (see photos opposite). Fold every other strip in half. Place a strip of dough perpendicularly in the middle of the pie, then unfold the strips back over. Next, fold up the strips you haven't folded yet, leaving the first-time folded strips down. Add another strip of dough perpendicularly, then continue this process, alternating with strips of dough you're weaving, until you create a lattice pattern.

8 Use scissors to trim off any excess overhang of dough, then use your fingers to tuck the rim of the dough under itself (be sure to tuck both the bottom pie crust and the lattice strips), creating a thick edge around the rim of the pie pan. Lightly squeeze the edge together using your fingers, sealing it in place. Then use your index finger on one hand and your "peace fingers" on the other hand to create a crimp around the edges of the pie crust.

9 In a small bowl, whisk the egg with 2 tablespoons water. Use a pastry brush to brush the top of the pie with the egg wash. Place the pie in the fridge to chill while your oven preheats (this will keep the pie dough from becoming too soft at room temperature).

10 Preheat the oven to 350°F. Place a large metal sheet pan on the bottom rack of the oven to catch any drips.

11 Place the pie on the middle rack and bake until the crust is golden brown and the cherries are bubbling, about 1 hour. Remove the pie from the oven and allow it to cool on a cooling rack for at least 3 hours, then slice and serve.

Sugar Cookie Bars

MAKES 16 BARS

PREP TIME 30 MINUTES
(PLUS 30 MINUTES COOL TIME)
COOK TIME 25 MINUTES
TOTAL TIME 1 HOUR 25 MINUTES

FOR THE COOKIE BARS

½ cup (1 stick) unsalted butter, at room temperature

1 cup granulated sugar

1 large egg, at room temperature

1 tablespoon milk (any dairy or nondairy milk works)

2 teaspoons vanilla extract

¼ teaspoon almond extract (optional, but adds that true sugar cookie flavor)

1⅔ cups all-purpose flour

½ teaspoon salt

FOR THE FROSTING

½ cup (1 stick) unsalted butter, at room temperature

2 cups confectioners' sugar

2 to 3 tablespoons milk (any dairy or nondairy milk works)

2 teaspoons vanilla extract

½ teaspoon salt

3 tablespoons rainbow sprinkles

Let's skip to the good part. A truly great sugar cookie is all about that chewy, slightly underbaked bottom and a generous layer of vanilla frosting on top. The annoying thing, though, is having to roll and cut out the dough. So here, we embrace the lazy baker inside all of us. Easy and crowd-pleasing, these cookie bars come together almost too fast, which is why I make them only once a month, so that all my other recipes don't get jealous.

1 *First, make the cookie bars.* Preheat the oven to 350°F. Line an 8 × 8-inch square baking pan with parchment paper on all sides (see page 23).

2 In a stand mixer fitted with the paddle attachment, combine the butter and granulated sugar and beat on medium-high speed until light and fluffy, about 2 minutes. Use a silicone spatula to scrape down the sides and bottom of the bowl, then add the egg, milk, vanilla extract, and almond extract (if using). Beat on medium-high speed until the mixture is smooth and combined, about 30 seconds. Scrape down the sides and bottom of the bowl as needed.

3 Add the flour and salt. Mix on low speed until combined and no streaks of flour remain. Transfer the batter to the prepared pan, using the silicone spatula to spread it evenly to the edges.

4 Bake until the bars are golden brown and a butter knife inserted into the center comes out clean, 20 to 25 minutes. Place the pan on a cooling rack and allow the bars to cool slightly in the pan, then use the parchment paper to lift the bars from the pan and place directly on the cooling rack to cool completely, about 30 minutes.

5 *Once the bars have cooled, make the frosting.* In a stand mixer fitted with the paddle attachment, combine the butter and confectioners' sugar. Beat on low speed until combined, so the sugar doesn't fly everywhere. Gradually increase the speed to medium-high and beat until smooth, about 30 seconds. Add 2 tablespoons of the milk, the vanilla extract, and salt. Beat on medium-high speed, scraping down the sides and bottom of the bowl with the silicone spatula as needed, until the frosting is fluffy, about 1 minute. If the frosting is too thick, add another tablespoon of milk.

6 Use an offset spatula or spoon to frost the bars, spreading the frosting into an even layer. Top with sprinkles, cut into 16 squares, and serve.

Giant Peanut Butter Cup

MAKES ONE 9-INCH PEANUT
BUTTER CUP

PREP TIME 30 MINUTES (PLUS 40
MINUTES CHILL TIME)
TOTAL TIME 1 HOUR 10 MINUTES

FOR THE PEANUT BUTTER FILLING

1¼ cups creamy peanut butter
(such as Jif, Skippy, or Peter
Pan—*not* natural peanut butter)

6 tablespoons (¾ stick) unsalted
butter

1½ cups confectioners' sugar

¼ teaspoon salt

FOR THE CHOCOLATE

20 ounces semisweet or
bittersweet chocolate, chopped
into small pieces

2 tablespoons coconut oil
(refined or unrefined works)

I've known my sweet tooth is genetic since the moment my mom declared that she only eats the outsides of Reese's Peanut Butter Cups so she gets "the right chocolate-to-peanut-butter ratio." That's usually when I got to eat the inside of the cup, where the sticky peanut butter overwhelms the chocolate—*my* personal ratio preference—but her conviction stayed with me. So when I decided to create a giant tart-size peanut butter cup, I made sure there was a perfect proportion of chocolate throughout. To make it truly professional looking, I roll out my peanut butter filling and cut it into a circle (sounds difficult, is actually NBD). It's a little trick that goes a long way in making the final cup satisfyingly even. Make sure to snag a slice for yourself before your friends (and maybe your mom) eat every last bite.

1 Line a 9-inch round tart pan with parchment paper (see page 23) and set aside.

2 *Make the peanut butter filling.* In a medium saucepan over low heat, cook the peanut butter and butter until melted, using a silicone spatula to stir occasionally. Remove from the heat and stir in the confectioners' sugar and salt.

3 Place a large rectangle of parchment paper on a work surface, then turn the peanut butter filling out onto the parchment paper. Pretend it's Play-Doh and mold it into a rough circle. Place a sheet of parchment on top, then use a rolling pin to roll the filling into an evenly thick 9½-inch disk (a little bigger than the penciled circle).

4 Place the removable bottom of the tart pan on top of the peanut butter disk (for step-by-step photos, see page 103). Use the tip of a butter knife to press an indentation around the circle. Remove the top piece of parchment paper—there should be a circular trace mark from the knife.

5 Use the tracing to cut the filling into a perfect circle. Peel away the excess peanut butter filling (snack on it or discard—I prefer the former). Set the filling aside.

6 *Next, melt the chocolate.* Line the bottom of the tart pan with parchment paper (see page 23). Fill a medium pot with 1 inch of water and set over high heat until it boils. Reduce the heat to low. In a large heatproof bowl, add the chopped chocolate and set the bowl over the steaming water, creating a double boiler (make sure the bottom of the bowl doesn't touch the hot water). Using a silicone spatula, stir the chocolate occasionally, until the chocolate is fully melted. Remove the bowl from the double boiler and stir in the coconut oil until fully combined.

(Continued on page 102)

(Continued from page 101)

7 Pour roughly one-third of the melted chocolate into the tart pan, then lift it up and tilt it slightly to spread the chocolate evenly around the bottom. Place the pan completely flat in the freezer to firm up for about 20 minutes, and set the remaining melted chocolate aside.

8 Remove the tart pan from the freezer. Flip your peanut butter filling disk (still on the parchment paper) into the middle of the tart, pressing it gently into the chocolate to remove any air between the surfaces (see photos opposite). Remove the parchment paper from the top of the filling.

9 If your remaining chocolate is firmed up, microwave it for 20 seconds to remelt. Pour the melted chocolate over the peanut butter center and use an offset spatula or spoon to smooth the chocolate into an even layer over the top and sides of the peanut butter filling.

10 Place the tart pan back in the freezer to set for about 20 minutes. Once the chocolate has set, carefully remove the tart from the pan (once the chocolate is fully hardened, it should pop out pretty easily) and place on a serving plate. Use a sharp knife to cut into slices and serve.

Oatmeal Cream Cookies

MAKES 16 SANDWICH COOKIES

PREP TIME 30 MINUTES
(PLUS 30 MINUTES COOL TIME)
COOK TIME 11 MINUTES
TOTAL TIME 1 HOUR 11 MINUTES

FOR THE COOKIES

½ cup (1 stick) unsalted butter, at room temperature

1 cup packed light brown sugar

1 tablespoon molasses

1 large egg, at room temperature

1 teaspoon vanilla extract

1¼ cups all-purpose flour

½ cup old-fashioned oats

¾ teaspoon baking soda

½ teaspoon salt

FOR THE VANILLA CREAM FILLING

½ cup (1 stick) unsalted butter, at room temperature

3 cups confectioners' sugar

2 tablespoons heavy cream

2 teaspoons vanilla extract

Pinch of salt

These are a shout-out to Little Debbie's Oatmeal Creme Pies, two impossibly moist oatmeal cookies that sandwich a velvety vanilla "creme" filling (*mmm*, creme). In this uncomplicated and unadulterated copycat, I stayed true to the original flavors, because sometimes original is best. I love all cookies (surprise, surprise), but for me these Oatmeal Cream Cookies are a top-5-of-all-time recipe. An I'll-just-have-one-more recipe. A reason-I-wrote-this-cookbook recipe.

1 *First, make the cookies.* Preheat the oven to 325°F. Line two sheet pans with parchment paper.

2 In a stand mixer fitted with the whisk attachment, add the butter, brown sugar, and molasses and beat on low speed until combined. Gradually increase the speed to medium-high and beat until smooth and homogenous, about 2 minutes.

3 Use a silicone spatula to scrape down the sides and bottom of the bowl, then add the egg and vanilla extract. Beat on medium-high speed until combined.

4 Add the flour, oats, baking soda, and salt and beat on low speed until just combined and no streaks of flour remain.

5 Use a ½-ounce cookie scoop to portion out equal amounts of dough (a tablespoon measure also works). Roll the dough in your hands to smooth the edges, then place 2 inches apart on the prepared sheet pans (you may need to bake in batches).

6 Bake until the cookies have puffed up and are set and firm around the edges but still somewhat soft in the middle, 9 to 11 minutes. Remove the sheet pans from the oven and allow the cookies to rest on the sheet pans for 5 minutes, then use a metal spatula to transfer the cookies to a cooling rack to cool completely, about 25 minutes more.

7 *Once the cookies have cooled, make the filling.* In a stand mixer fitted with the paddle attachment, combine the butter, confectioners' sugar, cream, vanilla extract, and salt. Beat on low speed, gradually increasing the speed to high, until creamy and fully incorporated, about 45 seconds. If the filling is too dry, add a small splash of cream.

8 Once the cookies are completely cool, it's time to assemble. Use a small offset spatula or a butter knife to spread about 2 tablespoons of filling onto the bottom side of one cookie, then place a second cookie on top to sandwich. Repeat with the remaining cookies and serve.

Everybody Loves an Ice Cream Cake

MAKES ONE 9-INCH ICE CREAM CAKE

PREP TIME 30 MINUTES (PLUS 6 HOURS CHILL TIME)
TOTAL TIME 6 HOURS 30 MINUTES

2 cups chocolate wafer cookies (I use Oreo cookies with the cream scraped off)

1 quart (2 pints) vanilla ice cream, softened

8 ounces hot fudge topping, slightly warmed (I like Hershey's)

1 quart (2 pints) chocolate ice cream, softened

3 cups heavy cream

3 cups confectioners' sugar

1 teaspoon vanilla extract

Blue food coloring

Rainbow sprinkles, for topping

PRO TIP *To get superclean slices, warm a sharp knife under hot running water before cutting each slice.*

In high school I worked at an ice cream shop in my hometown, and my favorite part of the job was making ice cream cakes. I'd spend hours scooping ice cream out of giant tubs, pairing flavors together (Oreo + coffee = yes), and learning how to write HAPPY BIRTHDAY in neon icing. This version has layers of vanilla ice cream and ground chocolate wafer cookies mixed with hot fudge sauce and chocolate ice cream, all wrapped in a sweet whipped cream frosting. The final product looks remarkably professional, but make no mistake: ice cream cakes are one of the easiest summer desserts for a crowd.

1   In a food processor or high-powered blender, add the chocolate cookies and pulse until they form sandlike crumbs. You should end up with 1 cup of cookie crumbs; if you have less, pulse a few more cookies.

2   Line a 9-inch springform pan with parchment paper on the bottom (see page 23). Spoon the vanilla ice cream into the pan and use a large spoon or a sturdy spatula to spread it into a flat, even layer.

3   Spoon the warm hot fudge topping over the ice cream, leaving a 1-inch border around the edge (this is so your fudge doesn't seep out later on). Sprinkle the cookie crumbs on top of the hot fudge. Place, uncovered, in the freezer to chill for 15 minutes.

4   Remove the cake from the freezer and spoon the chocolate ice cream over the cookie crumbs, spreading it into a flat, even layer. Cover the entire cake tightly with plastic wrap and place in the freezer to set for at least 6 hours or up to 2 weeks.

5   In a stand mixer fitted with the whisk attachment, add the cream, confectioners' sugar, and vanilla extract. Beat on low speed to combine, so the cream doesn't fly everywhere, then gradually increase the speed to high and whip until medium peaks form.

6   Scoop out roughly one-quarter of the whipped cream and place it in a medium bowl. Use a silicone spatula to fold in the blue food coloring—start with just a few drops; you can always add more. Place the tinted whipped cream in a piping bag fitted with a medium star tip.

7   Remove the frozen ice cream cake from the freezer and carefully open up the springform pan. If the sides aren't pulling away from the cake, turn the springform upside down on a plate and run the sides of the pan under hot water for 5 to 10 seconds. Place the released cake on a cake stand and use an offset spatula to frost the entire cake with the uncolored whipped cream. Place back in the freezer for 15 minutes to firm up.

8   Remove from the freezer and pipe the top of the cake with the remaining blue whipped cream. Top with sprinkles. Place back in the freezer until ready to serve.

FLAVOR VARIATIONS

This ice cream cake works for so many flavor combinations. Here are some of my faves:

DULCE DE LECHE 2 cups Nilla wafers, crushed + dulce de leche middle + vanilla ice cream for both layers

CARAMEL S'MORES 16 graham cracker sheets, crushed (2 cups) + store-bought caramel middle + chocolate ice cream for one layer and vanilla for the other

CHOCOLATE–PEANUT BUTTER PRETZEL 2 cups pretzels, crushed + melted peanut butter middle + chocolate ice cream for one layer and peanut butter for the other

Lunch Lady Brownies

MAKES 16 BROWNIES

PREP TIME 20 MINUTES
(PLUS 30 MINUTES COOL TIME)
COOK TIME 30 MINUTES
TOTAL TIME 1 HOUR 20 MINUTES

FOR THE BROWNIES

1 cup (2 sticks) unsalted butter, melted

⅔ cup Dutch-processed cocoa powder

2 cups packed light brown sugar

4 large eggs, at room temperature

2 teaspoons vanilla extract

2 cups all-purpose flour

1 teaspoon salt

FOR THE ICING

¼ cup (½ stick) unsalted butter

⅓ cup Dutch-processed cocoa powder

2 cups confectioners' sugar

3 tablespoons milk (any dairy or nondairy milk works)

2 teaspoons vanilla extract

Maybe you're the type of person who meal preps a big batch of grains and stuff for a week of lunches—but what about lunch dessert? These brownies are a throwback to the 1990s' school cafeteria, where our lunch ladies (and I hope yours, too) made these super-chewy cocoa brownies topped with a thick layer of chocolate icing that keeps them moist all week. You don't need to eat your lunch on a partitioned tray to deserve a little something sweet to get you through the rest of the day. These brownies are *it*.

1 *First, make the brownies.* Preheat the oven to 350°F. Line a 9 × 13-inch rectangular baking pan with parchment paper on all sides (see page 23).

2 In a large bowl, whisk the melted butter and cocoa powder until smooth and no lumps of cocoa remain. Add the brown sugar and whisk until combined. Add the eggs and vanilla extract and whisk until smooth, about 1 minute.

3 Use a silicone spatula to scrape down the sides and bottom of the bowl, then add the flour and salt and whisk slowly until just combined.

4 Transfer the batter to the prepared baking pan, spreading it evenly to the edges. Bake until the surface is shiny, the edges are set, and a butter knife inserted into the center comes out mostly clean (a crumb or two attached is okay), 25 to 30 minutes. Remove from the oven and place the pan on a cooling rack to cool slightly while you make the icing.

5 *Next, make the icing.* In a microwave-safe bowl, add the butter and microwave until it's half melted (it should be just starting to melt, but still have some unmelted parts), about 30 seconds. Whisk in the cocoa powder, confectioners' sugar, milk, and vanilla extract until smooth.

6 Spread the icing over the brownies while the brownies are still warm, then allow to set until the icing is firm and the brownies are at room temperature, about 30 minutes. Cut the brownies directly from the pan to serve.

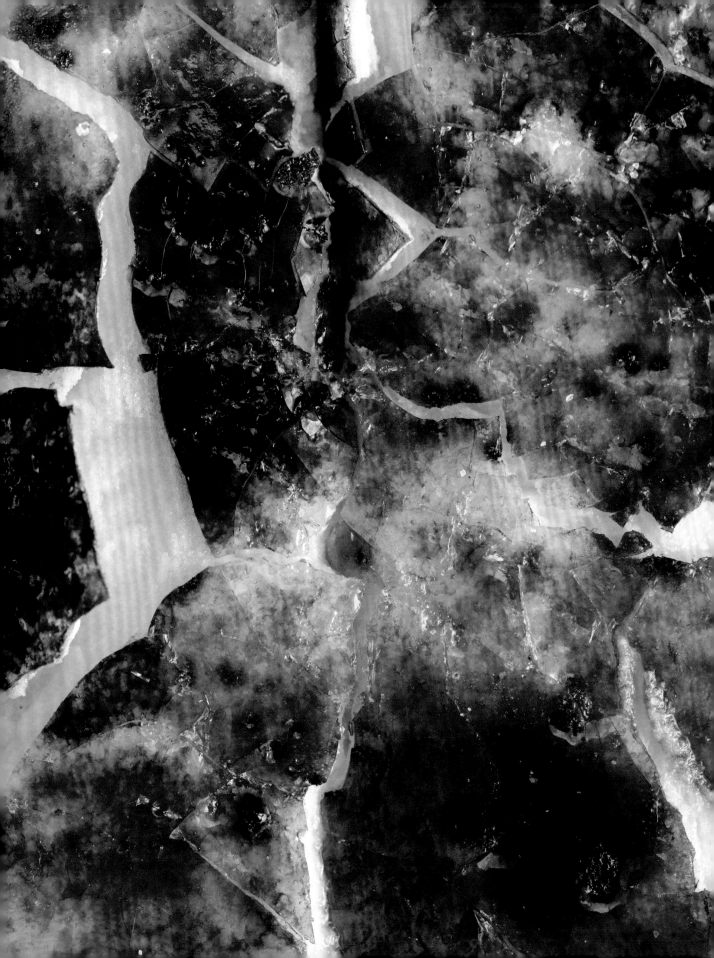

INVEN-TIVE SWEETS

There are only so many times you can bring chocolate chip cookies to the party/potluck/picnic/movie marathon before you start to feel like a one-hit wonder. You've got to keep the people on their toes. Surprise and delight them!

The recipes here do exactly that. They're classic flavors with a creative twist that will have everyone talking (between mouthfuls of Espresso Martini Cake). Forget blueberry pie; let's make Blueberry Pie Cookies. And what if strawberry shortcake was full-on cake-cake? See where I'm going with this? Someplace fun. You'll love it here.

Espresso Martini Cake

PREP TIME 1 HOUR
(PLUS 1 HOUR COOL TIME)
COOK TIME 30 MINUTES
TOTAL TIME 2 HOURS 30 MINUTES

FOR THE CAKE

½ cup (1 stick) unsalted butter, at room temperature

½ cup vegetable oil

1½ cups granulated sugar

4 large eggs, at room temperature

1 tablespoon vanilla extract

2½ cups all-purpose flour

¼ cup Dutch-processed cocoa powder

1 tablespoon instant espresso powder

2½ teaspoons baking powder

1 teaspoon salt

⅔ cup milk (any dairy or nondairy milk works)

⅔ cup coffee liqueur

FOR THE BOOZY COFFEE SYRUP

½ cup granulated sugar

½ cup coffee liqueur

¼ cup vodka

1 teaspoon vanilla extract

FOR THE ESPRESSO FROSTING

1½ cups (3 sticks) unsalted butter, at room temperature

5 cups confectioners' sugar

2 tablespoons instant espresso powder

2 tablespoons milk (any dairy or nondairy milk works)

2 tablespoons coffee liqueur

1 teaspoon vanilla extract

½ teaspoon salt

Espresso beans, for topping (optional)

Espresso martinis—brewed espresso, vodka, and coffee liqueur—are super popular for a reason: they're dangerously delicious. But let's be real, unless you feel like partying until 4 a.m. and nursing a massive hangover the next day, they might not be the drink you want more than one of. This coffee-flavored cake with an espresso frosting and boozy (but not *that* boozy) coffee syrup, on the other hand, is perfect for times you want to keep the party going … until a completely reasonable, responsible bedtime.

1 *First, make the cake.* Preheat the oven to 350°F. Line the bottoms of three 8-inch round cake pans with parchment paper (see page 23) and grease the sides with nonstick cooking spray.

2 In a stand mixer fitted with the whisk attachment, add the butter and vegetable oil and beat on low speed until combined, so the oil doesn't fly everywhere. Gradually increase the speed to medium-high and beat until smooth, about 2 minutes.

3 With the mixer running, slowly pour in the granulated sugar and continue to beat on medium-high speed until the mixture is light, fluffy, and turns a very pale yellow color, about 2 minutes.

4 Use a silicone spatula to scrape down the sides and bottom of the bowl, then add the eggs and vanilla extract. Beat on medium-high speed until the mixture is light and fluffy, about 2 minutes, scraping down the bowl as needed.

5 In a separate bowl, whisk together the flour, cocoa powder, espresso powder, baking powder, and salt. In a third bowl, combine the milk and coffee liqueur. With the mixer on low speed, alternate adding the dry ingredients and the wet ingredients in 3 additions (you'll add half the dry, then all of the wet, then the other half of the dry). It's okay if the batter still has a few lumps in it—you don't want to overmix.

6 Divide the cake batter evenly among the prepared pans. Bake until the cakes have risen, the tops spring back to the touch, and a butter knife inserted into the centers of the cakes comes out mostly clean (a crumb or two attached is okay), 20 to 25 minutes.

7 Place the cake pans on cooling racks and allow them to cool slightly. To remove the cakes from the pans, drag a butter knife around the edges of each cake, then carefully flip each cake out onto a plate, peel away the parchment paper, and re-invert each cake, right-side up, onto the cooling racks to cool completely, about 30 minutes.

(Continued on page 115)

(Continued from page 112)

8 *Once the cakes have cooled, make the coffee syrup.* In a small saucepan over medium heat, combine the granulated sugar, coffee liqueur, and vodka. Bring the mixture to a simmer, stirring constantly with the silicone spatula, until the mixture has thickened and coats the back of the spatula, about 5 minutes. Remove from the heat and stir in the vanilla extract. Set aside to cool, about 30 minutes.

9 *Last, make the frosting.* In a stand mixer fitted with the paddle attachment, combine the butter and confectioners' sugar and beat on low speed for 30 seconds. Add the espresso powder, milk, coffee liqueur, vanilla extract, and salt. Beat on medium speed, scraping down the sides and bottom of the bowl with the silicone spatula as needed, until the frosting is fluffy, about 1 minute.

10 Place the first cake layer on a cake stand or plate. Use a pastry brush to soak the top of the cake with about one-third of the coffee syrup, gently pressing the brush into the cake to help it absorb the syrup. Top with a large dollop of frosting, spreading it evenly to the edges of the cake. Repeat with the second and third cake layers, soaking the cakes in syrup, then topping with frosting. Last, frost the sides of the cake with the remaining frosting. If desired, top with espresso beans.

Coffee Cake Cookies

MAKES 15 COOKIES

PREP TIME 30 MINUTES
COOK TIME 13 MINUTES
TOTAL TIME 43 MINUTES

FOR THE COOKIES

½ cup (1 stick) unsalted butter, at room temperature

½ cup granulated sugar

½ cup packed light brown sugar

1 large egg, at room temperature

2 teaspoons vanilla extract

1¾ cups all-purpose flour

½ teaspoon baking powder

¼ teaspoon baking soda

½ teaspoon salt

FOR THE CINNAMON SWIRL

¼ cup packed light brown sugar

2 teaspoons ground cinnamon

FOR THE STREUSEL

½ cup all-purpose flour

3 tablespoons packed light brown sugar

Pinch of salt

3 tablespoons unsalted butter, melted

FOR THE VANILLA ICING

1 cup confectioners' sugar

3 tablespoons whole milk

½ teaspoon vanilla extract

Pinch of salt

Growing up, there were three desserts my mom loved to bake: brownies (for lunch boxes), cookies (for snacking), and coffee cake (for breakfast). As in, our whole household would snag slices of cinnamon–chocolate chip coffee cake as we headed out the door for school or work. Now, I love to reimagine coffee cake as a cookie. Specifically, a soft brown sugar and cinnamon–swirled cookie topped with a crunchy streusel and vanilla icing. It'll leave you wondering why putting streusel on your cookies isn't standard practice. And for the record, I like them at any time of day.

1 *First, make the cookies.* Preheat the oven to 350°F. Line two sheet pans with parchment paper.

2 In a stand mixer fitted with the paddle attachment, combine the butter, granulated sugar, and brown sugar and beat on medium-high speed until light and fluffy, about 2 minutes.

3 Use a silicone spatula to scrape down the sides and bottom of the bowl, then add the egg and vanilla extract. Beat on medium-high until smooth and fluffy, about 1 minute. Add the flour, baking powder, baking soda, and salt and beat on low speed until just combined and no streaks of flour remain.

4 *Then, mix the cinnamon swirl.* In a small bowl, use a fork to mix together the brown sugar and cinnamon for the swirl. Sprinkle the mixture over the cookie dough, then use the silicone spatula to fold it into the dough a few times. Do not overmix—you'll lose your swirls!

5 *Next, make the streusel.* In a small bowl, combine the flour, brown sugar, and salt. Add the melted butter and use a fork or your fingers to stir everything together until it resembles wet sand and clumps together.

6 Use a 1½-ounce cookie scoop to portion out equal amounts of dough (a large spoon also works; the ball should be about 3 tablespoons). Roll the dough in your hands to smooth the edges, then place 2 inches apart on the prepared sheet pans and flatten the top of the balls gently with your palm. Top each cookie with about 1 teaspoon of streusel topping, gently pressing the streusel into the top and sides of the dough so it sticks. You'll have extra streusel remaining; we'll use that in a bit.

7 Bake the cookies for 6 minutes, then take them out of the oven and sprinkle the remaining streusel on top of each cookie. Return the cookies to the oven and bake until they've puffed up and are set and firm around the edges but still soft in the middle, 6 to 7 minutes more. Remove the sheet pans from the oven and allow the cookies to rest on the pans for 5 minutes, then use a metal spatula to transfer the cookies to a cooling rack to cool completely.

8 *Last, make the icing.* In a small microwave-safe bowl, combine the confectioners' sugar, milk, vanilla extract, and salt and whisk until smooth. The mixture will be thick. Microwave for 15 seconds—this will thin the icing out and help it harden once it dries on top of your cookies. Use a spoon to drizzle the cookies with the icing. Allow the icing to set before serving the cookies.

Lemon Meringue Pie Macarons

MAKES 20 MACARONS

PREP TIME 45 MINUTES (PLUS 45 MINUTES REST/COOL TIME)
COOK TIME 15 MINUTES
TOTAL TIME 1 HOUR 45 MINUTES

FOR THE MACARONS

- 100 grams egg whites
- 75 grams granulated sugar, divided
- ½ teaspoon lemon extract (make sure it's not oil-based)
- 5 to 10 drops yellow food coloring
- Pinch of salt
- 100 grams superfine almond flour
- 100 grams confectioners' sugar
- ¼ cup graham cracker crumbs (about 2 sheets, crumbled)

FOR THE FILLING

- 6 tablespoons (¾ stick) unsalted butter, at room temperature
- 2 cups confectioners' sugar
- 2 tablespoons milk (any dairy or nondairy milk works)
- 1 teaspoon vanilla extract
- Pinch of salt
- ½ cup store-bought lemon curd

No cookie comes close to the transportive experience of biting into a French macaron. This version, with a crispy, airy exterior and lemon curd filling, blends the classic French pastry with Americana flavors. And if you've ever been intimidated about making them at home, let me be your guide. I've perfected my recipe over the years to be nearly foolproof, but you'll need to whip out an electric scale to measure the ingredients in grams (because precision is *key* in macaron-ing). A sprinkle of graham cracker crumbs on top makes these look straight out of a patisserie case, and while you'll definitely impress your friends, you'll impress yourself even more.

1 *First, make the macarons.* Line two sheet pans with parchment paper.

2 Fill a medium saucepan with 1 inch of water and set it over high heat until the water boils. Reduce the heat to low.

3 In the metal bowl of a stand mixer, combine the egg whites and 3 tablespoons of the granulated sugar. Whisk to combine, then place the bowl over the steaming saucepan, creating a double boiler (make sure the bottom of the bowl doesn't touch the hot water—you can also use a regular mixing bowl instead of the stand mixer bowl).

4 Whisk the egg whites and granulated sugar constantly and vigorously until the egg whites become light and frothy, about 1 minute. Remove the bowl from the double boiler and place it on the stand mixer.

5 Fit the stand mixer with the whisk attachment and whisk on high speed while slowly adding in the remaining granulated sugar. Add the lemon extract, food coloring, and salt. Continue to beat until the meringue forms stiff peaks, 3 to 4 minutes. Congratulations, you just made a Swiss meringue!

6 Next, use a fine-mesh sieve to sift together the almond flour and confectioners' sugar, then gently pour the mixture into the meringue bowl. Turn the mixer to medium speed and whisk until combined, no more than 10 seconds.

7 Remove the bowl from the stand mixer and use a silicone spatula to hand mix the batter from here on out. Use your spatula to gently fold the batter from the outside edges into the center in a spiral motion. Repeat this folding technique until you can make a figure-eight out of the batter dripping off the spatula without the batter breaking (it should be long and ribbony). The consistency should be thick, like slow-moving lava. It should give, but only slightly.

(Continued on page 120)

(Continued from page 119)

8 Scoop the batter into a large pastry bag fitted with a ½-inch tip. Pipe 1½-inch circles onto the prepared sheet pans, keeping about 1 inch between each macaron. Bang the sheet pans on the counter 2 or 3 times to remove any air bubbles. Sprinkle the tops of the macarons with a few graham cracker crumbs to garnish. Let the macarons sit on the sheet pans until the tops are dry to the touch, 15 to 30 minutes.

9 While the macarons are drying, preheat the oven to 300°F.

10 Bake the macarons for 15 minutes, turning the sheet pans around halfway through, until the macarons have puffed up, have "feet," and the tops of the macarons have hardened. Remove the sheet pans from the oven and allow the macarons to cool completely on the pans before filling them, about 15 minutes.

11 *Once the macarons have cooled, make the filling.* In a stand mixer fitted with the whisk attachment, add the butter, confectioners' sugar, milk, vanilla extract, and salt and beat on low speed until combined. Gradually increase the speed to medium and beat until light and fluffy, about 1 minute.

12 Scoop the filling into a piping bag fitted with a ¼-inch tip. Pipe a circle around the bottom of a macaron, then use a small spoon (or another piping bag) to dollop about ½ teaspoon lemon curd into the center of the macaron. Sandwich with another macaron. Repeat with all the macarons, then serve.

FLAVOR VARIATIONS

This macaron base works for so many flavor combinations; here are some of my faves.

RASPBERRY MACARONS
Red food coloring + ½ teaspoon almond extract + vanilla filling + raspberry jam middle

PEACH MACARONS
Orange food coloring + ½ teaspoon vanilla extract + vanilla filling + peach jam middle

COOKIE BUTTER MACARONS
No food coloring + cinnamon filling (add 1 teaspoon ground cinnamon to the vanilla filling) + store-bought cookie butter middle

Banoffee Cake

MAKES ONE 3-LAYER 8-INCH CAKE

PREP TIME 1 HOUR (PLUS
30 MINUTES COOL TIME)
COOK TIME 30 MINUTES
TOTAL TIME 2 HOURS

FOR THE CAKE

¾ cup (1½ sticks) unsalted butter,
  at room temperature

1½ cups granulated sugar

3 large eggs, at room
  temperature

2 teaspoons vanilla extract

1½ cups mashed overripe
  bananas (about 3 large)

½ cup full-fat sour cream (plain
  Greek yogurt also works)

2¾ cups all-purpose flour

2 teaspoons baking powder

½ teaspoon baking soda

1 teaspoon ground cinnamon

½ teaspoon salt

1 cup buttermilk (get my
  homemade version on page 28)

FOR THE CREAM CHEESE FROSTING

1 cup (2 sticks) unsalted butter, at
  room temperature

8 ounces cream cheese, at room
  temperature

5½ cups confectioners' sugar

2 teaspoons vanilla extract

½ teaspoon salt

FOR THE REST

2 large bananas, peeled and
  sliced into roughly ¼-inch
  rounds

1 (13-ounce) jar dulce de leche

Banoffee pie is a decadent layered banana and toffee dessert that we have England to thank for (banana + toffee = banoffee). But we're not making homemade crust, caramel, or dealing with water baths here. This cake-ified version is as if banana bread were upgraded into the beautiful layer cake it's always wanted to be, complete with cream cheese frosting and topped with swirls of dulce de leche (store-bought!). It's celebratory and unexpected, which is why it's one of my favorite cakes to make for birthdays.

1 *First, make the cake.* Preheat the oven to 350°F. Line the bottoms of three 8-inch round cake pans with parchment paper (see page 23) and grease the sides with nonstick cooking spray.

2 In a stand mixer fitted with the whisk attachment, combine the butter and granulated sugar and beat on medium-high speed until light and fluffy, about 2 minutes.

3 Use a silicone spatula to scrape down the sides and bottom of the bowl, then add the eggs and vanilla extract and beat on medium-high speed until the mixture is light and fluffy, about 2 minutes. Add the mashed bananas and sour cream (or yogurt) and beat to combine, about 30 seconds.

4 In a separate bowl, whisk together the flour, baking powder, baking soda, cinnamon, and salt. With the mixer on low speed, alternate adding the dry ingredients and the buttermilk in 3 additions (you'll add half the dry, then all of the buttermilk, then the other half of the dry). It's okay if the batter still has a few lumps in it—you don't want to overmix.

5 Divide the cake batter evenly among the prepared pans. Bake until the cakes are risen, the tops spring back to the touch, and a butter knife inserted into the centers of the cakes comes out mostly clean (a crumb or two attached is okay), 25 to 30 minutes

6 Place the cake pans on cooling racks and allow the cakes to cool slightly. To remove the cakes from the pans, drag a butter knife around the edges of each cake, then carefully flip each cake out onto a plate, peel away the parchment paper, and re-invert each cake, right-side up, onto the cooling racks to cool completely, about 30 minutes.

7 *Once the cakes have cooled, make the frosting.* In a stand mixer fitted with the paddle attachment, combine the butter and cream cheese and beat on low speed for 30 seconds. Add the confectioners' sugar, vanilla extract, and salt. Beat on medium speed, scraping down the sides and bottom of the bowl with a silicone spatula as needed, until the frosting is fluffy, about 1 minute. Scoop roughly one-third of the frosting into a large piping bag fitted with a 1-inch tip.

8 Place the first cake layer on a cake stand or plate. Top with about ½ cup of the frosting, spreading the frosting evenly to the edges of the cake. Use the piping bag to pipe a border of frosting around the top of the cake (this helps

PRO TIP *This cake is best served day-of. If you plan to make it ahead of time, omit the banana slices in the cake layers, because they can brown with time.*

keep the dulce de leche filling from coming out the sides). Use a large spoon to dollop ¼ cup of the dulce de leche in the center, spreading it to the edges. Place rounds of banana on top of the dulce de leche. Top with the second cake layer and repeat the process, frosting the top, piping the border, spreading the dulce de leche, and topping with bananas. Top with the third cake layer, then use the remaining frosting to frost the top and sides of the cake.

9 Using an offset spatula or dull knife, dab the remaining dulce de leche randomly along the top and sides of the cake, kind of like putting globs of paint onto a paint palette. Use the offset spatula or knife to gently smear the dabs so that they blend slightly into the frosting.

Strawberry Cheesecake Muffins

MAKES 12 MUFFINS

PREP TIME 45 MINUTES
COOK TIME 23 MINUTES
TOTAL TIME 1 HOUR 8 MINUTES

FOR THE CHEESECAKE SWIRL

8 ounces cream cheese, at room temperature

1 large egg yolk, at room temperature

¼ cup granulated sugar

1 teaspoon vanilla extract

FOR THE STREUSEL

⅔ cup all-purpose flour

¼ cup packed light brown sugar

2 tablespoons granulated sugar

Pinch of salt

¼ cup (½ stick) unsalted butter, melted

FOR THE MUFFINS

½ cup (1 stick) unsalted butter, melted

1 cup granulated sugar

2 large eggs, at room temperature

6 tablespoons full-fat sour cream (plain Greek yogurt also works)

6 tablespoons buttermilk (get my homemade version on page 28)

1 teaspoon vanilla extract

2 cups all-purpose flour

1 tablespoon baking powder

½ teaspoon salt

2 cups quartered fresh strawberries

⅓ cup strawberry preserves

Too many muffins are what I call *meh* muffins: dry, crumbly, *meh*. These Strawberry Cheesecake Muffins are my antidote. A fluffy vanilla muffin base folded with fresh strawberries, swirled with cheesecake batter *and* strawberry preserves, and topped with brown sugar streusel. They're maximalist muffins, through and through. The juicy strawberries, plus the cheesecake and jam, hydrate the batter and ensure there isn't a dry bite in the building.

1 Preheat the oven to 425°F. Line the muffin cups of a standard muffin tin with muffin liners, then spray the muffin liners and the top of the tin with nonstick cooking spray.

2 *First, make the cheesecake swirl.* In a medium bowl, whisk the cream cheese, egg yolk, granulated sugar, and vanilla extract until smooth and no lumps remain. Set aside.

3 *Next, make the streusel.* In a medium bowl, combine the flour, brown sugar, granulated sugar, and salt. Add the melted butter and use a fork or your fingers to stir everything together until it resembles wet sand and clumps together. Set aside.

4 *Then, make the muffins.* In a large bowl, whisk the melted butter and granulated sugar until combined. Add the eggs, sour cream (or yogurt), buttermilk, and vanilla extract and whisk until well combined.

5 Add the flour, baking powder, and salt. Use a silicone spatula to fold until combined and no streaks of flour remain. Gently fold in the strawberries. Drop large spoonfuls of strawberry preserves into the batter and use the silicone spatula to fold the preserves into the batter once or twice, creating streaks of preserves. Do not overmix—you want the batter to be marbled.

6 Scoop the batter evenly into the muffin cups, filling about three-quarters of each cup. If you want to get fancy, use a 3-ounce cookie scoop to create evenly domed scoops.

7 Spoon about 1 tablespoon of the cheesecake mixture on top of each muffin, then use a toothpick, chopstick, or butter knife to drag the cheesecake through the muffin batter, creating a swirl. Sprinkle about 1 tablespoon of the streusel topping on top of each muffin, pressing it in gently with your fingers so it doesn't fall off when baked.

8 Bake the muffins for 5 minutes at 425°F, then reduce the oven temperature to 375°F. Continue baking until the tops of the muffins are golden brown and spring back to the touch, about 18 minutes more. Place the muffin tin on a cooling rack and allow the muffins to cool slightly in the pan before serving.

Tiramisu Icebox Cake

MAKES ONE 8 × 8-INCH CAKE

PREP TIME 30 MINUTES
(PLUS 4 HOURS CHILL TIME)
TOTAL TIME 4 HOURS 30 MINUTES

3 cups heavy cream

1 cup confectioners' sugar

1 teaspoon vanilla extract

16 ounces mascarpone cheese, at room temperature

2 cups strongly brewed coffee

2 tablespoons granulated sugar

2 tablespoons dark rum

1 (14.4-ounce) box graham crackers (3 wrapped sleeves)

Dutch-processed cocoa powder, for topping

Icebox cakes are my summer secret weapon. These no-bake refrigerator cakes from the 1930s consist of layers of cookie wafers and whipped cream that blur the line between cake and ice cream. It's a dessert that's creamy yet light, refreshing, and a little retro. This tiramisu version uses rum and coffee–soaked graham crackers that get cushioned by clouds of mascarpone cream—all we could ever want after dinner, right?

1 Line an 8 × 8-inch square baking pan with plastic wrap or parchment paper on all sides (see page 23).

2 In a stand mixer fitted with the whisk attachment, add the cream, confectioners' sugar, and vanilla extract and beat on low speed until combined, so the cream doesn't fly everywhere. Gradually increase the speed to high and beat until medium peaks form, about 2 minutes. Add the mascarpone and beat on low speed until smooth and combined, about 30 seconds.

3 In a shallow, wide bowl, combine the coffee, granulated sugar, and rum. Quickly dip the graham cracker sheets into the coffee mixture one at a time (otherwise they'll get soggy and fall apart!), then layer them in a single layer in the bottom of the prepared pan (you may need to break apart a few graham cracker sheets to fully cover the bottom of the pan).

4 Scoop 1 cup of the mascarpone whipped cream mixture on top of the graham crackers and use a silicone spatula to spread it evenly to the edges. Repeat this layering process of soaked graham crackers and 1 cup mascarpone whipped cream so you end up with 5 layers of graham crackers and 5 layers of mascarpone whipped cream, with the mascarpone whipped cream being the top layer.

5 Transfer the remaining mascarpone whipped cream to a piping bag fitted with a 1-inch round tip (if you don't have a piping bag, place the filling in a large resealable plastic bag and cut off a corner with scissors). Pipe 1-inch circles of mascarpone whipped cream over the entire surface of the cake.

6 Place the pan, uncovered, in the fridge to chill for at least 4 hours and up to 2 days (if serving longer than 4 hours away, refrigerate the cake, uncovered, for 4 hours, then lightly cover it with plastic wrap). When you're ready, take the cake out of the fridge, generously dust the top of the cake with cocoa powder, slice it, and serve.

White Chocolate Brownies

MAKES 9 BROWNIES

PREP TIME 15 MINUTES
COOK TIME 30 MINUTES
TOTAL TIME 45 MINUTES

½ cup (1 stick) unsalted butter

1 cup white chocolate chips

1 (14-ounce) can sweetened condensed milk

1 large egg, at room temperature

1 tablespoon vanilla extract

1 teaspoon salt

1½ cups all-purpose flour

Confectioners' sugar, for topping

Some people (not me, but some) prefer white chocolate to regular chocolate, and those people deserve a brownie as much as the rest of us. Make no mistake: these aren't blondies. Blondies are pretty much cookie dough that's spread into bar form. These white chocolate brownies have the consistency of a chewy, dense brownie, but with the milkier flavor profile of white chocolate. Plus, if you let them cool in the fridge, they'll take on an even fudgier texture. While I made these for the white chocolate lovers, I admit that I do have room in my heart for them, too. Lots of room.

1 Preheat the oven to 350°F. Line an 8 × 8-inch square baking pan with parchment paper on all sides (see page 23).

2 In a large microwave-safe bowl, combine the butter and white chocolate chips. Microwave for 20 seconds, then remove from the microwave and use a silicone spatula to stir. Repeat, microwaving in 20-second increments and stirring after each, until the white chocolate is fully melted. Remove the bowl from the microwave.

3 Using the silicone spatula, stir in the sweetened condensed milk, egg, vanilla extract, and salt. Fold in the flour, mixing until just combined. Scrape the batter into the prepared pan, spreading it evenly to the edges and smoothing out the top.

4 Bake until the brownies have puffed up in the center, have taken on a pale color, and a butter knife inserted into the center of the brownies comes out mostly clean (a crumb or two attached is okay), 25 to 30 minutes. Place the pan on a cooling rack and allow the brownies to cool completely in the pan. Use the parchment paper to lift the brownies from the pan, then transfer them to a cutting board. Dust the top with confectioners' sugar, then cut into 9 squares and serve.

Blueberry Pie Cookies

PREP TIME 25 MINUTES
COOK TIME 30 MINUTES
TOTAL TIME 55 MINUTES

1 unbaked store-bought pie crust

½ cup (1 stick) unsalted butter,
  at room temperature

½ cup granulated sugar

½ cup packed light brown sugar

1 large egg, at room temperature

2 teaspoons vanilla extract

1⅔ cups all-purpose flour

¾ teaspoon baking powder

¼ teaspoon baking soda

½ teaspoon salt

1 cup frozen blueberries

I love pie. I include recipes for three in this very book. But hey, I admit, making, chilling, rolling, and crimping pie dough, cooking your filling to the exact right consistency, then getting that glowing, golden crust . . . can be a lot of work! But pie is beloved. Pie is life. Therefore, pie must be had. These salty-sweet Blueberry Pie Cookies have a chewy brown sugar cookie base and are bursting with blueberries and crunchy pie crust pieces (made from store-bought dough). These are throw-together cookies that never fail to blow people's minds—"Is that pie crust in here?!"—and bring in the big bucks at bake sales. If blueberries aren't your thing, try these with raspberries, blackberries, or even apples.

1 Preheat the oven to 350°F. Line two sheet pans with parchment paper.

2 Unroll the store-bought pie crust, place it flat on one of the sheet pans, and bake until golden brown and fully cooked, 12 to 15 minutes. Allow it to cool slightly, then use your hands to break the crust into dime-size pieces. Measure out 1 cup of pieces to go into your cookie batter later (sprinkle the leftovers into your oatmeal or yogurt—you're welcome). Set the sheet pan aside (with the parchment still on it) to bake the cookies on later.

3 In a stand mixer fitted with the paddle attachment, beat together the butter, granulated sugar, and brown sugar on low speed until combined. Gradually increase the speed to medium-high and beat until light and fluffy, about 2 minutes.

4 Add the egg and vanilla extract. Beat on medium-high speed until the mixture is smooth and combined, about 1 minute, scraping down the sides and bottom of the bowl as needed.

5 Add the flour, baking powder, baking soda, and salt and beat on low speed until just combined and no streaks of flour remain.

6 Remove the bowl from the stand mixer and use a silicone spatula to fold in the blueberries and the 1 cup of pie crust pieces, mixing gently until just combined.

7 Use a 1½-ounce cookie scoop to portion out equal amounts of dough (a large spoon also works; the ball should be about 3 tablespoons). Roll the dough in your hands to smooth the edges, then place the dough balls 2 inches apart on the prepared sheet pans.

8 Bake until the cookies have puffed up and are set and firm around the edges but still somewhat soft in the middle, 12 to 15 minutes. Remove the sheet pans from the oven, allow the cookies to cool completely on the sheet pans, then serve.

No-Churn Peach Crumble Ice Cream

MAKES 1 QUART ICE CREAM

PREP TIME 45 MINUTES (PLUS 8 HOURS CHILL TIME)
COOK TIME 30 MINUTES
TOTAL TIME 9 HOURS 15 MINUTES

FOR THE CRUMBLE

½ cup all-purpose flour

¼ cup packed light brown sugar

⅛ teaspoon salt

3 tablespoons unsalted butter, melted

FOR THE PEACH SWIRL

2 medium peaches, peeled, pitted, and cut into small cubes, or 8 ounces frozen chopped peaches

¼ cup packed light brown sugar

¼ cup water

2 tablespoons bourbon

FOR THE ICE CREAM

2 cups heavy cream

1 (14-ounce) can sweetened condensed milk

1 tablespoon vanilla extract

¼ teaspoon salt

If you haven't made no-churn ice cream, welcome to the first day of the rest of your life. Whereas many traditional ice cream recipes require an egg custard base and an ice cream machine, no-churn ice cream is their low-maintenance twin. All you have to do is combine lightly whipped heavy cream and sweetened condensed milk, then freeze to create practically the same creamy consistency as churned ice cream. Science, baby! Here I add juicy summer peaches and a buttery crumble topping; it's kind of the inverted version of a peach crisp à la mode.

1 *First, make the crumble.* Preheat the oven to 350°F. Line a sheet pan with parchment paper.

2 In a small bowl, combine the flour, brown sugar, and salt. Add the melted butter and use a fork or your fingers to stir everything together until the mixture resembles wet sand and clumps together.

3 Spread the crumble into an even layer on the prepared sheet pan and bake until golden brown, about 15 minutes. Place the sheet pan on a cooling rack to cool completely.

4 *While the crumble bakes, make the peach swirl.* In a saucepan over medium-low heat, combine the peaches, brown sugar, water, and bourbon. Cook the mixture, stirring constantly with a silicone spatula, until the peaches have broken down completely, about 15 minutes. Remove the pan from the heat and set aside to cool, about 30 minutes.

5 *Then, mix the ice cream.* In a stand mixer fitted with the whisk attachment, add the cream and beat on low speed, gradually increasing the speed to high, until soft peaks form, about 1 minute.

6 Remove the bowl from the stand mixer and add the sweetened condensed milk, vanilla extract, and salt. Use the silicone spatula to gently fold until combined and no streaks of condensed milk remain.

7 Spoon half of the ice cream mixture into a quart container (a plastic container works well, so does a 1-pound loaf pan or a paper ice cream container). Spoon half the peach mixture over the ice cream, then top with half of the crumble. Repeat the process, topping with the second halves of the ice cream, peaches, and crumble. Use a butter knife to gently swirl everything together (this will create ribbons of peach and crumble through your ice cream). Cover tightly with plastic wrap and place in the freezer to set for at least 8 hours before serving. When tightly covered, the ice cream will keep in the freezer for up to 2 months.

FLAVOR VARIATIONS

This vanilla ice cream base works for so many flavor combinations. Keep the crumble and swap the peach swirl in favor of:

STRAWBERRY CRUMBLE ICE CREAM ½ cup strawberry jam

PUMPKIN PIE ICE CREAM ½ cup pumpkin butter

APPLE CRUMBLE ICE CREAM ¾ cup apple pie filling

S'MORES ICE CREAM ¼ cup hot fudge sauce + ¼ cup Marshmallow Fluff

Cinnamon Roll Cookies

MAKES 14 COOKIES

PREP TIME 30 MINUTES (PLUS 1 HOUR 20 MINUTES CHILL TIME)
COOK TIME 10 MINUTES
TOTAL TIME 2 HOURS

FOR THE COOKIE DOUGH

½ cup (1 stick) unsalted butter, at room temperature

½ cup packed light brown sugar

1 large egg, at room temperature

1 teaspoon vanilla extract

1¼ cups all-purpose flour, plus more for rolling out the dough

1 teaspoon baking powder

½ teaspoon ground cinnamon

¼ teaspoon salt

FOR THE CINNAMON SUGAR FILLING

2 tablespoons (¼ stick) unsalted butter, melted

¼ cup packed light brown sugar

2 teaspoons ground cinnamon

FOR THE CREAM CHEESE ICING

1 tablespoon cream cheese

2 tablespoons milk (any dairy milk works)

1 cup confectioners' sugar

1 teaspoon vanilla extract

Pinch of salt

I've described these as "if sugar cookies and cinnamon rolls had a baby," and I stand by that. They're buttery cookies slathered in cinnamon sugar, then rolled into a spiral that you easily slice and bake. And it wouldn't be complete without a drizzle of cream cheese icing on top, which makes them as much of a party to look at as they are to eat. The way these cookies satisfy two of my sugary loves is heaven on earth to me, which is why I had to test and retest these . . . so many times.

1 *First, make the cookie dough.* In a stand mixer fitted with the paddle attachment, combine the butter and brown sugar and beat on medium-high speed until light and fluffy, about 2 minutes. Add the egg and vanilla extract. Beat on medium-high until the mixture is fluffy and pale in color, about 1 minute.

2 Stop the mixer and scrape down the bowl, then add the flour, baking powder, cinnamon, and salt and beat on low speed until just combined and no streaks of flour remain.

3 Set the cookie dough onto a large sheet of plastic wrap, lightly pat it into a flat rectangle (the size doesn't matter, just get it rectangle-shaped), then wrap it fully in the plastic and refrigerate until it's firm, about 1 hour.

4 *Once the dough is chilled, make the filling.* In a small bowl, use a silicone spatula to mix the melted butter, brown sugar, and cinnamon until combined. The mixture should resemble wet sand.

5 Place a large rectangle of plastic wrap on a work surface and dust it with flour. Unwrap the chilled dough and place it on the surface. Use a rolling pin to roll out the dough into an 8 × 11-inch rectangle, dusting the top with more flour as needed. Use an offset spatula or knife to spread the filling on top of the dough all the way to the edges.

6 Working from the short side of your dough, roll the dough into a tight log, using the plastic wrap beneath the dough to lift it up and into a spiral. Wrap the log tightly in the plastic wrap, roll it on the counter a little to seal the edges, and place in the freezer until it's firm to the touch, about 20 minutes.

7 While the dough firms up, preheat the oven to 350°F. Line two sheet pans with parchment paper. Once the dough is firm, remove it from the freezer. Using a sharp knife, slice off the ends of the log, then slice the log into ½-inch-thick cookies. Place the cookies 2 inches apart on the prepared sheet pans.

8 Bake until the cookies have puffed up and are light golden brown all over, 9 to 10 minutes. Remove the sheet pans from the oven and allow the cookies to rest on the sheet pans for 5 minutes, then use a metal spatula to transfer the cookies to a cooling rack to cool slightly while you make the icing.

9 *Last, make the cream cheese icing.* In a small microwave-safe bowl, add the cream cheese. Microwave until it's very soft, about 15 seconds. Whisk in the milk, confectioners' sugar, vanilla extract, and salt. Drizzle the icing over the cookies and allow the icing to set before serving.

Coconut Caramel Thumbprint Cookies

MAKES 22 COOKIES

PREP TIME 40 MINUTES
COOK TIME 20 MINUTES
TOTAL TIME 1 HOUR

¾ cup sweetened shredded coconut

1 cup (2 sticks) unsalted butter, at room temperature

¾ cup granulated sugar

¼ cup packed light brown sugar

2 teaspoons vanilla extract

1 large egg, at room temperature

2⅔ cups all-purpose flour

½ teaspoon salt

20 soft caramels, unwrapped

3 tablespoons heavy cream

4 ounces semisweet or bittersweet chocolate, coarsely chopped

Flaky sea salt, for topping (optional)

Everyone loves Samoas Girl Scout cookies, but they're nowhere to be found in the height of cookie season—the holidays! Let's right that wrong. And while I've tried to make them religiously true-to-form before, I wouldn't wish that labor on my worst enemies. This recipe takes a few shortcuts but retains the cookies' ingenious layering of buttery short-bread, drizzles of chocolate and caramel, and toasty coconut. It's instantly recognizable, and instantly devour-able.

1 Preheat the oven to 350°F. Line two sheet pans with parchment paper.

2 Spread the shredded coconut evenly onto one of the sheet pans. Bake until light golden brown, 5 to 7 minutes, stirring halfway through. Transfer the toasted coconut to a small bowl and set the sheet pan aside—you can bake the cookies on it later.

3 In a stand mixer fitted with the paddle attachment, beat the butter, granulated sugar, brown sugar, and vanilla extract on low speed until combined. Gradually increase the speed to medium-high and beat until light and fluffy, about 2 minutes.

4 Separate the egg yolk from the egg white. Add the yolk to the batter (reserve the white for later). Beat the batter on medium-high speed until the mixture is smooth and combined, about 1 minute. Add the flour and salt to the bowl and beat on low speed until just combined and no streaks of flour remain. The dough will be dry.

5 Use a 1-ounce cookie scoop to portion out equal amounts of dough (a large spoon also works; the ball should be about 2 tablespoons). Roll the dough in your hands to smooth the edges. Dip each dough ball in the reserved egg white, then roll the dough in the toasted coconut, evenly coating the outside of the ball. Place the dough balls 1 inch apart on the prepared sheet pans. Firmly press your thumb into the center of each cookie, making an indent. Bake the cookies for 5 minutes while you heat up your caramel.

6 In a small microwave-safe bowl, combine the caramels and cream. Microwave for 30 seconds, then whisk to combine. If the caramels are not fully melted, microwave for 30 seconds more and whisk again.

7 Once the cookies have baked for 5 minutes, remove them from the oven and place on a heatproof surface. Spoon about ½ teaspoon of the caramel mixture into the indentation in each cookie, then return the cookies to the oven. Bake until the cookies are light golden brown and are set and firm around the edges, 6 to 8 minutes more. Remove the sheet pans from the oven and allow the cookies to cool completely on the sheet pans.

8 Once the cookies have cooled, melt the chocolate. In a small microwave-safe bowl, add the chopped chocolate, and microwave in 15-second increments, using a silicone spatula to stir between each, until the chocolate is fully melted. Use a small spoon to drizzle the melted chocolate over the cookies, top with flakey sea salt (if using), and allow the chocolate to set before serving.

Strawberry Shortcake Cake

MAKES ONE 8-INCH CAKE

PREP TIME 30 MINUTES (PLUS
45 MINUTES COOL TIME)
COOK TIME 40 MINUTES
TOTAL TIME 1 HOUR 55 MINUTES

FOR THE CAKE

2 cups all-purpose flour

1 cup granulated sugar

1 tablespoon plus 1 teaspoon
baking powder

½ teaspoon salt

½ cup (1 stick) unsalted butter,
cold and cut into cubes

1 cup whole milk

1 teaspoon vanilla extract

¼ cup Demerara sugar (optional)

FOR THE STRAWBERRIES AND
WHIPPED CREAM

1 pint fresh strawberries, hulled
and cut into thin slices

2 tablespoons granulated sugar

1 cup heavy cream

2 tablespoons confectioners'
sugar

1 teaspoon vanilla extract

This recipe comes from the brilliant mind of Sofi's (the second-in-command at *Broma Bakery*) mom, Cathy. One day, Sofi came into work with the idea of re-creating her mom's Strawberry Shortcake Cake, which tastes like the love child of a shortcake biscuit and the best vanilla cake you've ever had. She uses an eggless biscuit technique to create a wonderfully unique texture that's crunchy on the top and sublimely tender in the middle. Top that baby with whipped cream and a heaping pile of lightly macerated strawberries and you've got your new summer blockbuster.

1 *First, make the cake.* Preheat the oven to 350°F. Line the bottom of an 8-inch round cake pan with parchment paper (see page 23) and grease the sides with nonstick cooking spray.

2 In a large bowl, add the flour, granulated sugar, baking powder, and salt and whisk to combine. Use a pastry cutter or your fingers to work the butter into the dry ingredients until the mixture starts to clump together and resembles wet sand.

3 Make a well in the center of the bowl and pour in the milk and vanilla extract. Use a silicone spatula to fold everything together into a thick, lumpy batter.

4 Transfer the batter to the prepared pan and use the silicone spatula to spread it all the way to the edges. Sprinkle the top with Demerara sugar (if using). Bake until the cake is puffed up, lightly golden brown on top, and a butter knife inserted into the center comes out mostly clean (a crumb or two attached is okay), 35 to 40 minutes.

5 Place the cake pan on a cooling rack and allow the cake to cool completely in the pan, about 45 minutes. To remove the cake from the pan, drag a butter knife around the edges of the cake, then carefully flip the cake out onto a plate, peel away the parchment paper, and re-invert the cake, right-side up, onto a serving plate.

6 *Last, prepare the strawberries and make the whipped cream.* In a medium bowl, toss together the strawberries and granulated sugar. Set aside while you whip your cream.

7 In a stand mixer fitted with the whisk attachment, beat the cream, confectioners' sugar, and vanilla extract on low speed until combined, so the cream doesn't fly everywhere. Gradually increase the speed to high and mix until medium peaks form and the whipped cream holds its shape, about 1 minute. Spoon the whipped cream over the top of the cake and top with the strawberries. Serve immediately.

Crème Brûlée
Cheesecake Bars

MAKES 16 BARS

PREP TIME 30 MINUTES (PLUS
3 HOURS 30 MINUTES COOL/CHILL
TIME)
COOK TIME 40 MINUTES
TOTAL TIME 4 HOURS 40 MINUTES

FOR THE CRUST

1½ cups graham cracker crumbs
(about 12 sheets, crumbled)

½ cup (1 stick) unsalted butter,
melted

5 tablespoons granulated sugar

¼ teaspoon salt

FOR THE CHEESECAKE

16 ounces cream cheese (two
8-ounce blocks), at room
temperature

½ cup full-fat sour cream, at
room temperature

1 cup granulated sugar, divided,
plus more as needed

2 large eggs, at room
temperature

1 tablespoon vanilla extract

½ teaspoon salt

PRO TIP *These bars
are best served right
after brûlée-ing, as the
sugar will soak into
the bars over time.*

If it were up to me, I'd brûlée everything. And since this book is up to me, we're doing it: we're brûlée-ing cheesecake bars (hey, if you've bought a kitchen torch, you want to use it as much as possible). These bars have a feel similar to traditional crème brûlée, with a creamy base and a slightly smoky, caramelized top. But they're less delicate and more party-friendly. Plus, the cheesecake's graham cracker crust gives the whole dessert a s'mores vibe, no campfire required.

1 *First, make the crust.* Adjust the oven racks to the lower third and middle of the oven. Fill a large baking dish with 2 inches of water and place on the bottom rack of your oven. Preheat the oven to 325°F. Line a 9 × 9-inch square baking pan with parchment paper on all sides (see page 23).

2 In a medium bowl, combine the graham cracker crumbs, melted butter, sugar, and salt. Use a silicone spatula to mix until the mixture begins to clump together and resembles wet sand. Transfer the mixture to the prepared pan and use a measuring cup (or something else with a flat bottom) to really pack the crust into an even layer.

3 *Next, make the cheesecake.* In a stand mixer fitted with the paddle attachment, combine the cream cheese, sour cream, and ¾ cup of the granulated sugar on medium-low speed until smooth, about 30 seconds.

4 Add the eggs, vanilla extract, and salt. Beat on medium-low speed until the batter is smooth, about 45 seconds, scraping down the sides and bottom of the bowl as needed.

5 Transfer the batter to the prepared pan and smooth it out to an even layer. Place the pan on the middle rack of the oven. Bake until the cheesecake is puffed up slightly and set around the edges but still a little wobbly in the center, 35 to 40 minutes.

6 Turn off the oven and open the oven door a crack. Leave the cheesecake in the turned-off oven for 30 minutes (this allows the cheesecake to cool down gradually and helps to prevent cracks). Remove the cheesecake from the oven and run a butter knife along the outer edge to separate it from the sides of the pan. Transfer the cheesecake, still in the pan, to the fridge to cool completely, about 3 hours and up to overnight.

7 Once the cheesecake is chilled, remove it from the fridge, use the parchment paper to lift the cheesecake from the pan, then carefully slide the cheesecake off of the parchment paper and onto a heatproof surface (such as a sheet pan).

8 Sprinkle the remaining ¼ cup granulated sugar over the cheesecake's surface. Use a kitchen torch to caramelize the sugar, moving the torch around constantly so as not to burn the sugar. Use the back of a large spoon to lightly "crack" the sugar on top before cutting the cheesecake into 16 bars.

Cherry Danish Cake

MAKES ONE 9 × 13-INCH CAKE

PREP TIME 25 MINUTES
COOK TIME 45 MINUTES
TOTAL TIME 1 HOUR 10 MINUTES

FOR THE CAKE

½ cup (1 stick) unsalted butter, at room temperature

⅔ cup granulated sugar

2 large eggs, at room temperature

2 teaspoons vanilla extract

½ teaspoon almond extract

1⅓ cups full-fat sour cream (plain Greek yogurt also works)

1½ cups all-purpose flour

1 tablespoon baking powder

½ teaspoon salt

¾ cup cherry jam or preserves of choice

¼ cup sliced almonds, for topping

FOR THE CREAM CHEESE ICING

2 tablespoons cream cheese, at room temperature

1 cup confectioners' sugar

2 tablespoons whole milk

½ teaspoon vanilla extract

⅛ teaspoon salt

Cherry Danishes are one of those desserts that I'll immediately point to at the bakery case but that I don't want to attempt to make at home. Braid puff pastry? I can barely braid my own hair, thank you. And while I'm being a little dramatic, turns out that nonconfrontation leads to innovation: this Cherry Danish Cake. It's 100% of the flavors and 10% of the work. It's a buttery vanilla cake swirled with cherry jam and topped with a cream cheese icing and sliced almonds, just like a traditional Danish. And yet, it's cake. Heaven.

1 *First, make the cake.* Preheat the oven to 350°F. Line a 9 × 13-inch rectangular baking pan with parchment paper on all sides (see page 23).

2 In a stand mixer fitted with the paddle attachment, combine the butter and granulated sugar and beat on medium-high speed until light and fluffy, about 2 minutes.

3 Use a silicone spatula to scrape down the sides and bottom of the bowl. Add the eggs, vanilla extract, and almond extract and beat until smooth. Add the sour cream (or yogurt) and beat until combined.

4 Add the flour, baking powder, and salt. Beat on low speed until combined and no streaks of flour remain. The batter will be thick. Transfer the batter to your prepared pan and use the silicone spatula to spread it evenly to the edges.

5 Drop 10 to 12 spoonfuls of the cherry jam on top of the cake batter. Use a butter knife to swirl the jam into the batter.

6 Bake until the cake is lightly golden brown on top and a butter knife inserted into the center of the cake comes out mostly clean (a crumb or two attached is okay), 40 to 45 minutes. Place the pan on a cooling rack and allow the cake to cool slightly in the pan.

7 *Last, make the cream cheese icing.* In a medium bowl, whisk the cream cheese, confectioners' sugar, milk, vanilla extract, and salt until combined. If the mixture is too thick, put it in the microwave for 10 to 15 seconds. Use the parchment paper to lift the cake from the pan, then transfer the cake to a cutting board. Drizzle the icing over the warm cake, then sprinkle with sliced almonds before slicing and serving.

BRUNCH BAKES

Sunday morning is arguably the best time to bake. You've slept in, you've got the whole day ahead of you, and you deserve something fluffy, glazed, and/or streusel-ed. Well, this chapter delivers. From Blueberry Pancakes and Pistachio Croissants to coffee-dunking donuts and irresistible Vanilla Bean–Blackberry Scones, there's a range of brunch classics and modern twists, none of which require your changing out of your pajamas.

Vanilla Bean–Blackberry Scones

MAKES 8 SCONES

PREP TIME 40 MINUTES
COOK TIME 25 MINUTES
TOTAL TIME 1 HOUR 5 MINUTES

FOR THE SCONES

2 vanilla beans

½ cup granulated sugar

2 cups all-purpose flour, plus
  more for rolling out the dough

1 tablespoon baking powder

½ teaspoon salt

½ cup (1 stick) unsalted butter,
  cold and cut into small cubes

6 tablespoons full-fat sour cream
  (plain Greek yogurt also works)

6 to 8 tablespoons heavy cream,
  plus more for brushing

2 teaspoons vanilla extract

1½ cups frozen blackberries
  (if your blackberries are huge,
  cut your large ones in half)

FOR THE VANILLA BEAN GLAZE

1 vanilla bean

1 cup confectioners' sugar

2 tablespoons whole milk

1 teaspoon vanilla extract

Pinch of salt

PRO TIP *If you can't
find frozen blackberries,
buy fresh ones and freeze
them ahead of time.
You can also use fresh
blackberries, but frozen
ones hold up a lot
better when folded into
your scone dough.*

Scones are the PR nightmare of the dessert world. They have a rep for being dry, crumbly messes that get everywhere (please tell me I'm not the only one who's found scone crumbs in her bra). But in reality, when you bite into the *right* scone, it can be a dream: pockets of butter folded into flour create layers of flaky pastry that's crunchy on the outside and pillowy soft on the inside—sweeter than a biscuit, less sweet than a muffin. Here, vanilla beans create a more present flavor than vanilla extract can on its own, while the addition of sour cream keeps the scones tender and moist.

1 *First, make the scones.* Preheat the oven to 400°F. Line a sheet pan with parchment paper.

2 Use a paring knife to open the vanilla bean pods in half lengthwise, being careful not to cut all the way through. Use the back of your knife to run down the length of the pod, scraping out the vanilla bean seeds. Place the seeds into a large freezer-safe bowl along with the granulated sugar. Use your fingers to rub the mixture together until combined.

3 Add the flour, baking powder, and salt to the bowl with the sugar and whisk to combine. Place in the freezer for 10 minutes (keeping all your ingredients cold will help to produce a fluffy, thick, and buttery scone).

4 After 10 minutes, remove the bowl from the freezer and add the butter. Use a pastry cutter or your fingers to work the butter into the dry ingredients, until the mixture resembles wet sand.

5 In a separate bowl, combine the sour cream (or yogurt), 6 tablespoons of the cream, and the vanilla extract, whisking until smooth. Working quickly, pour the wet ingredients into the flour mixture and use your hands to mix everything together until it forms a dry dough. If the dough is too dry or crumbly, add 1 tablespoon of cream at a time until the dough comes together. Use a silicone spatula to fold in the blackberries until just combined. Do not overmix.

6 Turn the dough out onto a well-floured surface. Generously flour your hands, then form the dough into a roughly 9-inch circular disk. Use a sharp knife to cut the dough into 8 equal wedges. Place the wedges on your prepared sheet pan, spacing them 2 inches apart.

7 Place a few tablespoons of cream in a bowl and use a pastry brush to brush the tops and sides of the scones. Bake the scones until they are just starting to turn golden brown around the edges and they feel dry to the touch, 22 to 25 minutes. Place the sheet pan on a cooling rack and allow the scones to cool slightly on the pan.

8 *While the scones cool, make the vanilla bean glaze.* Split and scrape the vanilla bean pod as instructed in Step 2. In a small bowl, whisk together the confectioners' sugar, milk, vanilla extract, scraped vanilla bean seeds, and salt. Use a large spoon to drizzle about 2 tablespoons of the glaze over each scone. Allow them to sit until the glaze is set, then serve.

Lemon–Poppy Seed Sweet Rolls

MAKES 12 ROLLS

PREP TIME 1 HOUR (PLUS 2 HOURS
RISE TIME)
COOK TIME 30 MINUTES
TOTAL TIME 3 HOURS 30 MINUTES

FOR THE DOUGH

4½ cups all-purpose flour,
   divided, plus more for rolling
   out the dough

⅓ cup granulated sugar

1 tablespoon freshly grated
   lemon zest (from about 1 lemon)

1 packet (2¼ teaspoons) instant
   yeast

1 teaspoon salt

1½ cups whole milk

6 tablespoons (¾ stick) unsalted
   butter

1 large egg, at room temperature

2 tablespoons poppy seeds

FOR THE LEMON FILLING

⅔ cup granulated sugar

1 tablespoon freshly grated
   lemon zest (from about 1 lemon)

¼ cup (½ stick) unsalted butter,
   at room temperature

FOR THE CREAM CHEESE
FROSTING

4 ounces cream cheese, at room
   temperature

½ cup (1 stick) unsalted butter,
   at room temperature

3 cups confectioners' sugar

2 to 3 tablespoons whole milk

1 teaspoon vanilla extract

Pinch of salt

1 tablespoon freshly grated
   lemon zest (from about 1 lemon)

These swirly, lemony rolls are a guaranteed crowd-pleaser, known to impress even the judgiest in-laws/grandmothers/friends . . . or so I've been told by my recipe testers. A sweet yeasted bread is folded with poppy seeds, then slathered in a buttery lemon filling before being rolled and baked like a cinnamon roll. It's topped with a cream cheese frosting that complements the lemon in that creamsicle kind of way. There are millions of recipes for traditional cinnamon rolls, but I love how much these delight people when I make them. You'll see what I mean when you do, too.

1 *First, make the dough.* In a stand mixer fitted with the paddle attachment, add 2 cups of the flour with the granulated sugar, lemon zest, yeast, and salt and beat on low speed until combined.

2 In a microwave-safe bowl, add the milk and butter. Microwave until the mixture is warm to the touch and the butter is melted, about 45 seconds (you don't want the mixture to be steaming or too hot, because this can kill the yeast).

3 Pour the milk mixture into the flour mixture, add the egg, and beat everything together on low speed until combined. Gradually increase the speed to high and beat for 2 minutes. The dough will look more like batter, but this is correct! This step kicks off the gluten development.

4 After 2 minutes, change the paddle attachment to the dough hook attachment. Add 1½ cups of the remaining flour and knead on low speed until combined. Add the remaining 1 cup flour and the poppy seeds and knead on low speed, stopping the mixer occasionally to redistribute the dough, until the dough starts to pull away from the sides of the bowl and forms a ball around the dough hook.

5 Increase the speed to medium-low and knead until the dough becomes smooth and supple, about 10 minutes. If the dough gets wrapped around the hook too much, turn off the mixer, pull the dough off, flip over the dough, and turn on the mixer again. The dough is ready when you can stretch a quarter-size piece of dough between your fingers and see light through it (without it breaking). This means the gluten has developed enough. If your dough breaks, knead for a few more minutes and try again.

6 Transfer the dough to a large bowl sprayed with nonstick cooking spray and cover the bowl with a dish towel or plastic wrap. Let rise in a warm place until the dough has doubled in size, about 1 hour.

(Continued on page 150)

(Continued from page 149)

PRO TIP *Want to split up the work? Do everything through Step 11 except the second rise, then wrap your pan tightly in plastic wrap and place it in the fridge overnight. In the morning, take the pan out and allow the rolls to do their second rise at room temperature until they puff up slightly, about 2 hours. Then bake as instructed.*

7 *Once the dough has risen, make the lemon filling.* In a small bowl, combine the granulated sugar and lemon zest. Use your fingers to rub the mixture together to infuse the sugar with lemon flavor.

8 Line a 9 × 13-inch rectangular baking pan with parchment paper on all sides (see page 23).

9 Turn the dough out onto a well-floured surface. Use a rolling pin to roll the dough into a 12 × 18-inch rectangle, with the wider side closest to you.

10 Using your hands or the silicone spatula, spread the butter all the way to the edges of the dough. Sprinkle the lemon sugar mixture on top, then use your fingers to spread it into the butter.

11 From the 18-inch side closest to you, roll the dough into a tight log. Press the dough along the outside seam to seal everything together. Use a very sharp knife (or floss . . . yes, seriously!) to cut the dough into 12 even rolls (for step-by-step photos, see page 208). Place the rolls in the prepared pan. Cover the pan with a dish towel or plastic wrap and allow to rise in a warm place until doubled in size, about 1 hour.

12 Preheat the oven to 350°F. Uncover the dough. Bake the rolls until they are golden brown all over, about 30 minutes. Place the pan on a cooling rack to cool slightly while you make the cream cheese frosting.

13 *Last, make the cream cheese frosting.* In a stand mixer fitted with the whisk attachment, combine the cream cheese, butter, confectioners' sugar, 2 tablespoons of the milk, the vanilla extract, and salt. Beat on low speed until combined, then gradually increase the speed to medium-high and beat until light and fluffy, about 1 minute. If the frosting is too thick, add another tablespoon of milk and beat to combine. Spread the frosting evenly over the warm rolls. Enjoy warm!

Sunday Waffles

MAKES 5 LARGE ROUND BELGIAN WAFFLES OR 10 STANDARD SQUARE WAFFLES

PREP TIME 20 MINUTES
COOK TIME ABOUT 15 MINUTES (TIME WILL VARY BASED ON WAFFLE MAKER MANUFACTURER'S DIRECTIONS)
TOTAL TIME ABOUT 35 MINUTES

2 large eggs, at room temperature

⅓ cup granulated sugar

½ cup (1 stick) unsalted butter, melted and cooled slightly

1¾ cups milk (any dairy or nondairy milk works)

1 tablespoon vanilla extract

2 cups all-purpose flour

1 tablespoon baking powder

½ teaspoon salt

Maple syrup, for serving

If you want my ideal Sunday, here it is: these waffles. Notice I didn't say a walk in the park, or a two-hour afternoon nap, or a trip to Target. I just really want waffles. I call these Sunday Waffles because they aren't your average pancake-batter-into-waffle-maker recipe. The wee bit of extra effort makes these more delicious by leaps and bounds; whipping the egg whites and sugar creates absurdly fluffy waffles, with a thin, crisp exterior. They're my go-to any time visitors are in town and I want to re-create that feeling of a long, lazy breakfast after a sleepover at a friend's house.

1 Preheat your waffle maker according to the manufacturer's instructions.

2 Separate the egg whites from the yolks, placing the egg whites in the bowl of a stand mixer fitted with the whisk attachment, and placing the yolks in a large bowl for later. Beat the egg whites on high speed until they form stiff peaks, 3 to 5 minutes. Set aside.

3 Add the sugar and butter to the bowl with the egg yolks and whisk until combined. Pour in the milk and vanilla extract, whisking to combine. Add the flour, baking powder, and salt and whisk until just combined (some small lumps of batter may remain). Do not overmix.

4 Add roughly half of the whipped egg whites to the batter, using a silicone spatula to gently fold them in. Add the remaining half of the egg whites and fold again until the batter is completely homogenous.

5 Spray the waffle iron with nonstick cooking spray and spoon in the amount of batter recommended by the manufacturer. Cook according to the manufacturer's instructions until the waffles are golden brown, then serve them along with a healthy drizzle of maple syrup.

Funfetti Crumb Cake

MAKES ONE 8-INCH CRUMB CAKE

PREP TIME 30 MINUTES
COOK TIME 50 MINUTES
TOTAL TIME 1 HOUR 20 MINUTES

FOR THE CAKE

½ cup (1 stick) unsalted butter, at room temperature

½ cup granulated sugar

2 large eggs, at room temperature

1 teaspoon vanilla extract

½ teaspoon almond extract

1½ cups all-purpose flour

½ teaspoon baking powder

½ teaspoon baking soda

½ teaspoon salt

½ cup full-fat sour cream (plain Greek yogurt also works)

½ cup rainbow sprinkles

FOR THE CRUMB TOPPING

½ cup (1 stick) unsalted butter, melted

1 cup all-purpose flour

½ cup packed light brown sugar

¼ cup granulated sugar

½ teaspoon almond extract

¼ teaspoon salt

3 tablespoons rainbow sprinkles

Confectioners' sugar, for topping (optional)

Close your eyes and try to remember a time when Funfetti didn't make you happy. Can't think of one, right? This Funfetti Crumb Cake is complete and utter joy. It's a simple vanilla cake studded with rainbow sprinkles—the crucial ingredient to happiness. Thanks to a high butterfat content in both the crumb and the cake, it'll stay moist for days, making it yet another stellar lunch dessert. And don't skip the almond extract in the batter; it's almost undetectable until you find yourself coming back for more, trying to pinpoint that extra something.

1 *First, make the cake.* Preheat the oven to 325°F. Line an 8 × 8-inch square baking pan with parchment paper on all sides (see page 23).

2 In a stand mixer fitted with the paddle attachment, combine the butter and granulated sugar and beat on medium speed until light and fluffy, about 2 minutes.

3 Turn off the mixer, then add the eggs, one at a time, and beat on low speed, scraping down the sides and bottom of the bowl with a silicone spatula after each addition. Add the vanilla extract and almond extract and beat well to combine.

4 In a separate bowl, whisk together the flour, baking powder, baking soda, and salt. With the mixer on low speed, alternate adding the dry ingredients and the sour cream (or yogurt) in 3 additions (you'll add half the dry, then all of the sour cream, then the other half of the dry). It's okay if the batter still has a few lumps in it—you don't want to overmix. Fold in the sprinkles. Transfer the batter to the prepared pan, using the silicone spatula to spread it into an even layer.

5 *Next, make the crumb topping.* In a large bowl, combine the melted butter, flour, brown sugar, granulated sugar, almond extract, and salt. Use a fork or your hands to cut the mixture together until the mixture is pebbly. Add the sprinkles and mix to combine. Sprinkle the crumb evenly over the batter in the pan.

6 Bake the cake until the top is golden brown and a butter knife inserted into the center comes out mostly clean (a crumb or two attached is okay), 45 to 50 minutes. Place the pan on a cooling rack and allow the cake to cool slightly in the pan. Use the parchment paper to lift the cake from the pan, then transfer the cake to a cutting board. Dust the top with confectioners' sugar (if using), slice into squares, and serve.

Ginger Apricot Muffins

MAKES 12 MUFFINS

PREP TIME 20 MINUTES
COOK TIME 23 MINUTES
TOTAL TIME 43 MINUTES

½ cup (1 stick) unsalted butter, melted

½ cup granulated sugar

½ cup packed light brown sugar

2 large eggs, at room temperature

1 tablespoon peeled and finely grated fresh ginger (or 2 teaspoons ground ginger)

1 teaspoon vanilla extract

6 tablespoons full-fat sour cream (plain Greek yogurt also works)

6 tablespoons buttermilk (get my homemade version on page 28)

2 cups all-purpose flour

1 tablespoon baking powder

½ teaspoon salt

3 large apricots, pitted and cut into small cubes (if fresh apricots aren't in season, you can substitute 1 cup chopped dried apricots)

1 cup sliced almonds (optional)

Confectioners' sugar, for topping (optional)

PRO TIP *For sky-high muffins, only line every other muffin cup in a standard muffin tin with muffin liners (it should look like a checkerboard). You'll have to bake in batches, but it'll give you an even better rise.*

Why is it that coffee shop muffins are so gigantic and gorgeous, yet when we make them at home, it's next to impossible to replicate that hot air balloon shape? Just me? Well, not anymore. These muffins are guaranteed to be fluffy, moist, and dramatically domed muffins the size of your fist. The secret? You bake them for the first 5 minutes at 425°F to kick-start their rise. The spicy-sweet combination of freshly grated ginger and apricot also has a sophisticated, coffee shop–worthy flavor that helps this muffin reach new elevations, too.

1 Preheat the oven to 425°F. Line the muffin cups of a standard muffin tin with muffin liners, then spray the muffin liners and the top of the tin with nonstick cooking spray.

2 In a large bowl, combine the melted butter, granulated sugar, and brown sugar and mix together using a silicone spatula. Add the eggs, ginger, vanilla extract, sour cream (or yogurt), and buttermilk and mix well.

3 Add the flour, baking powder, and salt. Mix until combined and no streaks of flour remain. Fold in the apricots, mixing only until combined. Do not overmix.

4 Scoop the batter evenly into the prepared muffin cups. If you want to get fancy, use a 3-ounce cookie scoop to create perfectly domed scoops. Top with sliced almonds (if using).

5 Bake the muffins for 5 minutes at 425°F, then reduce the oven temperature to 375°F. Continue baking until the tops of the muffins are golden brown and spring back to the touch, about 18 minutes more. Place the muffin tin on a cooling rack and allow the muffins to cool slightly in the pan before dusting the tops with confectioners' sugar (if using) and serving.

Old-Fashioned Chocolate Cake Donuts

MAKES 8 DONUTS AND
DONUT HOLES

PREP TIME 30 MINUTES (PLUS
1 HOUR CHILL TIME)
COOK TIME 10 MINUTES
TOTAL TIME 1 HOUR 40 MINUTES

FOR THE DONUTS

½ cup granulated sugar

3 tablespoons unsalted butter,
at room temperature

2 large egg yolks, at room
temperature

⅔ cup full-fat sour cream, at
room temperature

2 cups cake flour, plus more for
rolling out the dough

½ cup Dutch-processed cocoa
powder

1½ teaspoons baking powder

1 teaspoon salt

2 quarts vegetable oil, for deep-
frying

FOR THE GLAZE

2 cups confectioners' sugar

¼ cup whole milk

1 teaspoon vanilla extract

Everyone's hometown seems to have one unassuming bakery that made the best _____ in the world. For me, it was Linda's Donuts in Belmont, Massachusetts, and they made the best *ever* chocolate cake donuts. They were hefty and moist (not crumbly), with a crunchy exterior from sitting in the fryer for who knows how long. After years of testing, I'm proud to say I've finally perfected a recipe that rivals Linda's. By using only egg yolks in the dough, these donuts stay dense and delicious, while the sour cream keeps them moist and imparts a slight tang. From now on, call me Linda.

1 *First, make the donuts.* In a stand mixer fitted with the paddle attachment, add the granulated sugar and butter and beat on low speed until combined. Gradually increase the speed to medium and beat until light and fluffy, about 30 seconds.

2 Turn off the mixer, add the egg yolks, and beat until the mixture lightens in color, about 1 minute, scraping down the sides and bottom of the bowl with a silicone spatula as needed. Add the sour cream and mix on medium speed for 30 seconds more.

3 Add the cake flour, cocoa powder, baking powder, and salt. Mix on low speed until just combined.

4 Remove the dough from the mixer, flatten it into an oval disk, and wrap the disk tightly in plastic wrap. Refrigerate for 1 hour.

5 Turn the chilled dough onto a well-floured surface. Use a rolling pin to roll the dough out to a ½-inch thickness. Use a 3½-inch donut cutter to cut out the donuts, saving the donut holes. Use a pastry brush to gently brush off any excess flour on each donut. Gather the scraps into a ball and gently knead them together. Roll out and cut the dough again—you should end up with 8 donuts and 8 holes.

6 In a large pot, heat the vegetable oil over medium-low heat to 325°F. Place a cooling rack on top of a sheet pan.

7 *While the oil heats, make the glaze.* In a medium bowl, combine the confectioners' sugar, milk, and vanilla extract and whisk to combine. Set aside.

8 Fry 2 or 3 donuts at a time (being careful not to overcrowd the pot) for 2 minutes. At this point, you should be able to see the edges begin to look crisp. Flip the donuts and continue cooking until the donuts have expanded and have craggy edges all over, about 1 minute more. Use a metal slotted spatula to transfer the donuts to the prepared cooling rack. Repeat frying the remaining donuts and donut holes (the donut holes will fry in about half the time).

9 Once the donuts are cool enough to the touch (but still warm), dip the top half of each fried donut into the glaze, then place back on the cooling rack until the glaze has set. Serve within 4 hours of frying.

Lemon Blueberry Dutch Baby

MAKES ONE 9-INCH DUTCH BABY

PREP TIME 15 MINUTES
COOK TIME 20 MINUTES
TOTAL TIME 35 MINUTES

3 large eggs, at room
  temperature

½ cup milk (any dairy or
  nondairy milk works)

½ cup all-purpose flour

¼ cup granulated sugar

¼ teaspoon salt

2 teaspoons vanilla extract

1 tablespoon freshly grated
  lemon zest (from about
  1 lemon), plus more for topping

¼ cup (½ stick) unsalted butter

⅓ cup fresh blueberries, plus
  more for topping

Confectioners' sugar, for topping

Maple syrup, for serving

Can someone explain why a Dutch baby is called a Dutch baby, because I can't help but think of a tiny infant from Holland covered in lemon zest and blueberries. It needs a name that better reflects its wonderful texture, somewhere between a pancake and custard, but I'm coming up blank. Semantics aside, I still love 'em because they can feed a group without your having to stand at the stove and flip endless pancakes. In the oven, this blueberry-packed baby rises, puffs up, and falls back on itself, creating a gloriously soufflé-like center. The lemon imparts a bright acidity that wakes you up, but so will the giant carafe of coffee you should 100% serve with it.

1 Place a 9-inch cast-iron skillet in the oven. Preheat the oven to 425°F. (A hot skillet helps your Dutch baby rise.)

2 In a high-powered blender (or a food processor), combine the eggs, milk, flour, granulated sugar, salt, vanilla extract, and lemon zest. Blend on high speed until the mixture is fully combined and begins to froth, about 1 minute.

3 Carefully remove the skillet from the oven and add the butter to the hot pan. Place the skillet back in the oven until the butter is fully melted, 3 to 5 minutes.

4 Carefully remove the skillet from the oven and swirl it around so the butter evenly coats the bottom and sides of the skillet. Pour the prepared batter into the center of the skillet, then sprinkle it evenly with the blueberries.

5 Bake until the Dutch baby puffs up and is a light golden brown, about 20 minutes. Remove the skillet from the oven and allow it to cool slightly on the stovetop or a cooling rack. Top with more blueberries, lemon zest, and confectioners' sugar, then serve immediately alongside a healthy drizzle of maple syrup.

Pistachio Croissants

MAKES 8 CROISSANTS

PREP TIME 30 MINUTES
COOK TIME 15 MINUTES
TOTAL TIME 45 MINUTES

FOR THE CROISSANTS

8 day-old croissants

1½ cups shelled, roasted unsalted pistachios, divided

⅓ cup unsalted butter, at room temperature

½ cup granulated sugar

1 large egg, at room temperature

1 teaspoon vanilla extract

½ teaspoon almond extract

¼ teaspoon salt

Confectioners' sugar, for topping (optional)

FOR THE ORANGE SYRUP

½ cup water

½ cup honey

1 tablespoon freshly grated orange zest (from about 1 orange)

½ teaspoon almond extract

PRO TIP *If you're craving a more classic flavor, swap the pistachios with 1 cup almond flour in the filling, omit the orange zest, and use ¼ cup slivered almonds on top.*

Did you know that bakeries use leftover croissants to make those dreamy almond ones? It's because the dry croissant dough soaks up the almond filling in a way that fresh ones can't. But where they're using their *own* day-old croissants, we're outsourcing. Wherever you pick up croissants, give them a day (you might even be able to buy them at a discount if they're day-old), then cut them in half and stuff them with a pistachio paste you could and should eat by the spoonful. As the croissants bake, their dough comes back to life with a shattering crust and flaky interior—as good as new. Oh wait, *better.*

1 *First, make the croissants.* Preheat the oven to 350°F. Line two sheet pans with parchment paper.

2 Slice the croissants in half lengthwise and place, cut-side up, on the prepared sheet pans.

3 In a food processor or high-powered blender, add 1 cup of the pistachios and pulse until finely ground and resembling wet sand, about 30 seconds.

4 Transfer the ground pistachios to a large bowl. Add the butter, granulated sugar, egg, vanilla extract, almond extract, and salt. Use a silicone spatula to stir together until combined. Set aside.

5 *Next, make the orange syrup.* In a medium microwave-safe bowl, combine the water, honey, orange zest, and almond extract. Microwave for 1 minute, then remove from the microwave and whisk until combined. Use a pastry brush to generously soak the cut sides of the croissants with the syrup (save some for Step 7).

6 Scoop about 1 tablespoon of the pistachio filling onto the bottom half of each croissant, spreading it evenly to the edges with the silicone spatula. Place the top halves on top of the bottom halves, sandwiching the croissants together.

7 Brush the tops of the croissants with the remaining orange syrup and then spread the remaining pistachio filling over the tops. Coarsely chop the remaining ½ cup pistachios and sprinkle them over the tops as well.

8 Bake the croissants until they are golden brown all over, 12 to 15 minutes. Remove the sheet pans from the oven and allow the croissants to cool slightly on the pans before dusting the tops with confectioners' sugar (if using) and serving.

London Fog Loaf

MAKES ONE 8½-INCH LOAF

PREP TIME 30 MINUTES
COOK TIME 1 HOUR
TOTAL TIME 1 HOUR 30 MINUTES

FOR THE LOAF

⅓ cup milk (any dairy or nondairy milk works)

4 Earl Grey tea bags

1 cup (2 sticks) unsalted butter, at room temperature

½ cup granulated sugar

½ cup packed light brown sugar

⅓ cup honey

4 large eggs, at room temperature

1 teaspoon vanilla extract

¼ teaspoon lemon extract

2 cups all-purpose flour

1½ teaspoons baking powder

½ teaspoon salt

FOR THE GLAZE

1½ cups confectioners' sugar

2 tablespoons milk (any dairy or nondairy milk works)

¼ teaspoon lemon extract

2 tablespoons dried edible flowers (optional)

If quiet luxury were a dessert, it would be this unassuming Earl Grey loaf cake drizzled with lemon glaze. Its flavors are based on my favorite deep-winter café drink, a London Fog. A loaf cake is always going to look a little like a brick, but the flavor here is as refined as a royal wedding. Soaking your tea bags in milk infuses the bergamot-scented Earl Grey flavor deep into your cake without having to stir in actual Earl Grey tea leaves. The lemon glaze enhances the citrus notes in the cake and provides a lovely pop of brightness. Serve this on your finest china or a paper towel … either way, eat with your pinky up.

1 *First, make the loaf.* Preheat the oven to 350°F. Line a 1-pound loaf pan with parchment paper on all sides (see page 23).

2 In a small saucepan over low heat, add the milk and cook, swirling occasionally, until the milk is steaming but not boiling. Remove from the heat and add the tea bags, soaking them completely in the milk. This will seem like very little liquid, but it's correct. Allow the tea bags to steep in the milk while you make the rest of your batter.

3 In a stand mixer fitted with the paddle attachment, combine the butter, granulated sugar, brown sugar, and honey and beat on medium speed until light and fluffy, about 2 minutes.

4 Use a silicone spatula to scrape down the sides and bottom of the bowl. Add the eggs, one at a time, and beat at low speed, scraping down the bowl after each addition. Add the vanilla extract and lemon extract and beat well. At this stage, this batter has a tendency to look a little curdled. If this happens, it's okay! Just keep going.

5 In a separate bowl, whisk together the flour, baking powder, and salt. Squeeze the soaked tea bags over the milk in the saucepan to collect as much liquid as possible, then discard the tea bags. With the mixer on low speed, alternate adding the dry ingredients and the infused milk in 3 additions (you'll add half the dry, then all of the milk, then the other half of the dry).

6 Use the silicone spatula to transfer the batter to the prepared loaf pan and spread it evenly to the edges. Bake until the cake is golden brown (if it starts to take on too much color, cover it lightly with aluminum foil), the center of the loaf springs back to a light touch, and a butter knife inserted into the center comes out mostly clean (a crumb or two attached is okay), 55 to 60 minutes. Place the pan on a cooling rack set on top of a sheet pan and let the loaf cool slightly in the pan.

7 *While the loaf cools, make the glaze.* In a small bowl, whisk the confectioners' sugar, milk, and lemon extract until smooth. Use the parchment paper to lift the loaf from the pan, then set it back onto the cooling rack. Drizzle the glaze on top of the warm loaf, top with edible flowers (if using), and allow it to sit until the glaze is set before serving.

Raspberry Croissant Bread Pudding

MAKES ONE 9 × 13-INCH BREAD
PUDDING

PREP TIME 20 MINUTES
(PLUS 1 HOUR REST TIME)
COOK TIME 40 MINUTES
TOTAL TIME 2 HOURS

3 tablespoons unsalted butter, at
room temperature

12 cups day-old croissants (from
about 6 large croissants)

1 cup fresh raspberries, divided

4 large eggs, at room
temperature

5 cups milk (any dairy or
nondairy milk works)

½ cup granulated sugar

½ cup packed light brown sugar

1 tablespoon vanilla extract

Confectioners' sugar, for topping
(optional)

If I were to run for president of the United States, this would be my platform: Americans aren't eating enough bread pudding, and I am going to change that. With its soft, custardy texture in the center and craggy, almost caramelized top, bread pudding has the power to unite us, spread happiness, and bring about world peace, probably . . . if the pan is big enough. But let's start small here, with a bread pudding made of day-old croissants that soak up the custard like a champ, while adding a buttery flakiness, too. And remember: a vote for me is a vote for bread pudding everywhere.

1 Generously grease the bottom and sides of a 9 × 13-inch rectangular baking pan with the butter.

2 Coarsely chop the croissants (I cut mine in half lengthwise, then chop those into thirds!) and place half of them in the prepared pan. Sprinkle in ½ cup of the raspberries. Top with the remaining croissants and most of the remaining raspberries, reserving a small handful of raspberries to use later as a topping.

3 In a large bowl, whisk together the eggs, milk, granulated sugar, brown sugar, and vanilla extract. Carefully pour the mixture over the croissants, then use your hands to squish the croissants just slightly to soak up all the liquid. Cover the pan with plastic wrap and place in the fridge for at least 1 hour and up to overnight to allow the mixture to really soak into the croissants.

4 Once the croissants have soaked, preheat the oven to 350°F.

5 Bake the croissant mixture until golden brown on top and fully baked, about 40 minutes. Place the pan on the stove or a cooling rack to cool slightly, then top with the reserved raspberries, dust with confectioners' sugar (if using), and serve.

Blueberry Pancakes

PREP TIME 10 MINUTES
COOK TIME 20 MINUTES
TOTAL TIME 30 MINUTES

2 cups all-purpose flour

3 tablespoons granulated sugar

2 teaspoons baking powder

1 teaspoon baking soda

1 teaspoon salt

2 cups buttermilk, at room temperature (get my homemade version on page 28)

2 large eggs, at room temperature

3 tablespoons unsalted butter, melted, plus more for cooking the pancakes

1 tablespoon vanilla extract

1 cup fresh or frozen blueberries

Maple syrup, for serving

Growing up with divorced parents, my mom was a pro baker, while my dad relied on microwave dinners. Except on weekends, when he'd whip up a batch of blueberry pancakes that I'd eat in stacks as high as my head. But once I got older and started making them with him, I found out that the homemade pancakes I loved all my life were Krusteaz pancake mix (iconic, but still). And while I will never fault you for using pancake mixes, if you *are* looking for a recipe that gives the box a run for its money and that requires only a bowl and a whisk, these might take the (pan)cake (guys, I *had* to). The combination of baking powder and baking soda makes them extra light and fluffy, while the double dose of vanilla deepens the flavor.

1 In a large bowl, whisk the flour, granulated sugar, baking powder, baking soda, and salt until combined.

2 In a separate bowl, whisk the buttermilk, eggs, melted butter, and vanilla extract until combined.

3 Make a well in the center of the flour mixture, then pour in the wet ingredients. Whisk until just a few small lumps of flour remain, being careful not to overmix the batter. Use a silicone spatula to fold in the blueberries.

4 Heat a large skillet or griddle over medium heat (don't turn the heat up too high—you want a nice, even heat). Once the skillet is hot, liberally grease it with butter (I like about 1 tablespoon for every 3 pancakes).

5 Pour ¼ cup of the batter per pancake onto the hot surface (leave about 1 inch between each pancake to account for spread and easy flipping). Cook on one side until bubbles form on the top and the edges begin to look dry, 1 to 2 minutes. Flip and cook the other side for about 1 minute more. If at any time you notice the pancakes getting too dark, reduce the heat. Serve immediately with a waterfall of maple syrup.

FLAVOR VARIATIONS

Swap out the blueberries in favor of one of the following:

LEMON–POPPY SEED PANCAKES
1 tablespoon poppy seeds + 1 teaspoon lemon extract

CINNAMON–CHOCOLATE CHIP PANCAKES
1 cup chocolate chips + 1 teaspoon ground cinnamon

BIRTHDAY CAKE PANCAKES
2 tablespoons rainbow sprinkles + ½ teaspoon almond extract

Zebra Bundt Cake

PREP TIME 30 MINUTES
COOK TIME 50 MINUTES
TOTAL TIME 1 HOUR 20 MINUTES

½ cup (1 stick) unsalted butter, at room temperature

½ cup vegetable oil

2 cups granulated sugar

3 large eggs, at room temperature

1 cup full-fat sour cream, at room temperature (plain Greek yogurt also works)

2 teaspoons vanilla extract

2½ cups all-purpose flour, divided

1½ teaspoons baking powder

½ teaspoon baking soda

1 teaspoon salt

½ cup Dutch-processed cocoa powder

PRO TIP *Using piping bags will create the most vivid stripes, but if you don't have any, a gallon-size resealable plastic bag with a hole cut into the corner works in a pinch!*

Inspired by black-and-white marble cakes and that feeling of not being able to make up your mind, this recipe is a two-for-one, winner-takes-all-the-cake kind of deal. You begin with a sour cream cake base, split it between two bowls, doctor one with cocoa powder to create a chocolate batter and the other with more flour to create a vanilla batter, then layer them like zebra stripes in a Bundt pan. It's visually striking, deceptively easy, and delicious with a cup of milky black tea.

1 Preheat the oven to 350°F. Generously grease a 10-inch Bundt pan with nonstick cooking spray.

2 In a stand mixer fitted with the whisk attachment, combine the butter, vegetable oil, and granulated sugar and beat on medium-high speed until light and fluffy, about 2 minutes.

3 With the mixer still going, add the eggs, one at a time, beating well after each addition. Add the sour cream (or yogurt) and vanilla extract and beat until smooth.

4 Add 2 cups of the flour, the baking powder, baking soda, and salt. Beat on low speed, scraping down the sides and bottom of the bowl with the silicone spatula as needed, until just combined and no streaks of flour remain.

5 Remove the bowl from the stand mixer. Scoop 3 cups of the batter into a large bowl. You should now have two bowls with equal halves of batter.

6 Add the remaining ½ cup flour to one bowl of batter and use the silicone spatula to fold it in until no streaks of flour remain—this will be your vanilla batter.

7 Add the cocoa powder to the other bowl of batter and use the silicone spatula to fold it in until no streaks of cocoa remain—this will be your chocolate batter.

8 Transfer the batters to two large piping bags, creating one vanilla piping bag and one chocolate piping bag. Use scissors to cut a ¾-inch opening at the tip of each bag. Starting with the vanilla piping bag, pipe a circle of batter in the bottom of your Bundt pan. It won't fill the bottom of the pan—that's okay; the batters will melt into each other in the oven. Switch to the chocolate piping bag and pipe a circle of batter on top of the vanilla. Repeat this process, creating concentric circles of chocolate and vanilla, until you're out of both batters.

9 Bake until the cake has risen and a butter knife inserted into the center comes out mostly clean (a crumb or two attached is okay), 45 to 50 minutes.

10 Place the cake on a cooling rack to cool completely in the pan. To remove the cake from the pan, flip the cake onto a serving plate. Slice and serve.

Bumbleberry Tart

MAKES ONE 9-INCH TART

PREP TIME 25 MINUTES
COOK TIME 45 MINUTES
TOTAL TIME 1 HOUR 10 MINUTES

FOR THE DOUGH

1 cup all-purpose flour

1 cup superfine almond flour

⅔ cup packed light brown sugar

½ cup (1 stick) unsalted butter, cold and cut into cubes

½ teaspoon salt

FOR THE FILLING

2 cups fresh or frozen mixed berries (such as blueberries, raspberries, blackberries, and strawberries)

2 tablespoons cornstarch

¼ cup packed light brown sugar

1 tablespoon freshly grated lemon zest (from about 1 lemon)

1 teaspoon vanilla extract

Pinch of salt

¼ cup sliced almonds

Confectioners' sugar, for topping (optional)

Bumbleberry is an old-fashioned term for "mixed berry," but isn't it more fun to say? Yes, yes it is. Don't let this tart's simple presentation fool you; there's a toasty yet tender brown sugar–almond crust and a cozy crumble topping (made from the same dough!). The mixed berries—oh sorry, the *bumbleberries*—add a rich, jammy layer that's lovely for spring and summer brunch soirées. And yeah, it's the kind of dessert that makes you call parties soirées.

1 *First, make the dough.* Preheat the oven to 350°F. Line the bottom of a 9-inch round tart pan with parchment paper (see page 23) and grease the sides with nonstick cooking spray.

2 In a food processor, add the all-purpose flour, almond flour, brown sugar, butter, and salt. Pulse until the mixture starts to clump together and forms a dough ball.

3 Transfer two-thirds of the dough to the prepared tart pan and use your fingers to press the crust into an even layer along the bottom and sides of the pan. Then use a measuring cup (or something else with a flat bottom) to really pack the crust in. Set aside.

4 *Next, make the filling.* In a large bowl, combine the berries, cornstarch, brown sugar, lemon zest, vanilla extract, and salt. Toss together until the berries are evenly coated. Spread the berry mixture on top of the prepared crust. Crumble the remaining one-third of the dough on top of the berries, then top with the sliced almonds.

5 Bake until the crust is golden brown and the berries are bubbling, about 45 minutes.

6 Place the tart pan on a cooling rack and allow the tart to cool completely in the pan. Once the tart is cooled, remove it from the pan and place on a serving plate. Dust the top with confectioners' sugar (if using), slice, and serve.

Orange Pull-Apart Bread

PREP TIME 30 MINUTES
(PLUS 2 HOURS RISE TIME)
COOK TIME 45 MINUTES
TOTAL TIME 3 HOURS 15 MINUTES

FOR THE DOUGH

3 cups all-purpose flour, plus more for rolling out the dough

¼ cup granulated sugar

1 packet (2¼ teaspoons) instant yeast

1 teaspoon salt

⅔ cup whole milk

¼ cup (½ stick) unsalted butter

2 large eggs, at room temperature

2 teaspoons vanilla extract

FOR THE ORANGE FILLING

½ cup granulated sugar

2 tablespoons freshly grated orange zest (from about 2 oranges)

¼ cup (½ stick) unsalted butter, at room temperature

FOR THE ORANGE GLAZE

1½ cups confectioners' sugar

2 tablespoons freshly squeezed orange juice (from about 1 orange)

1 tablespoon whole milk

½ teaspoon vanilla extract

1 tablespoon freshly grated orange zest (from about 1 orange) (optional)

The year? 2012. The latest cultural culinary trend? Pull-apart bread (at least for me, anyway). And like rip-off sweatpants, I'm on a one-woman mission to bring it back into relevancy. This recipe begins with a soft yeasted dough that gets cut into rectangles and stacked in a loaf pan like pages in a book. Once baked, the layers swell into perfectly imperfect slices of orange-scented sweet bread. It's like the center of a cinnamon roll, but throughout the entire loaf. Don't even try to slice this thing—just reach in and grab a piece with your hands.

1 *First, make the dough.* In a stand mixer fitted with the dough hook attachment, combine the flour, granulated sugar, yeast, and salt and beat on low speed until well combined.

2 In a microwave-safe bowl, combine the milk and butter. Microwave until the mixture is warm to the touch and the butter is melted, about 45 seconds (you don't want the mixture to be steaming or too hot, as this can kill the yeast). Pour the milk mixture into the flour mixture, then add the eggs and vanilla extract.

3 Turn the mixer to low speed and knead for 8 to 10 minutes. Every minute or two, turn off the mixer, pull the dough from the hook, and flip it upside down. This will help knead the dough evenly. Knead until the dough is smooth, supple, and starts to pull away from the sides of the bowl. The dough is ready when you can stretch a quarter-size piece of dough between your fingers and see light through it (without it breaking). This means the gluten has developed enough. If your dough breaks, knead for a few minutes more and try again.

4 Transfer the dough to a large bowl sprayed with nonstick cooking spray and cover the bowl with a dish towel or plastic wrap. Let rise in a warm place until the dough has doubled in size, about 1 hour.

5 *Once the dough has risen, make the filling.* In a small bowl, combine the granulated sugar and orange zest. Use your fingers to rub the mixture together to infuse the sugar with orange flavor. Set aside.

6 Line a 1-pound loaf pan with parchment paper on all sides (see page 23).

7 Turn the dough out onto a well-floured surface. Use a rolling pin to roll it into a 12 × 19-inch rectangle. Using your hands or a silicone spatula, spread the butter all the way to the edges of the dough. Sprinkle the orange sugar mixture on top, then use your fingers to spread it into the butter.

(Continued on page 177)

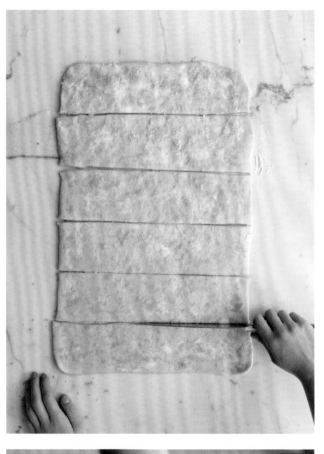

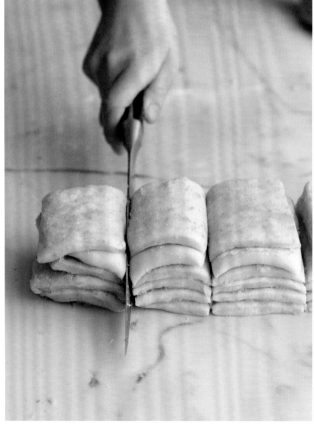

(Continued from page 174)

PRO TIP *If you want to get fancy, swap the vanilla extract for orange blossom water in the glaze for a fragrant, floral flavor.*

8 Using a sharp knife or pizza cutter, cut the dough crosswise into 6 even strips. Each strip should be about 3 inches wide (see photos opposite). Stack the strips on top of one another. Then, cut the stack of strips lengthwise into 6 equal pieces. You should end up with 6 stacks, each with 6 layers of dough.

9 Place the dough stacks in the prepared loaf pan. The end product should look like a dough accordion in your loaf pan. Cover the loaf with a dish towel or plastic wrap and let it rise in a warm place for 1 hour.

10 Preheat the oven to 350°F.

11 Uncover the dough. Bake the loaf until the dough is puffed up and the top is golden brown all over, about 45 minutes. Place the bread on a cooling rack on top of a sheet pan (to catch any drips of glaze you're about to create) and allow the bread to cool slightly in the pan.

12 *While the bread cools, make the glaze.* In a small bowl, whisk the confectioners' sugar, orange juice, milk, and vanilla extract until smooth.

13 Use the parchment paper to lift the bread from the pan, then transfer the bread to the cooling rack. Drizzle the glaze on top of the bread (it's okay if it's still a little warm!), top with the orange zest (if using), and serve.

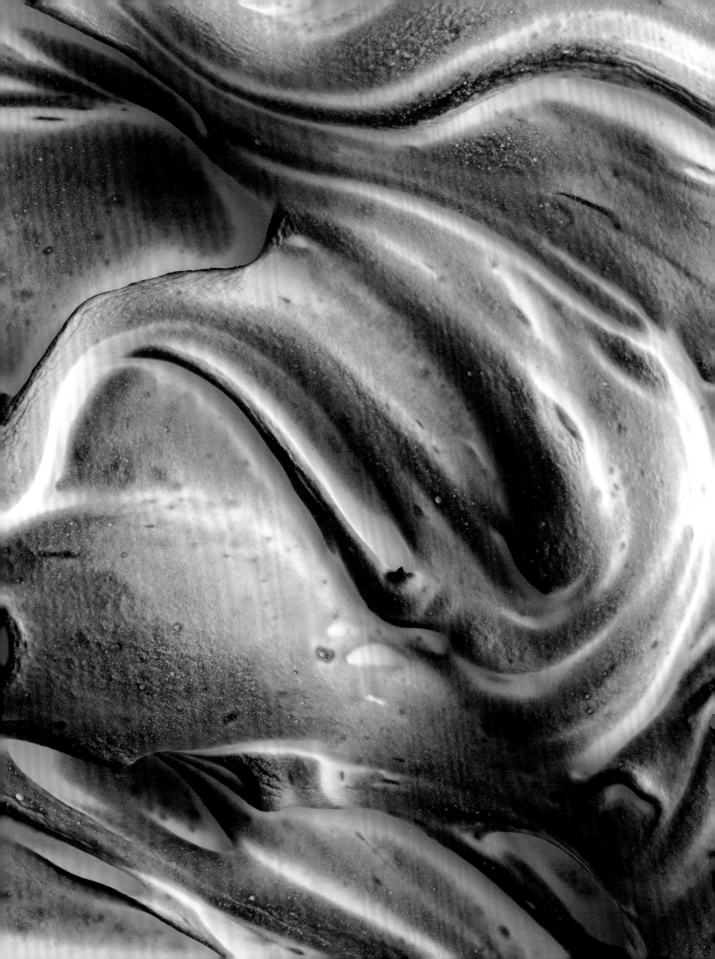

ALMOST TOO PRETTY TO EAT

This is the show-off chapter. The extra-special-occasion chapter. The shamelessly aesthetic chapter. We've got it all. From home-made custard ice cream to dramatic tarts and three-layer cakes for a crowd, these are the desserts to wow your audience and maybe even get a standing ovation (oh, you were just getting up to get a napkin? I'll count that).

Per usual, I'm here to walk you through every step, so that when you're whipping up egg whites for pavlova or dipping squares of cake into melted chocolate (are you drooling because I'm drooling), you'll know exactly what to do.

S'mores Tart

PREP TIME 45 MINUTES (PLUS
2 HOURS CHILL TIME)
COOK TIME 25 MINUTES
TOTAL TIME 3 HOURS 10 MINUTES

FOR THE GRAHAM CRACKER CRUST

1¾ cups graham cracker crumbs
(about 14 sheets, crumbled)

½ cup (1 stick) unsalted butter,
melted

⅓ cup granulated sugar

¼ teaspoon salt

FOR THE CHOCOLATE FILLING

6 ounces semisweet or
bittersweet chocolate, coarsely
chopped (or 1 cup semisweet
or bittersweet chocolate chips)

½ cup (1 stick) unsalted butter

3 large eggs, at room
temperature

½ cup granulated sugar

¼ teaspoon salt

FOR THE MERINGUE TOPPING

4 large egg whites, at room
temperature

1 cup granulated sugar

⅛ teaspoon salt

PRO TIP *You can bake
the crust and filling up to
2 days in advance. Just
cover the cooled tart with
plastic wrap and keep it
in the fridge. Right before
serving, make and top with
the meringue.*

No one asked for my feedback on s'mores, but here it is: the chocolate's too hard, the graham crackers are too breakable, and the hands . . . so sticky. This S'mores Tart is my revision. The crunchy graham cracker crust stays sturdy, thanks to our good friend butter; the fudgy chocolate filling has a hint of bitterness to balance the sweet; and the simple meringue is like a giant marshmallow cloud. To pretend you're at a bonfire, use a kitchen torch to char the meringue before serving.

1 *First, make the graham cracker crust.* Preheat the oven to 325°F. Line the bottom of a 9-inch round tart pan with parchment paper (see page 23) and grease the sides with nonstick cooking spray.

2 In a medium bowl, add the graham cracker crumbs, melted butter, granulated sugar, and salt, and use a silicone spatula to mix until the mixture resembles wet sand.

3 Transfer the mixture to the prepared pan and use your fingers to press the crust into an even layer along the bottom and sides of the pan. Then use a measuring cup (or something else with a flat bottom) to really pack the crust in.

4 *Next, make the filling.* In a small saucepan over low heat, combine the chocolate and butter and cook, stirring occasionally, until it melts completely. Remove from the heat and allow to cool slightly while you make the rest of the filling.

5 In a stand mixer fitted with the whisk attachment, combine the eggs, granulated sugar, and salt and beat on medium-high speed until light and fluffy, about 3 minutes.

6 Remove the bowl from the stand mixer and use the silicone spatula to fold one-third of the chocolate mixture (it's okay that it's still hot!) into the egg mixture until combined. Gently fold in the remaining two-thirds of the chocolate mixture.

7 Pour the chocolate filling into the prepared crust and use the silicone spatula to spread it into an even layer. Place the tart pan on a large sheet pan (this will ensure that you don't accidentally push the bottom of the tart pan up while handling it). Bake until the filling has puffed up slightly and is just beginning to crack around the edges, about 25 minutes. Place the tart on a cooling rack and allow it to cool to room temperature before transferring it to the fridge to cool completely, about 2 hours.

8 *When you're ready to serve, make the meringue topping.* In a stand mixer fitted with the whisk attachment, add the egg whites and beat on high speed until frothy. Continue beating while slowly streaming in the granulated sugar. Beat until the meringue is no longer gritty and holds stiff peaks when you lift up the whisk, 3 to 5 minutes. Mix in the salt.

9 Remove the tart from the tart pan and place it on a serving dish. Spread the meringue over the top of the tart, using a spoon to create big swirls and peaks. Use a kitchen torch to toast the exterior of the meringue. Enjoy!

Baklava Cheesecake

MAKES ONE 9-INCH CHEESECAKE

PREP TIME 1 HOUR (PLUS 5 HOURS CHILL TIME)
COOK TIME 1 HOUR
TOTAL TIME 7 HOURS

FOR THE CHEESECAKE

12 (9 × 14-inch) phyllo dough sheets, defrosted

½ cup (1 stick) unsalted butter, melted

24 ounces cream cheese (three 8-ounce blocks), at room temperature

1 cup full-fat sour cream, at room temperature

1⅓ cups granulated sugar

4 large eggs, at room temperature

¼ cup honey

2 teaspoons vanilla extract

FOR THE BAKLAVA TOPPING

⅓ cup water

¼ cup honey

1 tablespoon freshly squeezed lemon juice (from about 1 lemon)

½ cup chopped roasted unsalted walnuts

½ cup chopped roasted unsalted pistachios

I've made classic cheesecake enough times to know that it's delightful, yes, but forgettable. Sure, people enjoy it, but they won't be talking about it for weeks on end. This mash-up of baklava and cheesecake, however, they won't forget. Instead of a classic graham cracker crust, it uses layers of flaky phyllo dough to create a crunchy textural contrast to the creamy cheesecake. A baklava topping of walnuts, pistachios, and honey syrup adds even more crunch and sweetness. Not only will your friends be raving about it, but they'll beg you for the recipe. Go ahead, share it.

1 *First, make the cheesecake.* Adjust the oven racks to the lower third and middle of the oven. Fill a large baking dish with 2 inches of water and place on the bottom rack of your oven. Preheat the oven to 325°F. Line the bottom of a 9-inch springform pan with parchment paper (see page 23) and grease the sides with nonstick cooking spray.

2 Drape a phyllo dough sheet onto the bottom and up the edges of the springform pan, then use a pastry brush to brush it with some of the melted butter so it's coated but not soaked (for step-by-step photos, see page 184). Repeat the process, laying all of the phyllo dough sheets across the bottom and up the sides of the pan, brushing butter in between each layer, until the bottom and sides are fully lined. It'll be messy, sheets will overlap, and it might remind you of doing papier-mâché in art class—all good; it will look (and taste) amazing. Set aside.

3 In a stand mixer fitted with the paddle attachment, combine the cream cheese, sour cream, and granulated sugar and beat on medium-low speed until smooth, about 1 minute.

4 Use a silicone spatula to scrape down the sides and bottom of the bowl, then add the eggs, honey, and vanilla extract. Beat on medium-low speed until the batter is smooth, about 45 seconds, scraping down the sides and bottom of the bowl as needed.

5 Transfer the batter to the prepared pan and use the silicone spatula to smooth it out to an even layer. Place the cheesecake on the middle rack of the oven. Bake until it's puffed up slightly and set around the edges but still a little wobbly in the center, 55 to 60 minutes.

6 Turn off the oven and open the oven door a crack. Leave the cheesecake in the turned-off oven for 1 hour (this allows the cheesecake to cool down gradually and helps to prevent cracks). After an hour, remove the cheesecake from the oven and transfer it, still in the pan, to the fridge to cool completely, about 4 hours and up to overnight. Once the cheesecake is chilled, carefully remove the springform ring and base from the cheesecake and transfer the cheesecake to a serving dish.

(Continued on page 185)

(Continued from page 182)

7 *Make the baklava topping.* In a small saucepan over medium heat, combine the water, honey, and lemon juice and cook, stirring occasionally, until the mixture reduces by about half and is thick enough to coat the back of a spoon, about 5 minutes.

8 Remove from the heat and mix in the chopped walnuts and pistachios. Allow to cool completely in the pan, then pour over the cheesecake, using the back of a large spoon to spread it into an even layer. This cheesecake is best served within a day, as the phyllo will soften over time.

Nutella Smith Island Cake

MAKES ONE 9-LAYER 8-INCH CAKE

PREP TIME 1 HOUR 30 MINUTES
(PLUS 1 HOUR 45 MINUTES COOL
TIME)
COOK TIME 39 MINUTES
TOTAL TIME 3 HOURS 54 MINUTES

FOR THE CAKE

1 cup (2 sticks) unsalted butter,
  at room temperature

½ cup vegetable oil

2 cups granulated sugar

5 large eggs, at room
  temperature

1 tablespoon vanilla extract

3½ cups all-purpose flour

2 teaspoons baking powder

1 teaspoon salt

1¾ cups buttermilk, at room
  temperature (get my homemade
  version on page 28)

FOR THE NUTELLA ICING

6 tablespoons (¾ stick) unsalted
  butter, at room temperature

2¼ cups granulated sugar

¾ cup milk (any dairy milk works)

¼ teaspoon salt

1½ cups Nutella

This cake is such a star that it got invited to the Oscars, but turned it down because it had something more important to do that night (be the centerpiece on your dinner table). But let's back up: if you haven't been graced with a Smith Island Cake in your life, I will explain. This showstopping cake, hailing from a small island off the coast of Maryland, is made of nine thin layers of yellow cake alternating with a thick chocolate icing. This version's filling is enhanced with our good friend Nutella, because everything is better with Nutella. And if you're thinking, *Nine layers?!* Don't worry, you got this.

1 *First, make the cake.* Preheat the oven to 350°F. Line the bottom of three 8-inch round cake pans with parchment paper (see page 23) and grease the sides with nonstick cooking spray. You're going to use these cake pans three times each (totaling 9 layers of cake), so take this time to cut out 6 more circles of parchment paper for later. (If you have only two cake pans, that works, too. You'll just bake in more batches.)

2 In a stand mixer fitted with the whisk attachment, beat the butter and vegetable oil on low speed until combined, so the oil doesn't fly everywhere. Gradually increase the speed to medium-high and beat until smooth, about 2 minutes.

3 With the mixer running, slowly pour in the granulated sugar and continue to beat on medium-high speed until the mixture is light, fluffy, and turns a pale yellow color, about 2 minutes.

4 Use a silicone spatula to scrape down the sides and bottom of the bowl, then add the eggs and vanilla extract. Beat on medium-high speed until the mixture is light and fluffy, about 2 minutes.

5 In a separate bowl, combine the flour, baking powder, and salt. With the mixer on low speed, alternate adding the dry ingredients and the buttermilk in 3 additions (you'll add half the dry, then all of the buttermilk, then the other half of the dry). It's okay if the batter still has a few lumps in it—you don't want to overmix.

6 Use a 1-cup measure to scoop 1 cup of batter into each of the prepared cake pans. You want to be super precise here for those lovely even layers—use the back of a butter knife to level off the cup measurement and use the silicone spatula to scrape all of the batter out into the pan. Use the spatula to spread the batter to the edges of the pan. The layer will be very thin, but this is correct. Bake until the cakes have risen and the tops spring back to the touch, 11 to 13 minutes.

(Continued on page 188)

(Continued from page 187)

7 Place the cake pans on cooling racks and allow the cakes to cool until just warm to the touch. To remove the cakes from the pans, drag a butter knife around the edges of each cake, then carefully flip each cake out onto a plate, peel away the parchment paper, and re-invert each cake, right-side up, onto the cooling rack to cool completely, about 20 minutes.

8 Use a paper towel to wipe away any crumbs inside the cake pans, then place a new sheet of parchment paper on the bottom and grease the sides again with nonstick cooking spray. Pour another cup of batter into each of the cake pans and repeat the baking process until all 9 cake layers are baked and cooled.

9 *While the cakes cool, make the Nutella icing.* In a medium saucepan over medium-low heat, add the butter, granulated sugar, milk, and salt and cook until the sugar granules melt completely, 3 to 5 minutes. Add the Nutella, bring the icing to a low boil, then reduce the heat to a simmer for 1 minute. Remove the icing from the heat and let it cool to room temperature, about 45 minutes.

10 When you're ready to assemble, place a cooling rack on top of a sheet pan to catch any drips of icing you're about to create. Place the first cake layer in the middle of the cooling rack. Top with ¼ cup of the icing (again, be precise! Measure this out with a ¼-cup measure and level it off with the back of a butter knife so all your icing layers are even). Then use an offset spatula or a butter knife to spread the icing evenly to the edges of the cake. Repeat this process, layering cake and ¼ cup icing. If your icing begins to harden and set, microwave it for 10 to 15 seconds; this should get it nice and spreadable again.

11 For the final layer, pour the remaining icing over the top of the cake, using an offset spatula or butter knife to spread it evenly to the edges and allowing the icing to fall off the sides of the cake. Use the silicone spatula to spread the icing around the sides to fully coat. Allow the cake to set until the icing firms up, about 1 hour, then use two large spatulas (or whatever large flat tool you have) to carefully pick up the cake from the bottom and transfer it to a cake stand or plate and serve.

Coffee, Caramel, Cookies and Cream Ice Cream

MAKES 1 QUART ICE CREAM

PREP TIME 45 MINUTES (PLUS
9 HOURS CHILL/CHURN TIME)
COOK TIME 10 MINUTES
TOTAL TIME 9 HOURS 55 MINUTES

FOR THE ICE CREAM

2 cups heavy cream

1 cup whole milk

½ cup granulated sugar

2 tablespoons instant coffee (instant espresso powder works, too)

2 teaspoons vanilla extract

½ teaspoon salt

5 large egg yolks

12 Oreo cookies, coarsely chopped

FOR THE SALTED CARAMEL

½ cup granulated sugar

3 tablespoons unsalted butter

3 tablespoons heavy cream

½ teaspoon salt

PRO TIP *To make this recipe no-churn, follow the ingredients and instructions for the ice cream base of the No-Churn Peach Crumble Ice Cream (page 132), mixing in 2 tablespoons instant coffee dissolved in 2 tablespoons water in the final moments of whipping your cream. Stir in the Oreos and caramel as instructed.*

This ice cream reminds me of ordering the most ridiculous Frappuccino at Starbucks as a teen, and I love re-creating that feeling. Homemade coffee ice cream gets folded with Oreos, and together they achieve an almost mocha flavor—marrying bitter and sweet—that I can't get enough of. Then we're swirling in thick ribbons of homemade salted caramel because, why not? In this recipe, an ice cream maker is necessary for that churned texture (I use a Cuisinart), but I've also included a note for a no-churn version below, which is a slightly firmer texture but is still an undisputed joy.

1 *First, make the ice cream.* In a medium saucepan over low heat, combine the cream, milk, granulated sugar, coffee, vanilla extract, and salt and cook, using a silicone spatula to stir occasionally, until the sugar dissolves completely, about 3 minutes.

2 In a medium heatproof bowl, add the egg yolks. Whisking constantly, pour ½ cup of the hot cream mixture into the yolks. Whisk the yolk mixture back into the pan with the cream. Cook the mixture over low heat, using the silicone spatula to stir slowly and constantly, until the mixture thickens enough to coat the back of the spatula, 3 to 5 minutes.

3 Pour the mixture into a gallon-size resealable plastic bag and seal it tightly. Place the bag in the freezer until it's cool to the touch, about 30 minutes.

4 *While the custard cools, make the caramel.* In a small saucepan over medium-low heat, add the granulated sugar and cook until it melts completely. Use a silicone spatula to stir the sugar occasionally, scraping down the sides and bottom of the pan. First the sugar will form clumps, then it will begin to melt and take on a light golden color. After 5 to 7 minutes, it will become fully melted and be a medium gold hue. As soon as your last bit of sugar has melted, turn off the heat and immediately stir in the butter—use caution because the mixture will violently bubble. Use a whisk to stir the butter and melted sugar together until combined, about 20 seconds. Whisk in the cream and salt until combined. Allow the caramel to cool in the pan to room temperature.

5 Once everything has chilled, churn your ice cream in an ice cream maker according to the manufacturer's instructions. Add the chopped Oreos during the last minute of churning.

6 Place half of the ice cream in a freezer-safe container, then drizzle half of the caramel on top (if your caramel is feeling firm, place it in a microwave for 15 seconds to loosen it). Add the second half of the ice cream, then top with the second half of the caramel. Use a knife to gently swirl the caramel through the ice cream. Cover tightly with plastic wrap and place in the freezer to set for at least 8 hours before serving. When tightly covered, the ice cream will keep in the freezer for up to 2 months.

Pistachio Layer Cake with White Chocolate Frosting

MAKES ONE 3-LAYER 8-INCH CAKE

PREP TIME 40 MINUTES
(PLUS 30 MINUTES COOL TIME)
COOK TIME 27 MINUTES
TOTAL TIME 1 HOUR 37 MINUTES

FOR THE CAKE

1½ cups roasted unsalted pistachios, plus chopped pistachios for topping (optional)

½ cup (1 stick) unsalted butter, at room temperature

¼ cup vegetable oil

1½ cups granulated sugar

2 large eggs plus 2 large egg whites, at room temperature

2 teaspoons vanilla extract

½ teaspoon almond extract

¾ cup full-fat sour cream (plain Greek yogurt also works)

¾ cup milk (any dairy or nondairy milk works)

2 cups all-purpose flour

1 tablespoon baking powder

½ teaspoon baking soda

1 teaspoon salt

FOR THE WHITE CHOCOLATE FROSTING

12 ounces white chocolate, finely chopped

1½ cups (3 sticks) unsalted butter, at room temperature

1½ cups confectioners' sugar

1½ teaspoons vanilla extract

½ teaspoon salt

Blackberries, for topping (optional)

Almond flour is the popular kid at the alternative flour table, and for good reason: it creates a soft and moist crumb. But you know what else does that same thing, and arguably better? Pistachio flour that you can make in a food processor in under ten seconds. It results in an extremely tender cake with a playful green hue that reminds me of spring tulips. And—pause for dramatic effect—the white chocolate frosting! It pairs excellently with the delicate, slightly nutty flavor of the pistachios. It's unique and unexpected, not to mention utterly beautiful.

1 *First, make the cake.* Preheat the oven to 350°F. Line the bottoms of three 8-inch round cake pans with parchment paper (see page 23) and grease the sides with nonstick cooking spray.

2 In a food processor or high-powered blender, add the pistachios and pulse until they form sandlike crumbs. Set aside.

3 In a stand mixer fitted with the whisk attachment, beat the butter and vegetable oil on low speed until combined, so the oil doesn't fly everywhere. Gradually increase the speed to medium-high and beat until smooth, about 2 minutes.

4 With the mixer running, slowly pour in the granulated sugar and continue to beat on medium-high speed until the mixture is light, fluffy, and turns a pale yellow color, about 2 minutes.

5 Add the eggs, extra egg whites, vanilla extract, and almond extract. Beat on medium-high speed until the mixture is light and fluffy, about 2 minutes. Add the sour cream (or yogurt) and milk and mix on medium-high for 30 seconds more. At this stage, this batter has a tendency to look a little curdled. If this happens, it's okay! Keep going.

6 Stop the mixer and scrape down the sides and bottom of the bowl. Add the flour, ground pistachios, baking powder, baking soda, and salt and beat on low speed until just combined and no streaks of flour remain.

7 Divide the cake batter evenly among the prepared pans, spreading it evenly to the edges. Bake until the cakes have risen, the tops spring back to the touch, and a butter knife inserted into the centers comes out mostly clean (a crumb or two attached is okay), 22 to 27 minutes.

8 Place the cake pans on cooling racks and allow them to cool slightly. To remove the cakes from the pans, drag a butter knife around the edges of each cake, then carefully flip each cake out onto a plate, peel away the parchment paper, and re-invert each cake, right-side up, onto the cooling rack to cool completely, about 30 minutes.

(Continued on page 195)

(Continued from page 192)

9 *Once the cakes have cooled, make the frosting.* In a large microwave-safe bowl, add the chopped white chocolate. Microwave in 15-second increments, using a silicone spatula to stir between each, until the white chocolate is fully melted. Set aside to cool slightly, so it's warm but not hot to the touch, about 5 minutes.

10 In a stand mixer fitted with the paddle attachment, beat the butter, confectioners' sugar, vanilla extract, and salt on low speed until combined. With the mixer still running, slowly stream in the melted white chocolate. Once the white chocolate is incorporated, increase the speed to medium-high and beat until light and fluffy, about 1 minute, scraping down the sides and bottom of the bowl with the silicone spatula as needed.

11 Place the first cake layer, right-side up, on a cake stand or plate. Spread a large dollop of frosting on top, using an offset spatula to spread a thick layer evenly to the edges of the cake. Repeat with the second and third cake layers and dollops of frosting. Use the remaining frosting to frost the sides of the cake. Top with chopped pistachios and blackberries (if using) and serve.

Salted Caramel Pots-de-Crème

MAKES SIX 6-OUNCE
POTS-DE-CRÈME

PREP TIME 30 MINUTES
(PLUS 2 HOURS CHILL TIME)
COOK TIME 1 HOUR 7 MINUTES
TOTAL TIME 3 HOURS 37 MINUTES

1 cup granulated sugar

2 tablespoons (¼ stick) unsalted butter

1½ cups heavy cream, at room temperature

½ cup whole milk (2% milk also works), at room temperature

½ teaspoon salt

5 large egg yolks

2 teaspoons vanilla extract

Flaky sea salt, for topping

Apparently "pots-de-crème" means "jars of cream" in French, and I love that for us. While the traditional version is a chocolate custard, we're making ours with a velvety salted caramel (drool). The joy of pots-de-crème is that they have the silkiness of crème brûlée without the flashy torched topping. Also, can we talk about how, when baked, the custard naturally separates into two visually distinct layers that make it look like you did more work than you actually did? *Oui.* Good news for your next dinner party: if you wanna make these ahead, they hold up well when covered in the fridge overnight.

1 Preheat the oven to 325°F. Place six 6-ounce ramekins inside a baking pan (any pan size works as long as it's bigger and taller than your ramekins).

2 In a medium saucepan over medium-low heat, add the granulated sugar and cook until it melts completely. Use a silicone spatula to stir the sugar occasionally, scraping down the sides and bottom of the pan. First the sugar will form clumps, then it will begin to melt and take on color. After 5 to 7 minutes, it will become fully melted and be a medium-gold hue. As soon as your last bit of sugar has melted, turn off the heat and don't let the sugar continue to cook or it will burn.

3 Remove the saucepan from the heat and immediately stir in the butter—use caution as the mixture will violently bubble. Use a whisk to stir the butter and melted sugar together until combined, about 20 seconds. Whisk in the cream, milk, and salt until combined.

4 In a medium heatproof bowl, combine the egg yolks and vanilla extract. Whisking constantly, pour about ½ cup of the hot cream mixture into the yolks. Whisk the yolk mixture back into the pan with the cream. Cook the mixture over low heat, using the silicone spatula to stir slowly and constantly, until the mixture thickens enough to coat the back of the spatula, 3 to 5 minutes.

5 Divide the mixture evenly among the ramekins. Create a water bath for the pots-de-crème by carefully pouring boiling water into the larger baking pan until it comes halfway up the sides of the ramekins.

6 Bake the pots-de-crème until the edges are set but the centers of the custards jiggle slightly, about 1 hour. Use tongs to carefully remove the ramekins from the water bath and place them on a cooling rack to cool to room temperature before transferring them to the fridge for at least 2 hours and up to 3 days (if chilling for more than 2 hours, cover the tops of your ramekins tightly with plastic wrap or, eww, they'll get a skin!). To serve, top each pot-de-crème with flaky sea salt.

Apple Rose Tart

MAKES ONE 9-INCH TART

PREP TIME 1 HOUR 20 MINUTES
COOK TIME 50 MINUTES
TOTAL TIME 2 HOURS 10 MINUTES

FOR THE TART CRUST

1⅓ cups all-purpose flour

⅓ cup granulated sugar

⅓ cup packed light brown sugar

¼ teaspoon salt

½ cup (1 stick) unsalted butter, cold and cut into small cubes

FOR THE FRANGIPANE FILLING

½ cup (1 stick) unsalted butter, at room temperature

½ cup granulated sugar

1 large egg plus 1 large egg yolk, at room temperature

2 teaspoons almond extract

1 teaspoon vanilla extract

1 cup superfine almond flour

2 tablespoons all-purpose flour

¼ teaspoon salt

FOR THE APPLE TOPPING

7 or 8 medium red-skinned apples, such as Gala or Fuji, cored and cut into ¹⁄₁₆-inch slices (break out the mandoline if you have one)

2 cups water

¾ cup granulated sugar

2 tablespoons freshly squeezed lemon juice (from about 1 lemon)

Confectioner's sugar, for topping (optional)

This tart isn't just a pretty face. But also—look at that pretty face! Beneath the oh-so-beautiful surface, though, is a buttery almond frangipane that balances the apple's sweetness while insulating the tart dough from becoming soggy. Boiling the apple slices for a few minutes softens them so they can be rolled into delicate roselike petals (you don't even need to peel them). The result looks like a blushing bouquet of roses that is nearly impossible not to photograph, but make it quick—there are people who saved room for dessert here.

1 *First, make the tart crust.* Preheat the oven to 350°F. Line the bottom of a 9-inch round tart pan with parchment paper (see page 23).

2 In a food processor, add the all-purpose flour, granulated sugar, brown sugar, and salt and pulse to combine. Add the butter and pulse until the mixture forms a sandy dough, about 30 seconds.

3 Transfer the dough to the prepared tart pan and use your fingers to press the crust into an even layer along the bottom and sides of the pan. Then use a measuring cup (or something else with a flat bottom) to really pack the crust in. Place the pan in the fridge to chill slightly while you make your filling.

4 *Next, make the frangipane filling.* In a stand mixer fitted with the paddle attachment, combine the butter and granulated sugar and beat on medium-high speed until well mixed and slightly fluffy, about 1 minute.

5 Add the egg, extra egg yolk, almond extract, and vanilla extract. Beat on medium-high speed until combined, about 30 seconds. Stop the mixer and scrape down the bowl, then add the almond flour, all-purpose flour, and salt and beat on low speed until just combined and the mixture forms a thick paste.

6 Remove the tart crust from the fridge and use the silicone spatula to spread the filling into an even layer on the bottom of the tart. Place the tart pan back in the fridge while you make your apple topping.

7 *Make your apple topping.* In a large saucepan over medium-low heat, combine the apples, water, granulated sugar, and lemon juice and cook until the apples are soft and pliable, about 2 minutes. Drain the apples in a colander and allow them to cool until warm to the touch, about 10 minutes.

8 Next, it's time to roll some roses. Working on a clean work surface, line 5 apple slices slightly overlapping one another (for step-by-step photos, see pages 200–201). Roll the apple slices into a spiral "rose," then place carefully on top of the frangipane filling, pushing the roses down slightly so they stay in place. Repeat until the tart is full of roses, with some using more apple slices so they're bigger than others; this is how you get your roses to be all different sizes.

9 Place the tart pan on a large sheet pan (this will ensure that you don't accidentally push the bottom of the tart pan up while handling it). Bake until the frangipane filling has puffed up slightly and the tart crust is golden brown, 45 to 50 minutes. Place the tart on a cooling rack and allow it to cool to room temperature before dusting with confectioners' sugar (if using) and serving.

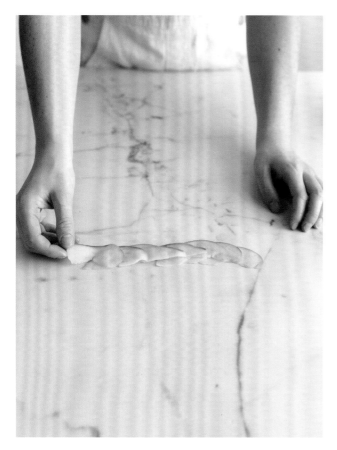
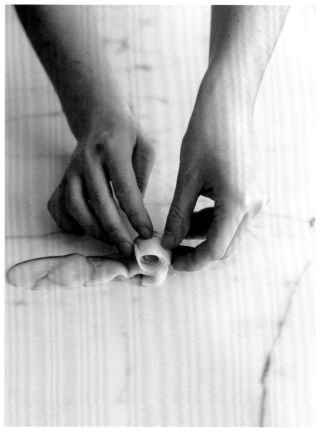

Chocolate Tiramisu

MAKES ONE 9 × 13-INCH PAN

PREP TIME 45 MINUTES
(PLUS 4 HOURS CHILL TIME)
TOTAL TIME 4 HOURS 45 MINUTES

1½ cups brewed coffee

¼ cup coffee liqueur or dark rum, divided

4 large eggs

⅔ cup granulated sugar, divided

16 ounces mascarpone cheese

2 teaspoons vanilla extract

½ teaspoon salt

12 ounces (1½ cups) hot fudge sauce (Hot fudge jars come in weird sizes. Some are 11.5 ounces, some are 12.4 ounces . . . anything close to 12 ounces will work.)

2 (7-ounce) packages ladyfingers

¼ cup Dutch-processed cocoa powder

I went through the first twenty-five years of life thinking I didn't like tiramisu. It always seemed to taste like a sponge. Then I went to Italy, had a traditional tiramisu, and I learned I actually *love* tiramisu. It's just that, unfortunately, so many American versions of tiramisu use whipped cream in the mascarpone filling, which leads to a dry and airy texture that is just. not. it. Authentic Italian tiramisu utilizes whipped egg whites in the filling, which are lightweight and yet velvety rich, a food science miracle. Oh, and obviously we're taking things one step further by adding a layer of chocolate fudge sauce.

1 In a wide shallow bowl, add the coffee and 2 tablespoons of the coffee liqueur and whisk to combine. Get out a 9 × 13-inch rectangular baking pan. Set both aside.

2 Separate the egg whites from the yolks. Place the egg whites in the bowl of a stand mixer fitted with the whisk attachment and place the yolks in a small bowl for later. Beat the egg whites on high speed until frothy, then keep the mixer going as you stream in ⅓ cup of the granulated sugar. Continue beating on high speed until your meringue forms stiff peaks, 3 to 5 minutes. Use a silicone spatula to scrape the meringue into a large bowl and set aside.

3 In the stand mixer bowl (no need to clean it), combine the reserved egg yolks and the remaining ⅓ cup granulated sugar. Beat on high speed (still using the whisk attachment) until light and pale in color, about 2 minutes. Add the mascarpone, the remaining 2 tablespoons coffee liqueur, the vanilla extract, and salt and whisk until combined, about 20 seconds. Remove the bowl from the stand mixer.

4 Scrape half of the meringue into the bowl with the egg yolk mixture. Use the silicone spatula to fold gently to combine. Add the remaining half of the meringue and fold until no streaks of meringue remain. Spread a thin coating of the mascarpone cream on the bottom of the baking pan.

5 In a microwave-safe bowl, add the hot fudge sauce. Microwave until the sauce is warm and a spreadable consistency. Quickly dunk the ladyfingers into the coffee mixture on both sides (they will fall apart if you soak them any longer) and place them in a single layer in the bottom of the baking pan. Top with half of the hot fudge sauce and spread it over the ladyfingers in an even layer. Use the spatula to spread about half of the mascarpone cream on top of the hot fudge sauce, smoothing the layer as evenly as possible.

6 Repeat the process with another layer of coffee-soaked ladyfingers. Top with the second half of the fudge sauce. This time, add a thin layer of mascarpone cream on top; it should be just thick enough to cover the hot fudge, but no thicker. Afterward, you should have a little less than half of the mascarpone cream remaining.

7 Transfer the remaining mascarpone cream to a piping bag fitted with a ½-inch round tip. Pipe 1-inch circles of mascarpone cream over the entire

PRO TIP *If you're a purist and want a classic tiramisu, omit the hot fudge sauce.*

surface of the tiramisu. Place the baking pan, uncovered, in the fridge to set for at least 4 hours and up to overnight (if refrigerating for longer than 4 hours, refrigerate the pan, uncovered, for the first 4 hours, then lightly cover it with plastic wrap, being careful not to smoosh down your mascarpone cream dollops).

8 When you're ready to serve, take the tiramisu out of the fridge. Generously dust the top with cocoa powder, then slice and serve.

Dulce de Leche Cheesecake Brownies

MAKES 16 BROWNIES

PREP TIME 30 MINUTES
(PLUS 1 HOUR CHILL TIME)
BAKE TIME 35 MINUTES
TOTAL TIME 2 HOURS 5 MINUTES

FOR THE DULCE DE LECHE

1 (13-ounce) jar dulce de leche

¼ teaspoon salt

FOR THE CHEESECAKE SWIRL

4 ounces cream cheese, at room temperature

¼ cup granulated sugar

1 large egg, at room temperature

1 teaspoon vanilla extract

FOR THE BROWNIES

½ cup (1 stick) unsalted butter

1 cup granulated sugar

4 ounces bittersweet chocolate, finely chopped

2 large eggs plus 1 large egg yolk

1 teaspoon vanilla extract

¾ cup all-purpose flour

¼ cup Dutch-processed cocoa powder

½ teaspoon salt

2 tablespoons water

I'm living up to the *Sweet Tooth* promise here to bring you desserts that go the extra mile. A mile made of swirly dulce de leche that, in addition to swirly cheesecake, creates an unapologetically fancy brownie. And yet brownies are a dessert that always feels casual to me, so when I eat these, they seem to elevate the everyday: noshing while folding a pile of laundry, taking one for the road on a walk, snacking while checking emails . . . mood, improved.

1 *First, mix the dulce de leche.* Open your jar of dulce de leche and stir in the salt. Separate out ⅓ cup dulce de leche to use for this recipe and set aside. (You will have some dulce de leche left over. Use it to top ice cream, drizzle over a cake, go wild!)

2 Preheat the oven to 350°F. Line a 9 × 9-inch square baking pan with parchment paper on all sides (see page 23).

3 *Next, make the cheesecake swirl.* In a stand mixer fitted with the paddle attachment, combine the cream cheese, granulated sugar, egg, and vanilla extract and beat until well mixed, about 30 seconds. Set aside.

4 *Then, make the brownie layer.* In a large microwave-safe bowl, add the butter and granulated sugar. Microwave until the butter is fully melted and the mixture is hot to the touch, about 1 minute, then remove from the microwave and whisk together. Add the chopped chocolate and microwave for 30 seconds more. Remove the bowl; the chocolate should be completely melted. If it isn't, microwave for another 15 seconds. Whisk again.

5 Add the eggs, extra egg yolk, and vanilla extract and whisk vigorously until the mixture becomes glossy, about 30 seconds. (Don't worry about cooling the chocolate mixture before adding your eggs; whisk them in immediately and you're good.) Add the flour, cocoa powder, and salt and whisk slowly until evenly incorporated. Remove ½ cup of the brownie batter and place it in a small bowl. Add the water and whisk to thin it out. This will become the brownie swirl on top.

6 Pour the larger amount of brownie batter into the prepared pan, spreading it to the edges. Pour the cheesecake batter on top. Drop spoonfuls of the dulce de leche on top of the batter (8 to 10 spoonfuls from the ⅓ cup measurement). Last, drop spoonfuls of the thinned-out brownie batter on top (8 to 10 spoonfuls). Use a butter knife to drag and swirl everything together.

7 Bake until the surface of the brownies is shiny, the edges are set, and a butter knife inserted into the center comes out mostly clean (a crumb or two attached is okay), 30 to 35 minutes. Place the pan on a cooling rack and allow the brownies to cool slightly in the pan before transferring them to the fridge to cool completely, about 1 hour. Once the brownies are chilled, use the parchment paper to lift them from the pan, transfer them to a cutting board, cut into 16 squares, and serve.

Cinnamon Roll Bread

MAKES ONE 8½-INCH LOAF

PREP TIME 1 HOUR (PLUS 2 HOURS RISE TIME)
COOK TIME 40 MINUTES
TOTAL TIME 3 HOURS 40 MINUTES

FOR THE DOUGH

4½ cups all-purpose flour, divided, plus more for rolling out the dough

⅓ cup granulated sugar

1 packet (2¼ teaspoons) instant yeast

1 teaspoon salt

1½ cups whole milk

6 tablespoons (¾ stick) unsalted butter

1 large egg, at room temperature

FOR THE CINNAMON SUGAR FILLING

⅔ cup packed light brown sugar

1 tablespoon ground cinnamon

¼ cup (½ stick) unsalted butter, at room temperature

FOR THE CREAM CHEESE ICING

2 tablespoons cream cheese

1 tablespoon unsalted butter

1½ cups confectioners' sugar

2 tablespoons whole milk

1 teaspoon vanilla extract

Pinch of salt

Just when you thought you couldn't love a cinnamon roll more, this bread comes along. It's a delicately spiced, sweetly yeasted loaf made from brioche-style bread that's rolled and cut into pieces as you would cinnamon rolls. But instead of going swirl-side up into a baking pan, the slices are lined up in a loaf pan, where they meld together while baking into lovely slices reminiscent of cinnamon swirl bread, only better. If you're going to toast the slices (nice move), keep the cream cheese icing on the side to spread on afterward.

1 *First, make the dough.* In a stand mixer fitted with the paddle attachment, combine 2 cups of the flour, the granulated sugar, yeast, and salt and beat on low speed until well mixed.

2 In a microwave-safe bowl, add the milk and butter. Microwave until the mixture is warm to the touch and the butter is melted, about 1 minute 15 seconds (you don't want the mixture to be steaming or too hot, because this can kill the yeast).

3 Pour the milk mixture into the flour mixture, add the egg, and beat everything together on low speed until combined. Gradually increase the speed to high and beat for 2 minutes. The dough will look more like batter, but this is correct! This step kicks off the gluten development.

4 After 2 minutes, change the paddle attachment to the dough hook attachment. Add 1½ cups of the remaining flour and knead on low speed until combined. Add the remaining 1 cup flour and knead on low speed, stopping the mixer occasionally to redistribute the dough, until the dough starts to pull away from the sides of the bowl and forms a ball around the dough hook.

5 Increase the speed to medium-low and knead until the dough becomes smooth and supple, about 10 minutes. If the dough gets wrapped around the hook too much, turn off the mixer, pull the dough off, flip over the dough, and turn on the mixer again. The dough is ready when you can stretch a quarter-size piece of dough between your fingers and see light through it (without it breaking). This means the gluten has developed enough.

6 Transfer the dough to a large bowl sprayed with nonstick cooking spray and cover the bowl with a dish towel or plastic wrap. Let rise in a warm place until the dough has doubled in size, about 1 hour.

7 *Once the dough has risen, make the cinnamon sugar filling.* In a small bowl, combine the brown sugar and cinnamon. Set aside.

8 Line a 1-pound loaf pan with parchment paper on all sides (see page 23).

(Continued on page 209)

(Continued from page 206)

9 Turn the dough out onto a well-floured surface. Use a rolling pin to roll it into a 12 × 20-inch rectangle, with the wider side closest to you.

10 Using your hands or a silicone spatula, spread the butter all the way to the edges of the dough. Sprinkle the cinnamon sugar mixture on top, then use your fingers to spread it into the butter.

11 From the 20-inch side closest to you, roll the dough into a tight log. Press the dough along the outside seam to seal everything together. Use a very sharp knife (or floss . . . yes, seriously!) to cut the dough into 12 even rolls (see photos opposite).

12 Add 8 of the rolls to the prepared loaf pan in 2 rows of 4, placing the rolls on their sides so the cut/swirled sides face the short sides of the pan.

13 Cut one of the 4 remaining rolls in half. Place the remaining 3 rolls on top of the first layer, again with the cut/swirled sides facing the short sides of the pan. Place the last roll cut in half on each end of the loaf. Slightly tuck the bottoms of the rolls in between the first layer of rolls so that they stay in place. Cover the dough with a dish towel or plastic wrap and allow to rise in a warm place for 1 hour.

14 Preheat the oven to 350°F. Uncover the dough. Bake the bread until it is puffed up and the top is golden brown all over, about 40 minutes. If the top of the bread starts to brown too quickly, loosely cover it with aluminum foil. Place the loaf pan on a cooling rack to cool slightly, about 15 minutes.

15 *While the bread cools, make the cream cheese icing.* In a medium microwave-safe bowl, combine the cream cheese and butter. Microwave until soft and slightly warm, 15 to 30 seconds. Add the confectioners' sugar, milk, vanilla extract, and salt and whisk until smooth.

16 Use the parchment paper to lift the bread from the pan, then transfer the bread to a cooling rack. Put a pan beneath the cooling rack to catch the drips, drizzle the icing on top of the bread (it's okay if it's still a little warm!), then allow the bread to sit until the icing is set and serve.

Black Forest Pavlova

MAKES 1 LARGE PAVLOVA

PREP TIME 30 MINUTES
(PLUS 2 HOURS COOL TIME)
COOK TIME 1 HOUR 30 MINUTES
TOTAL TIME 4 HOURS

FOR THE PAVLOVA

1 teaspoon distilled white vinegar

1½ teaspoons cornstarch

6 large egg whites, at room temperature

1½ cups granulated sugar

1 teaspoon vanilla extract

1 teaspoon almond extract

¼ teaspoon salt

FOR THE TOPPING

1½ cups heavy cream

¼ cup confectioners' sugar

1 teaspoon vanilla extract

14 ounces store-bought pitted Morello cherries in syrup (or any cherries in syrup)

1 ounce semisweet or bittersweet chocolate (in bar form)

Fresh cherries, for topping (optional)

I don't think pavlovas get enough hype. They combine the light, crunchy goodness of a meringue cookie with the ethereal fluffiness of a marshmallow. Plus, there's always a heaping pile of whipped cream on top. This version has flavors of a Black Forest cake (cherries and chocolate, with a hint of almond) counterbalancing the airy meringue with depth and richness. It's light, so much fun to eat, and the contrast of textures will keep you coming back for another bite, until the whole thing disappears.

1 *First, make the pavlova.* Adjust a rack to the lower third of the oven. Preheat the oven to 200°F. Line a sheet pan with parchment paper.

2 In a small bowl, combine the vinegar and cornstarch and stir together (you can use your finger or a fork). Set aside.

3 In a stand mixer fitted with the whisk attachment, add the egg whites and beat on high speed until frothy. Continue beating and slowly stream in the granulated sugar. Beat until the meringue forms stiff peaks, 5 to 7 minutes.

4 Turn the mixer off and add the vinegar mixture, vanilla extract, almond extract, and salt. Beat on high speed until the meringue is stiff, glossy, and you can't feel any granulated sugar when you rub the meringue between your fingers, about 5 minutes more.

5 Spoon the meringue onto the parchment paper. Use a silicone spatula to form the meringue into your desired shape. Use the spatula to create a slight divot in the center of the meringue (like a volcano with a shallow crater). Last, use the spatula to create cloudlike flourishes and swooshes around the meringue (you can't really go wrong; find your inner artist).

6 Bake the pavlova for 1 hour and 30 minutes. Turn off the oven and open the oven door a crack. Leave the pavlova in the turned-off oven for 1 hour (this allows it to dry out gradually and helps prevent it from sweating and deflating). After an hour, remove the pavlova from the oven and transfer the pan to a cooling rack to cool completely, about 1 hour more.

7 *Once the pavlova is cooled, make the topping.* In a stand mixer fitted with the whisk attachment, beat the cream, confectioners' sugar, and vanilla extract on low speed until combined. Gradually increase the speed to high and beat until soft peaks form and the whipped cream holds its shape, about 1 minute.

8 Spoon the whipped cream into the center of the pavlova, then top with the cherries in syrup. Use a vegetable peeler to create chocolate shavings on top of the pavlova by dragging the peeler along the edge of the chocolate bar. Top with fresh cherries (if using) and serve.

Triple Chocolate Cheesecake

MAKES ONE 9-INCH CHEESECAKE

PREP TIME 1 HOUR
(PLUS 5 HOURS CHILL TIME)
COOK TIME 55 MINUTES
TOTAL TIME 6 HOURS 55 MINUTES

FOR THE CRUST

¼ cup (½ stick) unsalted butter, melted

20 Oreo cookies, finely ground into crumbs (about 2 cups)

FOR THE CHOCOLATE CHEESECAKE

8 ounces bittersweet chocolate, finely chopped

24 ounces cream cheese (three 8-ounce blocks), at room temperature

1 cup full-fat sour cream, at room temperature

1¼ cups granulated sugar

¼ cup Dutch-processed cocoa powder

2 teaspoons instant espresso powder

4 large eggs, at room temperature

1 tablespoon vanilla extract

FOR THE CHOCOLATE GANACHE

6 ounces bittersweet chocolate, finely chopped

¾ cup heavy cream

Chocolate sprinkles, for topping (optional)

I can't help it. But when I'm eating something that I really like, I start to wiggle from side to side. I call it my Happy Food Dance (it's as silly as it sounds). And this Triple Chocolate Cheesecake gives me the Happy Food Dance every time. An Oreo cookie crust provides a crunchy base for the rich chocolate cheesecake that's then topped with a glossy ganache. It's a chocolate lover's fantasy, and if it doesn't make you wiggle, you might want to get those hips checked out.

1 *First, make the crust.* Adjust the oven racks to the lower third and middle of the oven. Fill a large baking dish with 2 inches of water and place on the bottom rack of your oven. Preheat the oven to 325°F. Line a 9-inch springform pan with parchment paper (see page 23) and grease the sides with nonstick cooking spray.

2 In a medium bowl, combine the butter and Oreo cookie crumbs. Use a silicone spatula to mix until it clumps together and resembles wet sand.

3 Transfer the mixture to the prepared pan and press the crust into an even layer along the bottom of the pan with your fingers. Then use a measuring cup (or something else with a flat bottom) to really pack the crust into an even layer.

4 *Next, make the cheesecake.* In a medium microwave-safe bowl, add the chopped chocolate. Microwave for 30 seconds, then remove from the microwave and use a silicone spatula to stir. Repeat, microwaving in 30-second increments and stirring after each, until the chocolate is fully melted. Set aside.

5 In a stand mixer fitted with the paddle attachment, combine the cream cheese, sour cream, and granulated sugar and beat on medium-low speed until smooth, about 30 seconds.

6 Use a silicone spatula to scrape down the sides and bottom of the bowl, then add the cocoa powder and espresso powder and mix on low speed until combined. Add the eggs and vanilla extract. Beat on medium-low speed until the batter is smooth, about 45 seconds, scraping down the sides and bottom of the bowl as needed.

7 With the mixer running on low speed, slowly pour in the melted chocolate and mix until fully combined. Pour the batter into the prepared pan and use the silicone spatula to smooth it evenly to the edges.

8 Place the cheesecake on the middle rack of the oven. Bake until the cheesecake is puffed up slightly and set around the edges but still a little wobbly in the center, 50 to 55 minutes.

(Continued on page 215)

(Continued from page 212)

9 Turn off the oven and open the oven door a crack. Leave the cheesecake in the turned-off oven for 1 hour (this allows the cheesecake to cool down gradually and helps to prevent cracks). After an hour, remove the cheesecake from the oven and transfer it, still in the pan, to the fridge to cool completely, about 4 hours and up to overnight. Once the cheesecake is chilled, carefully remove the springform ring and base from the cheesecake, transfer to a serving plate, and set aside while you make your ganache.

10 *Last, make the ganache.* In a small saucepan over medium heat, combine the chocolate and cream and cook, stirring constantly, until the chocolate is melted.

11 Remove the saucepan from the heat. Transfer about one-third of the ganache to a small bowl and place in the fridge for 30 minutes. You'll use this later for the ganache piping on top of the cheesecake.

12 Pour the remaining ganache over the cheesecake, allowing it to drip down the sides. Place the cheesecake back in the fridge to set for 30 minutes.

13 After 30 minutes, take the reserved ganache and the cheesecake out of the fridge. Transfer the ganache to a piping bag fitted with a small star tip. The ganache should hold its shape, but it should not be so cold that you can't pipe it (if it's too cold, place it in the microwave for 5 to 10 seconds). Pipe dollops of ganache on the edges of your cheesecake, then top the dollops with chocolate sprinkles, if desired (and aren't they always?), and serve.

Rhubarb and Almond Galette

MAKES ONE 10-INCH GALETTE

PREP TIME 30 MINUTES
(PLUS 30 MINUTES CHILL TIME)
COOK TIME 50 MINUTES
TOTAL TIME 1 HOUR 50 MINUTES

FOR THE PIE DOUGH

1¼ cups all-purpose flour, plus more for rolling out the dough

1 tablespoon granulated sugar

½ teaspoon salt

½ cup (1 stick) unsalted butter, cold and cut into cubes

2 to 3 tablespoons ice water or chilled vodka (water is standard in pie crust, but vodka will make your crust extra flaky!)

1 large egg, for egg wash

¼ cup sliced almonds

Demerara sugar, for topping (optional)

FOR THE FRANGIPANE FILLING

¼ cup (½ stick) unsalted butter, at room temperature

½ cup granulated sugar

1 large egg, at room temperature

½ teaspoon vanilla extract

½ teaspoon almond extract

¾ cup superfine almond flour

¼ teaspoon salt

FOR THE RHUBARB

1 pound rhubarb stalks, cut into 7-inch-long pieces

3 tablespoons granulated sugar

Rhubarb is such a sign that summer is here, you have to seize it—and make this galette. But when I first made this recipe for my family, my mom's reply when I mentioned bringing a rhubarb galette was: "I guess that's okay." Cut to six hours later, and both my husband and my mom are exclaiming between bites that it is the best galette they've ever had. I think their hesitancy about the sour rhubarb was erased once they tasted it with the creamy almond frangipane it sits atop. The next night, my mom called me. "The combination of the sweet almond, crunchy pie crust, and tart rhubarb . . . it was *incredible*, Sarah." It's officially Mom-approved.

1 *First, make the pie dough.* In a food processor, add the all-purpose flour, granulated sugar, and salt and pulse to combine. Add the butter and pulse until the mixture resembles wet sand and no big chunks of butter remain, about 20 seconds.

2 Add 2 tablespoons of the ice water, then pulse until a dough begins to form a ball around the blade, about 20 seconds. If your dough doesn't come together, add another tablespoon of water and pulse again.

3 Turn the dough out onto a clean work surface and flatten it into a 1-inch-thick oval disk. Wrap the disk tightly in plastic wrap and refrigerate for at least 30 minutes and up to 2 days.

4 *Next, make the frangipane filling.* In a stand mixer fitted with the paddle attachment, beat the butter and granulated sugar on medium-high speed until combined and slightly fluffy, about 1 minute.

5 Use a silicone spatula to scrape down the sides and bottom of the bowl, then add the egg, vanilla extract, and almond extract. Beat on medium-high speed until combined, about 30 seconds. Add the almond flour and salt and beat on low speed until just combined and the mixture forms a thick paste. Set aside.

6 Preheat the oven to 375°F. Line a sheet pan with parchment paper. Once the dough has chilled, remove it from the fridge and set it on the counter to soften for 5 minutes.

7 *While the dough is softening, prepare your rhubarb.* Place the rhubarb on a large cutting board and slice it vertically into ½-inch-thick strips. Sprinkle the granulated sugar over the rhubarb and rub it into the stalks.

8 Lightly dust a clean work surface with flour, unwrap the dough disk, and place it on the work surface. Dust with more flour and use a rolling pin to roll out the dough into a roughly 12-inch circle, dusting the top and underside with more flour as needed. Carefully roll the dough around your rolling pin like a scroll, then roll it out over the prepared sheet pan.

9 Spread the frangipane filling on the bottom of the pie dough, leaving a 2-inch border around the edges. Place the rhubarb strips on top of the frangipane, using your fingers to pat the rhubarb slightly into the frangipane.

PRO TIP *If you don't like rhubarb, you can swap it out for almost any fruit—1 cup berries; 2 cored and sliced apples or pears; or 2 or 3 halved, pitted, and sliced peaches or plums.*

Working your way around the galette in a series of folds, fold the pie dough up and over the rhubarb, pressing each fold down slightly to adhere.

10 In a small bowl, whisk the egg with 2 tablespoons water. Use a pastry brush to brush the top of the dough with the egg wash. Sprinkle the sliced almonds around the brushed dough and use your fingers to gently press the almonds down into the dough. Sprinkle the edges with demerara sugar, if using.

11 Bake the galette until the crust is golden brown and the rhubarb looks soft, 45 to 50 minutes. Remove the pan from the oven and allow the galette to cool slightly on the pan before serving.

Lamingtons

MAKES 24 LAMINGTONS

PREP TIME 1 HOUR (PLUS 1 HOUR
30 MINUTES CHILL TIME)
COOK TIME 40 MINUTES
TOTAL TIME 3 HOURS 10 MINUTES

FOR THE CAKE

¾ cup (1½ sticks) unsalted butter,
  at room temperature

1½ cups granulated sugar

3 large eggs, at room
  temperature

2 teaspoons vanilla extract

2½ cups cake flour

2 teaspoons baking powder

1 teaspoon salt

¾ cup milk (any dairy or nondairy
  milk works)

1 cup raspberry jam (I prefer a
  seedless jam)

FOR THE CHOCOLATE COCONUT COATING

1½ cups semisweet or
  bittersweet chocolate chips

½ cup milk (any dairy milk works)

3 cups confectioners' sugar

3 cups unsweetened shredded
  coconut

Tiny cakes. That's all that Lamingtons are, so don't be intimidated by the fancy name. These are Australia's national cake, but again, no pressure. We're making a fluffy yellow cake with raspberry jam filling, then slicing it into bite-sizes and dipping them in chocolate and coconut. I believe the correct number of Lamingtons per person is "I've lost count," so bring them to a bake sale, holiday party, or any occasion where you'd normally bring cupcakes or cookies but want to stand out from the crowd.

1 *First, make the cake.* Preheat the oven to 350°F. Line a 9 × 13-inch rectangular baking pan with parchment paper on all sides (see page 23).

2 In a stand mixer fitted with the paddle attachment, beat the butter and granulated sugar on low speed until combined. Gradually increase the speed to medium-high and beat until light and fluffy, about 2 minutes.

3 Use a silicone spatula to scrape down the sides and bottom of the bowl, then add the eggs and vanilla extract. Beat on medium-high speed until light and fluffy, about 2 minutes.

4 In a separate bowl, combine the cake flour, baking powder, and salt. With the mixer on low speed, alternate adding the dry ingredients and the milk in 3 additions (add half the dry, then all of the milk, then the other half of the dry).

5 Pour the batter into the prepared baking pan, using the silicone spatula to spread it evenly to the edges. Bake until the cake has risen, the top springs back to the touch, and a butter knife inserted into the center comes out mostly clean (a crumb or two attached is okay), 35 to 40 minutes.

6 Place the cake on a cooling rack to cool to room temperature. To remove the cake from the pan, carefully flip the cake out onto the cooling rack, peel away the parchment paper, and re-invert the cake, right-side up, onto a large cutting board.

7 Use a sharp knife to cut the cake in half horizontally, creating 2 layers. Spread the raspberry jam onto the bottom layer of cake, then carefully place the other cake layer on top, creating a jam sandwich. Use a sharp knife to cut the cake into 24 squares (4 rows by 6 rows) and arrange the squares, still on the cutting board, so they're slightly separated. Gently cover the squares with a dish towel or plastic wrap and place in the freezer to chill for 1 hour.

8 *Next, make the chocolate coconut coating.* In a large microwave-safe bowl, combine the chocolate chips and milk. Microwave for 30 seconds, then remove from the microwave and use a silicone spatula to stir. Repeat, microwaving in 30-second increments and stirring after each, until the chocolate is fully melted. Use a whisk to stir in the confectioners' sugar until combined.

9 Remove the cake from the freezer and make a cake dipping station: Place a cooling rack on top of a sheet pan. Pour the coconut flakes into a medium bowl.

10 Use two forks to dip each Lamington into the melted chocolate, coating all sides. Shake off any excess coating, then dip the Lamington into the shredded coconut, coating all sides. Place on the cooling rack, then repeat until the cake squares are all dipped and coated. Allow the chocolate coating to harden for about 30 minutes before serving.

HOLIDAY BAKING

September through December is the unofficial—but to me, very official—baking season. As soon as the temperature drops below 65°F, I abandon my habitual spot on our patio couch, put on a chunky sweater, and head to the kitchen to bake up a batch of Maple-Glazed Apple Blondies. The next few months are filled with Thanksgiving showstoppers like Caramel Pumpkin Layer Cake (because that holiday should have more cakes), Christmas cookies galore (Hot Chocolate Cookies, I'm looking at you), and wintry treats like Flourless Ginger Chocolate Cake.

The holiday desserts in this chapter are playful and festive, best baked alongside *A Charlie Brown Christmas* soundtrack on repeat, and meant to be shared around a table with people you love so much it hurts.

Gingerbread Crinkle Cookies

MAKES 16 COOKIES

PREP TIME 30 MINUTES
COOK TIME 15 MINUTES
TOTAL TIME 45 MINUTES

¾ cup (1½ sticks) unsalted butter, at room temperature

¾ cup packed light brown sugar

⅓ cup molasses

1 large egg, at room temperature

2 teaspoons vanilla extract

2⅓ cups all-purpose flour

½ teaspoon baking soda

¼ teaspoon baking powder

2 teaspoons ground ginger

2 teaspoons ground cinnamon

½ teaspoon ground cloves

¼ teaspoon ground nutmeg

½ teaspoon salt

½ cup granulated sugar

½ cup confectioners' sugar

If crinkle cookies aren't a holiday staple for you, we're gonna change that. They're named for the defined cracks all over the surface of the cookie—the result of rolling the dough in confectioners' sugar *and* granulated sugar before baking—that make them look permanently snow-dusted. And the texture? To die for. It's an almost brownie-like consistency with a little bit of crunch from the sugar coating that makes me happy as an elf. This gingerbread version is flavored with molasses, ginger, cinnamon, nutmeg, and cloves, resulting in a wonderfully chewy, spiced holiday cookie.

1 Preheat the oven to 350°F. Line two sheet pans with parchment paper.

2 In a stand mixer fitted with the paddle attachment, beat the butter and brown sugar on low speed until combined. Gradually increase the speed to medium-high and beat until light and fluffy, about 2 minutes.

3 Use a silicone spatula to scrape down the sides and bottom of the bowl, then add the molasses, egg, and vanilla extract. Beat on medium-high speed until the mixture is smooth and fluffy, about 1 minute, scraping down the bowl as needed.

4 In a separate bowl, whisk together the flour, baking soda, baking powder, ginger, cinnamon, cloves, nutmeg, and salt. Add the dry ingredients to the stand mixer and beat on low speed until just combined and no streaks of flour remain.

5 Pour the granulated sugar into a small bowl. Pour the confectioners' sugar into a second small bowl.

6 Use a 1½-ounce cookie scoop to portion out equal amounts of dough (a large spoon also works; the ball should be about 3 tablespoons). Roll the dough in your hands to smooth the edges. Roll the dough balls in the granulated sugar first, then roll them in the confectioners' sugar, evenly coating the outside of the cookies. Place the cookies 2 inches apart on the prepared sheet pans.

7 Bake until the cookies have formed cracks all over and are set and firm around the edges but still somewhat soft in the middle, 12 to 15 minutes. Remove the sheet pans from the oven and allow the cookies to cool completely on the sheet pans before serving.

Caramel Pumpkin Layer Cake

MAKES ONE 3-LAYER 8-INCH CAKE

PREP TIME 1 HOUR (PLUS
30 MINUTES COOL TIME)
COOK TIME 37 MINUTES
TOTAL TIME 2 HOURS 7 MINUTES

FOR THE CAKE

1½ cups pumpkin puree (not
   pumpkin pie filling)

1½ cups granulated sugar

1 cup vegetable oil

4 large eggs, at room temperature

2 teaspoons vanilla extract

2 cups all-purpose flour

2 teaspoons baking soda

1½ teaspoons baking powder

2 teaspoons ground cinnamon

1 teaspoon ground nutmeg

1 teaspoon ground ginger

1 teaspoon salt

FOR THE SALTED CARAMEL
(OPTIONAL, BUT IS IT?)

½ cup granulated sugar

3 tablespoons unsalted butter

¼ cup heavy cream

½ teaspoon salt

FOR THE CREAM CHEESE FROSTING

1 cup (2 sticks) unsalted butter,
   at room temperature

8 ounces cream cheese, at room
   temperature

7 cups confectioners' sugar

1 tablespoon vanilla extract

½ teaspoon salt

Fresh blackberries, figs,
   pomegranate seeds, or
   rust-colored edible flowers,
   for topping (optional)

Welcome to the fall flavor festival. Sit down, stay awhile, and have a slice of pumpkin cake. It's like pumpkin bread, only softer, lighter, and even more moist. It's layered with a cream cheese buttercream that complements the warm spices in the cake, and is then drizzled with a sticky-sweet salted caramel that transforms this dessert into an autumnal stunner. Because this cake is a little ~extra~ I go all-out with decorations like blackberries, figs, and pomegranate seeds. Or let the caramel drizzle do the talking— that works, too.

1 *First, make the cake.* Preheat the oven to 350°F. Line the bottoms of three 8-inch round cake pans with parchment paper (see page 23) and grease the sides with nonstick cooking spray.

2 In a medium bowl, whisk together the pumpkin puree, granulated sugar, vegetable oil, eggs, and vanilla extract. Set aside.

3 In a large bowl, whisk together the flour, baking soda, baking powder, cinnamon, nutmeg, ginger, and salt. Make a well in the center of the bowl and pour in the wet ingredients. Whisk until no streaks of flour remain.

4 Divide the cake batter evenly among the prepared pans. Bake until the cakes have risen, the tops spring back to the touch, and a butter knife inserted into the centers of the cakes comes out mostly clean (a crumb or two attached is okay), 25 to 30 minutes.

5 Place the cake pans on cooling racks and allow the cakes to cool slightly. To remove the cakes from the pans, drag a butter knife around the edges of each cake, then carefully flip each cake out onto a plate, peel away the parchment paper, and re-invert each cake, right-side up, onto a cooling rack to cool completely, about 30 minutes.

6 *While the cakes cool, make the caramel.* In a small saucepan over medium-low heat, add the granulated sugar and cook until it melts completely. Use a silicone spatula to stir the sugar occasionally, scraping down the sides and bottom of the pan. First the sugar will form clumps, then it will begin to melt and take on a light golden color. After 5 to 7 minutes, it will become fully melted and be a medium-gold hue. As soon as your last bit of sugar has melted, turn off the heat and don't let it continue to cook or it'll burn.

7 Remove the saucepan from the heat and immediately stir in the butter— use caution as the mixture will violently bubble. Use a whisk to stir the butter and melted sugar together until combined, about 20 seconds. Whisk in the cream and salt until combined. Allow the caramel to cool completely in the pan until you're ready to frost the cake.

8 *Last, make the cream cheese frosting.* In a stand mixer fitted with the paddle attachment, beat the butter and cream cheese on medium speed until combined, about 20 seconds. Add the confectioners' sugar, vanilla extract, and salt. Beat on medium speed until the frosting is fluffy, about 2 minutes.

9 Place the first cake layer, right-side up, on a plate or cake stand. Spread a large dollop of the frosting on top, using an offset spatula to spread the layer evenly to the edges of the cake. Repeat with the second and third cake layers and dollops of frosting. Frost the sides of the cake with the remaining frosting.

10 Once the caramel is cooled to room temperature, place it into a squeeze bottle or piping bag with a small tip (if it's too solid, microwave it for 10 seconds). Starting from the center of the cake, squeeze out the caramel in a tight spiral, going all the way to the edges of the cake. Once you're at the edges of the cake, make small zig-zag-like movements along the edges to allow the caramel to make those luscious drips. Keep the cake simple as is, or decorate the top with fresh blackberries, figs, and pomegranate seeds.

Peppermint Chocolate Mousse

MAKES 6 MOUSSES

PREP TIME 15 MINUTES (PLUS
2 HOURS CHILL TIME)
COOK TIME 5 MINUTES
TOTAL TIME 2 HOURS 20 MINUTES

⅔ cup plus ½ cup heavy cream,
  divided

2 teaspoons vanilla extract

¾ teaspoon peppermint extract

Pinch of salt

8 ounces semisweet or
  bittersweet chocolate, finely
  chopped

1 large egg, at room temperature

1 teaspoon instant espresso
  powder

¼ cup boiling water

Crushed peppermint candies
  or candy canes and whipped
  cream, for serving (optional)

Did you know you can make a chocolate mousse that would knock Julia Child's socks off using boiling water and a blender? It's true and it's awesome. This peppermint mousse is everything I want in a holiday dessert, from the dreamy texture to the flavor reminiscent of candy canes and hot chocolate at the mall after meeting Santa. It also keeps in the fridge for up to seven days, meaning you can mousse it up all week long.

1 In a small saucepan over low heat, add ⅔ cup of the cream and cook until hot but not boiling. Add the vanilla extract, peppermint extract, and salt and use a silicone spatula to stir to combine. Set aside.

2 In a high-powered blender, add the chocolate, egg, and espresso powder. Turn the blender to medium-high speed and, with the blender going, slowly stream in the boiling water. Blend until smooth, about 20 seconds.

3 With the blender still going, slowly stream in the cream mixture and blend on high speed for 1 minute. The mixture should be creamy and smooth with no pieces of chocolate remaining. Set aside.

4 In a medium bowl, add the remaining ½ cup cream and whisk until soft peaks form (about 3 minutes by hand or 1 minute with a hand mixer). Add the chocolate mixture to the bowl and use the silicone spatula to gently fold the two mixtures together until completely combined and no pockets of unmixed whipped cream remain.

5 Spoon the mousse into six 6-ounce ramekins or small bowls. Cover the ramekins with plastic wrap and place in the fridge to chill for at least 2 hours and up to 7 days before serving. Serve with crushed peppermint candies and fresh whipped cream (if using).

PRO TIP *If peppermint isn't your thing, or you want to make these as a plain chocolate mousse outside of the holiday season, omit it!*

Brown Sugar–Walnut Dutch Apple Pie

MAKES ONE 9-INCH PIE

PREP TIME 1 HOUR 15 MINUTES
(PLUS 30 MINUTES CHILL TIME)
BAKE TIME 1 HOUR
TOTAL TIME 2 HOURS 45 MINUTES

FOR THE PIE DOUGH

- 1¼ cups all-purpose flour, plus more for rolling out the dough
- 1 tablespoon granulated sugar
- ½ teaspoon salt
- ½ cup (1 stick) unsalted butter, cold and cut into cubes
- 2 to 3 tablespoons ice water or chilled vodka (water is standard in pie crust, but vodka will make your crust extra flaky!)

FOR THE APPLE FILLING

- 2 pounds Granny Smith apples (6 to 7 apples)
- ½ cup packed light brown sugar
- 3 tablespoons all-purpose flour
- 1 tablespoon freshly squeezed lemon juice (from about 1 lemon)
- 2 teaspoons vanilla extract
- 2 teaspoons ground cinnamon
- ½ teaspoon ground ginger
- ½ teaspoon ground nutmeg
- ¼ teaspoon salt

FOR THE STREUSEL TOPPING

- 1 cup all-purpose flour
- 1 cup packed light brown sugar
- ½ cup finely chopped roasted unsalted walnuts
- ¼ teaspoon salt
- ½ cup (1 stick) unsalted butter, melted

There are two types of Thanksgiving dessert people: those who want a fruit pie and those who want an indulgent, rich dessert. This streusel-topped apple pie satisfies both camps. A little technique talk to get you excited: Most pies call for cutting apples into thin slices, which can sadly leave gaps that make the pie fall apart on your plate. But if you cut those slices in half, your pie holds together ten times better. And a bonus for the less-experienced bakers? The streusel top is so much easier than learning to lattice.

1 *First, make the pie dough.* In a food processor, add the flour, granulated sugar, and salt and pulse to combine. Add the butter and pulse until the mixture resembles wet sand, about 20 seconds.

2 Add 2 tablespoons of the ice water, then pulse until a dough begins to form a ball around the blade, about 20 seconds. If your dough doesn't come together, add another tablespoon of water and pulse again.

3 Turn the dough out onto a clean work surface and pat it into an oval disk, then wrap it in plastic wrap. Refrigerate for at least 30 minutes and up to 2 days.

4 Once the dough has chilled, remove it from the fridge and set it on the counter to soften for 5 minutes. Lightly dust a clean work surface with flour, unwrap the disk, and place it on the surface. Use a rolling pin to roll out the dough into a roughly 12-inch circle, dusting the top and underside with more flour as needed. Carefully roll the dough around your rolling pin like a scroll, then roll it out over a 9-inch pie pan. Press the dough into the bottom and sides of the pie pan, then use scissors to trim around the edges of the pie dough, leaving a ½-inch overhang.

5 Tuck the overhang of the pie under itself, creating a thick edge around the rim of the pie pan. Lightly squeeze the edge together using your fingers, sealing it in place. Use your index finger on one hand and your "peace fingers" on the other hand to create a crimp around the edges of the pie (see page 96). Place the pie pan, uncovered, in the fridge to set while you make your pie filling.

6 *Next, make the apple filling.* Preheat the oven to 350°F. Peel and core the apples, then cut them into thin slices about ¼ inch thick and place into a large bowl. For a truly packed-in apple filling, cut those slices in half. Add in the brown sugar, flour, lemon juice, vanilla extract, cinnamon, ginger, nutmeg, and salt. Set aside.

7 *Last, make the streusel topping.* In a small bowl, combine the flour, brown sugar, walnuts, and salt. Add the melted butter and use a fork or your fingers to stir everything together until it resembles wet sand and clumps together.

8 Remove the prepared pie crust from the fridge and pour in the apple filling, using your fingers to gently pack the apples down into an even layer. The filling will be tall and should mound slightly. Use your hands to squeeze the streusel into your palms, then break it apart into big and small clusters, sprinkling it all over the apples and patting it into the apple layer slightly.

9 Cover the pie pan lightly with aluminum foil. Bake for 20 minutes with the foil on, then remove the foil and continue to bake, uncovered, until the topping is golden brown and the fruit is bubbling around the edges, 35 to 40 minutes more. Remove the pie from the oven and allow it to cool slightly on a cooling rack before serving.

Caramel Pecan Sticky Buns

MAKES 12 STICKY BUNS

PREP TIME 1 HOUR
(PLUS 2 HOURS RISE TIME)
COOK TIME 30 MINUTES
TOTAL TIME 3 HOURS 30 MINUTES

FOR THE DOUGH

4½ cups all-purpose flour, divided, plus more for rolling out the dough

⅓ cup granulated sugar

1 packet (2¼ teaspoons) instant yeast

1 teaspoon salt

1½ cups whole milk

6 tablespoons (¾ stick) unsalted butter

1 large egg, at room temperature

FOR THE CARAMEL PECAN SAUCE

1½ cups lightly chopped roasted unsalted pecans

1 cup packed light brown sugar

¼ cup light corn syrup

¼ cup (½ stick) unsalted butter

½ teaspoon salt

FOR THE CINNAMON SUGAR FILLING

2 tablespoons (¼ stick) unsalted butter, at room temperature

⅓ cup packed light brown sugar

1 tablespoon ground cinnamon

My family has a house on an island in Nova Scotia, and I always look forward to "island coffee hour," when the locals and vacationers gather over baked goods and plenty of coffee. When I was a kid, I always beelined for homemade sticky buns made by my grandfather's friend Earl—and I wasn't the only one. The buns were pillowy perfection. The gooey sauce melted into the crevices of each bun, truly sticky and so satisfying. My recipe is an ode to Earl's, with a brown sugar–caramel pecan sauce that soaks into the fluffiest yeasted rolls, along with just a hint of cinnamon sugar filling.

1 *First, make the dough.* In a stand mixer fitted with the paddle attachment, mix 2 cups of the flour with the granulated sugar, yeast, and salt and beat on low speed until combined.

2 In a microwave-safe bowl, combine the milk and butter. Microwave until the mixture is warm to the touch and the butter is melted, about 45 seconds (you don't want the mixture to be steaming or too hot, because this can kill the yeast).

3 Pour the milk mixture into the flour mixture, add the egg, and beat everything together on low speed until combined. Gradually increase the speed to high and beat for 2 minutes. The dough will look more like batter, but this is correct! This step kicks off the gluten development.

4 After 2 minutes, change the paddle attachment to the dough hook attachment. Add 1½ cups of the remaining flour and knead on low speed until combined. Add the remaining 1 cup flour and knead on low speed, stopping the mixer occasionally to redistribute the dough, until the dough starts to pull away from the sides of the bowl and forms a ball around the dough hook.

5 Increase the speed to medium-low and knead until the dough becomes smooth and supple, about 10 minutes. If the dough gets wrapped around the hook too much, turn off the mixer, pull the dough off, flip the dough over, and turn on the mixer again. The dough is ready when you can stretch a quarter-size piece of dough between your fingers and see light through it (without it breaking). This means the gluten has developed enough. If your dough breaks, knead for a few minutes more and try again.

6 Transfer the dough to a large bowl sprayed with nonstick cooking spray and cover the bowl with a dish towel or plastic wrap. Let rise in a warm place until the dough has doubled in size, about 1 hour.

7 *Toward the end of the dough's rise, make the caramel pecan sauce.* Line a 9 × 13-inch baking pan with parchment paper on all sides (see page 23). Spread the pecans evenly on the bottom of the pan.

(Continued on page 232)

(Continued from page 231)

8 In a small saucepan over medium heat, combine the brown sugar, corn syrup, butter, and salt and cook, using a silicone spatula to stir the mixture occasionally. As soon as the mixture starts to bubble, set a timer and let it bubble for 1 minute. Remove the saucepan from the heat, then pour the caramel over the pecans in your prepared pan, using the spatula to spread it evenly to the edges.

9 Turn the risen dough onto a well-floured surface. Use a rolling pin to roll it into a 12 × 18-inch rectangle, with the wider side closest to you.

10 *Next, add in the cinnamon sugar filling.* Using your hands or a silicone spatula, spread the butter all the way to the edges of the dough. Sprinkle the brown sugar and cinnamon over the butter, then use your fingers to spread it into the butter.

11 From the 18-inch-wide side closest to you, roll the dough into a tight log. Press the dough along the outside seam to seal everything together. Use a very sharp knife (or floss . . . yes, seriously!) to cut the dough into 12 even rolls (for step-by-step photos, see page 208). Place the rolls on top of the caramel pecan sauce. Cover the pan with a dish towel or plastic wrap and let rise until doubled in size, about 1 hour.

12 Preheat the oven to 350°F. Uncover the rolls. Bake the sticky buns until they are golden brown all over, about 30 minutes. Place the pan on a cooling rack to cool until warm to the touch, then carefully flip the pan over onto a large serving board. Peel away the parchment paper to reveal the gooey caramel pecan bottoms and serve.

Oatmeal Fudge Bars

MAKES 9 BARS

PREP TIME 20 MINUTES
BAKE TIME 30 MINUTES
TOTAL TIME 50 MINUTES

FOR THE OAT LAYER

½ cup (1 stick) unsalted butter, at room temperature

½ cup granulated sugar

¼ cup packed light brown sugar

1 large egg, at room temperature

2 teaspoons vanilla extract

1 cup all-purpose flour

1 cup old-fashioned oats

½ teaspoon baking soda

¼ teaspoon baking powder

½ teaspoon salt

FOR THE FUDGE LAYER

½ cup sweetened condensed milk (about half of a 14-ounce can)

½ cup semisweet or bittersweet chocolate chips

1 tablespoon unsalted butter

1 teaspoon vanilla extract

¼ teaspoon salt

Oats and fudge is one of those flavor combinations that doesn't get as much holiday press as, say, peppermint and chocolate, but oh my goodness, they are made for each other. These super-chewy oat bars have a thick layer of chocolate filling that's soft and fudgy. I love making these in the early fall when I'm craving something warm and nostalgic but am not ready for apple or pumpkin yet. They've got a homey, passed-down-for-generations quality, like a dessert that would win a blue ribbon at a county competition. Put them in front of a crowd and watch them disappear.

1 *First, make the oat layer.* Preheat the oven to 350°F. Line an 8 × 8-inch square baking pan with parchment paper on all sides (see page 23).

2 In a stand mixer fitted with the paddle attachment, combine the butter, granulated sugar, and brown sugar and beat on medium speed until light and fluffy, about 2 minutes.

3 Add the egg and vanilla extract and beat until combined. Scrape down the bowl, then add the flour, oats, baking soda, baking powder, and salt. Beat on low speed until just combined and no streaks of flour remain.

4 *Next, make the fudge layer.* In a small saucepan over medium-low heat, combine the sweetened condensed milk, chocolate chips, and butter. Use the silicone spatula to stir the mixture occasionally as it cooks until it's completely smooth. The mixture will be glossy and thick. Remove the saucepan from the heat and stir in the vanilla extract and salt.

5 Transfer half of the oat batter to the prepared pan, using the silicone spatula or your fingers to push it evenly to the edges. The layer will be thin, but this is correct!

6 Pour the fudge over the oat layer, using the spatula to spread it evenly to the edges. Use your fingers to crumble the remaining oat dough over the fudge layer, leaving some areas of fudge uncovered.

7 Bake until the bars are lightly golden brown and a butter knife inserted into the center comes out clean, 25 to 30 minutes. Place the pan on a cooling rack and allow the bars to cool completely in the pan. Use the parchment paper to lift the bars from the pan, then transfer them to a cutting board, cut into 9 bars, and serve.

Flourless Ginger Chocolate Cake

MAKES ONE 9-INCH CAKE

PREP TIME 30 MINUTES
COOK TIME 50 MINUTES
TOTAL TIME 1 HOUR 20 MINUTES

½ cup (1 stick) unsalted butter, cut into pieces, plus more for the pan

2 tablespoons Dutch-processed cocoa powder, plus more for the pan

8 ounces semisweet or bittersweet chocolate, coarsely chopped

5 large eggs, at room temperature

¾ cup granulated sugar

2 teaspoons vanilla extract

½ teaspoon salt

2 tablespoons peeled and finely grated fresh ginger

1 teaspoon ground ginger

½ teaspoon ground cloves

PRO TIP *If ginger isn't your thing, omit it (along with the cloves)! This cake is fabulous either way.*

This lovely number is a cross between a cake and a meringue. It has a light, fudgy interior and a crisp, delicate top that cracks in an effortlessly rustic way, like a dessert in a restaurant with wobbly farmhouse tables and flickering candlelight. Fresh ginger adds a bright, zippy bite that keeps the chocolate from getting too rich, which is why I love having this after a hearty fall braise or roast. And what do you know—it's gluten free.

1 Preheat the oven to 325°F. Line the bottom of a 9-inch springform pan with parchment paper (see page 23), generously butter the sides, then dust the sides with cocoa powder.

2 In a large microwave-safe bowl, combine the butter and chopped chocolate. Microwave in 30-second increments, using a silicone spatula to stir between each, until the chocolate is fully melted. Set aside to cool slightly, about 5 minutes.

3 While the chocolate cools, make the meringue. Separate the egg whites from the yolks, placing the egg whites in the bowl of a stand mixer fitted with the whisk attachment, and placing the yolks in a small bowl for later. Beat the egg whites on high speed until frothy, then keep the mixer going as you stream in the granulated sugar. Continue beating on high speed until your meringue forms stiff peaks, 3 to 5 minutes.

4 Whisk the reserved egg yolks into the chocolate mixture, one at a time. Add the cocoa powder, vanilla extract, and salt and whisk until combined. Add the fresh ginger, ground ginger, and cloves.

5 Drizzle roughly one-third of the chocolate mixture over the meringue, then use the silicone spatula to fold gently to combine. Repeat, folding in another one-third of the chocolate mixture, then repeat again until the batter is completely combined and homogenous.

6 Transfer the batter into the prepared pan, using the silicone spatula or the back of a large spoon to carefully spread it into an even layer (take care not to deflate the mixture).

7 Bake the cake until the edges of the cake start to pull away from the sides of the pan and a butter knife inserted into the center comes out mostly clean (a crumb or two attached is okay), 45 to 50 minutes. Place the pan on a cooling rack to cool to room temperature. Once the cake has cooled, carefully drag a butter knife around the edges of the cake, then remove the springform ring and base from the cake and transfer the cake to a serving dish.

Spiced Pumpkin Snickerdoodles

MAKES 14 COOKIES

PREP TIME 25 MINUTES
(PLUS 30 MINUTES CHILL TIME)
COOK TIME 13 MINUTES
TOTAL TIME 1 HOUR 8 MINUTES

FOR THE COOKIES

⅓ cup pumpkin puree (not pumpkin pie filling)

½ cup (1 stick) unsalted butter, melted

½ cup granulated sugar

½ cup packed light brown sugar

1 teaspoon vanilla extract

1¼ cups all-purpose flour

½ teaspoon baking soda

½ teaspoon cream of tartar

½ teaspoon salt

1 teaspoon ground cinnamon

1 teaspoon ground ginger

1 teaspoon ground cardamom

⅛ teaspoon ground nutmeg

⅛ teaspoon freshly ground black pepper

FOR THE SPICED SUGAR COATING

⅓ cup granulated sugar

1 teaspoon ground cinnamon

1 teaspoon ground ginger

1 teaspoon ground cardamom

⅛ teaspoon ground nutmeg

Pinch of salt

I'm truly amazed at how many holiday flavors I've crammed into this cookie. Cinnamon! Ginger! Pumpkin! Cardamom! Snickerdoodle! Is snickerdoodle a flavor? I think so. I put these cookies in the same holiday category as mistletoe, Christmas carolers, and eggnog. They're a cheerful treat you can put in a cookie box or place on a table where everyone will sneak seconds. This version swaps in pumpkin puree for the egg, a trick that keeps the cookies chewy, not puffy. A pinch of cream of tartar, while seemingly inconsequential, gives these cookies that signature snickerdoodle tang.

1 *First, make the cookies.* Place the pumpkin puree on a thick paper towel or piece of cheesecloth. Carefully wrap the paper towel around the pumpkin puree and squeeze it over a small bowl to remove excess moisture. You should end up with ¼ cup strained puree. This step removes excess water from your puree so the cookies don't bake up too puffy.

2 In a large bowl, whisk the melted butter, strained pumpkin puree, granulated sugar, brown sugar, and vanilla extract until combined.

3 In a separate bowl, whisk the flour, baking soda, cream of tartar, salt, cinnamon, ginger, cardamom, nutmeg, and black pepper until combined. Add the dry ingredients to the wet ingredients and use a silicone spatula to mix until a soft dough forms and no streaks of flour remain. Cover the bowl with a dish towel or plastic wrap and place it in the fridge to chill for at least 30 minutes and up to 1 day.

4 *While the dough chills, make the spiced sugar coating.* In a small bowl, combine the granulated sugar, cinnamon, ginger, cardamom, nutmeg, and salt.

5 Preheat the oven to 350°F. Line two sheet pans with parchment paper.

6 Use a 1-ounce cookie scoop to portion out equal amounts of dough (a large spoon also works; the ball should be about 2 tablespoons). Roll the dough in your hands to smooth the edges, then roll the dough in the sugar-spice mixture, evenly coating the outside of the dough. Place the dough balls 2 inches apart on the prepared sheet pans.

7 Bake until the cookies have puffed up, are slightly cracked on top, and are set and firm around the edges but still very soft in the middle, 11 to 13 minutes. Remove the sheet pans from the oven and allow the cookies to cool slightly on the sheet pans before serving.

Maple-Glazed Apple Blondies

MAKES 16 BLONDIES

PREP TIME 30 MINUTES
(PLUS 15 MINUTES COOL TIME)
COOK TIME 50 MINUTES
TOTAL TIME 1 HOUR 35 MINUTES

FOR THE APPLE LAYER

1 large apple, peeled, cored, and
   cut into ½-inch cubes (I prefer
   a tart Granny Smith)

¼ cup packed light brown sugar

2 teaspoons ground cinnamon

¼ teaspoon ground nutmeg

FOR THE BLONDIES

1 cup (2 sticks) unsalted butter,
   melted

1½ cups granulated sugar

½ cup packed light brown sugar

2 large eggs plus 1 large egg
   yolk, at room temperature

2 teaspoons vanilla extract

1 teaspoon maple extract

2 cups all-purpose flour

½ teaspoon baking powder

½ teaspoon salt

FOR THE MAPLE GLAZE

½ cup confectioners' sugar

1 tablespoon maple syrup

1 tablespoon milk (any dairy
   or nondairy milk works)

½ teaspoon vanilla extract

½ teaspoon maple extract

Pinch of salt

Crisp fall apples get to shine in pies, crumbles, and cakes, but I'm telling you, they belong in blondies, too. The juicy bits of chopped apples in these bars make them a dream snack to take on a long, leaf-peeping walk. The quick maple glaze complements the tart apples like flannel shirts and corduroys. Have I emphasized how fall-y these are yet?? And while I wish I could say the maple extract is optional, it's really not—it takes the blondies from basic to a flavor explosion that you just can't replicate with maple syrup alone.

1 *First, make the apple layer.* Preheat the oven to 350°F. Line a 9 × 9-inch square baking pan with parchment paper on all sides (see page 23).

2 In a small bowl, combine the chopped apple, brown sugar, cinnamon, and nutmeg. Toss together to evenly coat the apple. Set aside.

3 *Next, make the blondies.* In a large bowl, whisk the melted butter, granulated sugar, and brown sugar until combined. Whisk in the eggs, extra egg yolk, vanilla extract, and maple extract and beat until lightened in color, about 30 seconds.

4 Add the flour, baking powder, and salt. Use a silicone spatula to fold the batter until combined and no streaks of flour remain.

5 Transfer half of the batter to the prepared pan, using the silicone spatula to spread it evenly to the edges. The layer will be thin, but this is correct!

6 Sprinkle the apple mixture over the batter evenly to the edges, then use your fingers to gently press the apples into the batter in a flat, even layer. Use the silicone spatula to spread the remaining half of the blondie batter over the apples, spreading evenly to the edges.

7 Bake until the blondies are golden brown and a butter knife inserted into the center comes out clean, 40 to 50 minutes. Place the pan on a cooling rack and allow the blondies to cool slightly in the pan.

8 *While the blondies cool, make the maple glaze.* In a small bowl, whisk the confectioners' sugar, maple syrup, milk, vanilla extract, maple extract, and salt until smooth.

9 Pour the glaze over the blondies (it's okay if they're still a little warm!), using an offset spatula to spread a thick layer evenly to the edges. Once the glaze has set, about 15 minutes, use the parchment paper to lift the blondies from the pan, transfer the blondies to a cutting board, cut into 16 squares, and serve.

Cranberry Pie Bars

MAKES 16 BARS

PREP TIME 30 MINUTES
COOK TIME 1 HOUR
TOTAL TIME 1 HOUR 30 MINUTES

FOR THE CRUST

1 cup all-purpose flour

¾ cup (1½ sticks) unsalted butter, cold and cut into small cubes

⅓ cup granulated sugar

⅓ cup packed light brown sugar

1 teaspoon salt

1 large egg, at room temperature

1 teaspoon vanilla extract

FOR THE CRANBERRY LAYER

1 pound fresh or frozen cranberries (if you're using frozen cranberries, defrost and rinse them clean first)

½ cup granulated sugar

2 tablespoons cornstarch

2 tablespoons freshly grated orange zest (from about 2 oranges)

FOR THE CRUMB TOPPING

¼ cup (½ stick) unsalted butter, melted

¼ cup granulated sugar

¼ cup packed light brown sugar

¾ cup all-purpose flour

½ teaspoon salt

Confectioner's sugar, for topping (optional)

When bags of fresh cranberries are in stores, you know the holidays are near. I throw two in my cart, immediately, and make big plans to make these bars. They've got a buttery shortbread crust, a thick layer of cranberry pie filling, and a sweet crumble topping. You get all the flavor of a tart cranberry pie without making and chilling a crust or remembering where the rolling pin is. The combination of textures and the jolt of that puckering, bright filling get me every time.

1 *First, make the crust.* Preheat the oven to 350°F. Line a 9 × 9-inch square baking pan with parchment paper on all sides (see page 23).

2 In a stand mixer fitted with the paddle attachment, add the flour, butter, granulated sugar, brown sugar, and salt and beat on medium-low speed until combined, about 1 minute. The mixture will be thick. Add the egg and vanilla extract and beat on medium speed until the mixture forms a thick dough, about 45 seconds. Transfer the dough to the prepared pan and use a measuring cup (or something else with a flat bottom) to really pack the crust into an even layer.

3 *Next, make the cranberry layer.* In a large bowl, combine the cranberries, granulated sugar, cornstarch, and orange zest. Transfer the cranberry mixture over the crust and use a silicone spatula to spread it evenly to the edges.

4 *Last, make the crumb topping.* In a small bowl, combine the melted butter, granulated sugar, brown sugar, flour, and salt. Use a fork or your fingers to work everything together until the mixture resembles wet sand and clumps together.

5 Squeeze the crumb topping into your palm, then break it apart into big and small clusters, sprinkling them all over the cranberry layer like a fruit crisp (some pockets of exposed cranberries are okay!). Bake until the cranberries have burst completely and the top of the bars is light golden brown, about 1 hour.

6 Place the pan on a cooling rack and allow the bars to cool completely in the pan. Use the parchment paper to lift the bars from the pan, then transfer them to a cutting board. Dust the top with confectioners' sugar (if using), cut into 16 squares, and serve.

Hot Chocolate Cookies

MAKES 12 COOKIES

PREP TIME 30 MINUTES
(PLUS 15 MINUTES COOL TIME)
COOK TIME 14 MINUTES
TOTAL TIME 59 MINUTES

FOR THE COOKIES

½ cup (1 stick) unsalted butter, at room temperature

1 cup packed light brown sugar

1 large egg, at room temperature

2 teaspoons vanilla extract

1¼ cups all-purpose flour

⅓ cup Dutch-processed cocoa powder

½ teaspoon baking soda

½ teaspoon salt

FOR THE TOPPING

1 cup semisweet or bittersweet chocolate chips

12 large marshmallows

You know how happy you are when it's freezing outside and you're warming your hands around a mug of hot chocolate? That's how these cookies make me feel. They start with my favorite chewy chocolate-cookie base, which gets topped with melted chocolate and a giant marshmallow. Then pop them under the broiler for a (truly) hot second to get a top that looks just like a mug of cocoa with a marshmallow bobbing at the surface. Serve them after shoveling snow, in your holiday cookie box, or with a marathon of festive rom-coms.

1 *First, make the cookies.* Preheat the oven to 350°F. Line two sheet pans with parchment paper.

2 In a stand mixer fitted with the paddle attachment, add the butter and brown sugar and beat on medium-high speed until light and fluffy, about 2 minutes.

3 Add the egg and vanilla extract. Beat on medium-high speed until the mixture is light and pale in color, about 2 minutes, scraping down the bowl as needed.

4 Add the flour, cocoa powder, baking soda, and salt and beat on low speed until just combined and no streaks of flour remain.

5 Use a 1½-ounce cookie scoop to portion out equal amounts of dough (a large spoon also works; the ball should be about 3 tablespoons). Roll the dough in your hands to smooth the edges, then place 2 inches apart on the prepared sheet pans.

6 Bake until the cookies have puffed up and are set and firm around the edges but still somewhat soft in the middle, 10 to 12 minutes. Remove the sheet pans from the oven and allow the cookies to cool slightly on the sheet pans, about 15 minutes.

7 *Once the cookies have cooled slightly, make the topping.* Set the oven to broil on high.

8 In a small microwave-safe bowl, add the chocolate chips. Microwave in 30-second increments, using a silicone spatula to stir between each, until the chocolate is fully melted.

9 Spoon about 2 teaspoons of melted chocolate over each cookie, leaving a slight border along the outside edges of the cookie. Squish the marshmallows flat between your palms and place one marshmallow on top of each cookie.

10 Place the sheet pans, one at a time, on the middle rack of the oven and broil on high until the marshmallows are golden brown and melted, 1 to 2 minutes. Keep an eye on them because they will toast very quickly! Remove the sheet pans from the oven and allow the cookies to cool slightly on the pan before serving.

Jelly Donuts

MAKES 10 DONUTS

PREP TIME 45 MINUTES (1 HOUR
25 MINUTES RISE TIME)
COOK TIME 20 MINUTES
TOTAL TIME 2 HOURS 30 MINUTES

FOR THE DONUTS

3¼ to 3¾ cups all-purpose flour,
  divided, plus more for rolling
  out the dough

2 tablespoons granulated sugar

2 packets (4½ teaspoons) instant
  yeast

1 teaspoon salt

1 cup plus 2 tablespoons whole
  milk

¼ cup (½ stick) unsalted butter

3 large egg yolks, at room
  temperature

2 quarts vegetable oil, for
  deep-frying

FOR THE FILLING AND COATING

1 cup granulated sugar

½ cup fruit jam of choice
  (strawberry is my preference,
  but you can also use raspberry
  or blackberry)

These donuts are puffy balloons of joy and exactly what you want to bite into after lighting the Hanukkah candles (or after waking up on a cozy winter morning). They're rolled in a coating of granulated sugar (reminiscent of a gloriously wintry day) and filled with strawberry jam. And hey, did you know that stuffing a donut with jam is surprisingly easy? You just stick a piping bag into the side of the donut and squeeze. It's so satisfying.

1 *First, make the donuts.* In a stand mixer fitted with the paddle attachment, add 2 cups of the flour, the granulated sugar, yeast, and salt and beat on low speed until combined.

2 In a microwave-safe bowl, combine the milk and butter. Microwave until the mixture is warm to the touch and the butter is melted, about 45 seconds (you don't want the mixture to be steaming or too hot, because this can kill the yeast).

3 Pour the milk mixture into the flour mixture, add the egg yolks, and beat everything together on low speed until combined. Gradually increase the speed to medium and beat for 2 minutes. The dough will look more like batter, but this is correct! This step kicks off the gluten development.

4 After 2 minutes, change the paddle attachment to the dough hook attachment. Add 1¼ cups of the remaining flour and knead on low speed until combined and a soft dough forms. Knead on low speed, stopping the mixer occasionally to redistribute the dough, until the dough starts to pull away from the sides of the bowl and forms a ball around the dough hook, about 3 minutes. Increase the speed to medium-low and knead until the dough becomes smooth and supple, about 5 minutes. If the dough feels too wet, add the remaining ½ cup flour and mix for an additional minute or so.

5 Turn the dough onto a clean, lightly floured surface. Cover it loosely with a dish towel or plastic wrap and let rest for 10 minutes.

6 Line two sheet pans with parchment paper. Use a rolling pin to roll the dough out to a 12-inch circle about ½ inch thick. Use a 3-inch round cookie cutter to cut out as many donuts as possible, placing them on the prepared sheet pans and covering loosely with a dish towel or plastic wrap. Gather the remaining scraps together into a ball and gently knead them back together. Let the dough rest for 15 minutes, then roll out the scraps, cut the dough again, place the donuts onto the prepared sheet pans, and cover them with a dish towel or plastic wrap—you should end up with 10 donuts. Let rise in a warm place until the donuts have doubled in size, about 1 hour.

7 In a large pot, heat the vegetable oil over medium-low heat to 325°F. Place a cooling rack on top of a separate sheet pan.

8 *While the oil heats up, prepare the filling and coating.* In a medium bowl, add the granulated sugar. Place the jam in a piping bag fitted with a ½-inch metal tip.

9 Fry 2 or 3 donuts at a time (being careful not to overcrowd the pot) for 2 minutes on each side. You'll know to flip the donuts over when they float to the top of the oil and are golden brown around the bottom edge, right where it meets the oil. Use a slotted metal spatula to transfer them to the prepared cooling rack. Repeat with the remaining donuts.

10 Once the donuts are cool enough to the touch but still warm, toss them in the granulated sugar. Then, insert the piping bag tip into the side of each donut and firmly squeeze a few tablespoons of jam into the center of the donut. Serve within 4 hours of frying (but they're best while still warm, obviously).

Brûléed Pumpkin Pie

MAKES ONE 9-INCH PIE

PREP TIME 45 MINUTES (PLUS
4 HOURS 30 MINUTES CHILL TIME)
COOK TIME 1 HOUR
TOTAL TIME 6 HOURS 15 MINUTES

FOR THE PIE DOUGH

1¼ cups all-purpose flour, plus more for rolling out the dough

1 tablespoon granulated sugar

½ teaspoon salt

½ cup (1 stick) unsalted butter, cold and cut into cubes

2 to 3 tablespoons ice water or chilled vodka (water is standard in pie crust, but vodka will make your crust extra flaky!)

FOR THE PIE FILLING

1 cup granulated sugar, divided, plus more as needed

1 teaspoon ground cinnamon

½ teaspoon ground ginger

¼ teaspoon ground cloves

½ teaspoon salt

2 large eggs plus 1 large egg yolk

1 (15-ounce) can pumpkin puree (not pumpkin pie filling)

1 (12-ounce) can evaporated milk

1 teaspoon vanilla extract

This is the mash-up of pumpkin pie and crème brûlée you've been waiting for (you were waiting for it, right?). The custardy pumpkin filling gets topped with crackly caramelized sugar that looks like beautiful stained glass. It's barely any extra work from traditional pumpkin pie—you'll toss some granulated sugar over the top and use a kitchen torch to caramelize. (Remember when I told you to pick up a kitchen torch? This is another good reason why!) Plus, the all-butter pie crust is my staple for any home-made pie, not just pumpkin.

1 *First, make the pie dough.* In a food processor, add the flour, granulated sugar, and salt and pulse to combine. Add the butter and pulse until the mixture resembles wet sand, about 20 seconds.

2 Add 2 tablespoons of the ice water, then pulse until a dough begins to form a ball around the blade, about 20 seconds. If your dough doesn't come together, add another tablespoon of water and pulse again.

3 Turn the dough out onto a clean work surface and flatten it into a 1-inch-thick oval disk. Wrap the disk tightly in plastic wrap and refrigerate for at least 30 minutes and up to 2 days.

4 Once the dough has chilled, remove it from the fridge and set it on the counter to soften for 5 minutes. Lightly dust a clean work surface with flour, unwrap the disk, and place it on the surface. Use a rolling pin to roll out the dough into a roughly 12-inch circle, dusting the top and underside with more flour as needed. Carefully roll up the dough around your rolling pin like a scroll, then drape it into a 9-inch pie pan. Press the dough into the bottom and sides of the pie pan, then use scissors to trim around the edges of the dough, leaving a ½-inch overhang.

5 Tuck the overhang of the pie under itself, creating a thick edge around the rim of the pie pan. Lightly squeeze the edge together using your fingers, sealing it in place. Use your index finger on one hand and your "peace fingers" on the other hand to create a crimp around the edges of the pie (see photos on page 96). Place the pie pan, uncovered, in the fridge to chill while you make your pie filling.

6 *Next, make the pie filling.* Preheat the oven to 350°F.

7 In a large bowl, combine ¾ cup of the granulated sugar, the cinnamon, ginger, cloves, and salt. Add the eggs, extra egg yolk, and pumpkin puree and whisk until combined. Add the evaporated milk and vanilla extract, whisking until homogenous. Remove the prepared pie pan from the fridge and pour in the filling.

8 Bake until the pie is set around the edges but still slightly jiggly in the middle, about 1 hour. Remove the pie from the oven and allow it to cool to room temperature on a cooling rack. Place the pie, uncovered, in the fridge to cool completely, at least 4 hours and up to 1 day.

9 Once you're ready to serve, remove the pie from the fridge and sprinkle the remaining ¼ cup granulated sugar over the pie. Use a kitchen torch to melt and cook the sugar until it caramelizes, being careful not to burn the sugar. Use the back of a large spoon to lightly "crack" the sugar on top before cutting the pie into slices. This pie is best served right after brûlée-ing, as the sugar will soak into the pie over time.

Coconut Cake Snowballs

MAKES 30 CAKE BALLS

PREP TIME 30 MINUTES (PLUS
1 HOUR 30 MINUTES CHILL TIME)
COOK TIME ABOUT 30 MINUTES,
BUT WILL VARY BASED ON CAKE
MIX DIRECTIONS
TOTAL TIME ABOUT 2 HOURS 30
MINUTES

FOR THE CAKE BALLS

1 (15.25-ounce) box vanilla cake
mix (I love Betty Crocker)

4 to 6 tablespoons milk (any
dairy or nondairy milk works)

¾ teaspoon coconut extract

FOR THE COCONUT–WHITE
CHOCOLATE COATING

2 cups unsweetened shredded
coconut

2 cups white chocolate chips

2 tablespoons coconut oil

Cake pops feel like a fever dream from 2010, and while I spy them at Starbucks, I want to run into handheld cakes *way* more often. These Coconut Cake Snowballs prove that two to three bites of cake lead to increased happiness. They begin with packaged vanilla cake mix to speed up the process. Once baked, the cake is smashed up (it's a messy good time, especially if you have kids to help), mixed with milk and coconut extract, and rolled into balls that get coated in white chocolate and shredded coconut. They're ideal for holiday parties and cold-weather weekend baking activities . . . just don't throw them at your siblings.

1 *First, bake the cake mix.* Line the bottom of a 9 × 13-inch pan with parchment paper on all sides (see page 23) and prepare and bake the cake according to package directions. For best results, underbake the cake slightly so that your truffles end up extra moist.

2 *Once the cake is cool, make the cake balls.* Line a sheet pan with parchment paper. Set aside.

3 Transfer the cake to a large bowl and use your hands to break the cake into crumbly pieces in the bowl. Add 4 tablespoons of the milk and the coconut extract and use your hands or a silicone spatula to mix everything together until it forms a thick dough. If your dough is too dry, you may need an extra tablespoon or two of milk.

4 Use a 1-ounce cookie scoop to portion out equal amounts of dough (a large spoon also works; the ball should be about 2 tablespoons). Roll the dough in your hands to smooth the edges, then place 2 inches apart on the prepared sheet pan. Cover lightly with plastic wrap and refrigerate for at least 30 minutes and up to 1 day.

5 *When you're ready to assemble, make the coconut–white chocolate coating.* Place the shredded coconut in a small bowl. Set aside.

6 In a small microwave-safe bowl, combine the white chocolate and coconut oil. Microwave in 15-second increments, using a silicone spatula to stir between each, until the mixture is fully melted.

7 Use a fork to dip each cake ball into the melted white chocolate. Shake off any excess coating, then roll the ball in the shredded coconut, fully coating it. Place the balls back on the sheet pan to set completely, about 30 minutes. Serve.

DESSERT FOR ONE

Single recipes are often treated as a one-off, a novelty, with a tinge of oh-it's-so-sad-you-don't-have-fourteen-people-to-share-these-with. But it's not like that! It's more like: "I want a cupcake *now* and I don't want to use every bowl and measuring cup in the house. I might even mix the ingredients with a fork instead of a whisk." (Gasp!)

These recipes require minimal amounts of ingredients and time, and while most are designed to serve one, some actually make two of that thing, because frankly, scaling them down any more would ruin your cupcake texture—and who wants to halve an egg? I love it because it means you can either enjoy these with someone you love, or have your cake and eat it . . . twice.

P.S.: *Because these desserts are just that good, I've also included QR codes for scaled-up, "full-size" versions of each recipe. Ingredients or techniques may vary (that is, you might have to use an actual whisk), but the full-size recipe is true to its single-serve sibling.*

Single-Serve Double Chocolate Chip Cookies

PREP TIME 10 MINUTES
COOK TIME 12 MINUTES
TOTAL TIME 22 MINUTES

2 tablespoons (¼ stick) unsalted butter, at room temperature

¼ cup packed light brown sugar

1 large egg yolk, at room temperature

¼ teaspoon vanilla extract

¼ cup all-purpose flour

1½ tablespoons Dutch-processed cocoa powder

⅛ teaspoon baking soda

⅛ teaspoon salt

3 tablespoons semisweet or bittersweet chocolate chips

Flaky sea salt, for sprinkling (optional)

Chewy. Warm. Chocolate. Chocolate Chip. Cookie. Coming right up. The Dutch-processed cocoa powder gives these cookies an almost brownie-like consistency, and brown sugar adds depth and a fudgy chew. They pair beautifully with a tall glass of milk or a scoop of ice cream. And because the chemistry of baking often gives us what we didn't realize we wanted, this recipe makes two cookies. You're welcome.

1 Preheat the oven to 350°F. Line a sheet pan with parchment paper.

2 In a medium bowl, add the butter and brown sugar and use a silicone spatula to mix until combined (if it's not fully coming together, microwave the mixture for 3 seconds—and make sure your bowl is microwave safe!).

3 Add the egg yolk and vanilla extract and mix well. Add the flour, cocoa powder, baking soda, and salt and mix until combined and no streaks of flour remain. Use the silicone spatula to fold in the chocolate chips until just combined.

4 Divide the dough in half and roll each half into a ball between your palms. Place at least 3 inches apart on the prepared sheet pan.

5 Bake until the cookies have puffed up and are set and firm around the edges but still somewhat soft in the middle, 11 to 12 minutes. Remove the sheet pan from the oven, sprinkle the cookies with sea salt (if using), and allow the cookies to cool slightly on the sheet pan before serving.

FULL SIZE
For the full-size version of this recipe, scan the QR code above.

Single Lady Apple Crisp

MAKES 1 APPLE CRISP

PREP TIME 10 MINUTES
COOK TIME 30 MINUTES
TOTAL TIME 40 MINUTES

FOR THE APPLE

1 large apple, peeled, cored, and finely chopped (whatever variety you have on hand works!)

1 tablespoon packed light brown sugar

½ teaspoon ground cinnamon

⅛ teaspoon ground ginger

⅛ teaspoon ground nutmeg

Pinch of salt

FOR THE OAT CRISP

4 teaspoons all-purpose flour

1 tablespoon old-fashioned oats

1 tablespoon packed light brown sugar

¼ teaspoon ground cinnamon

Pinch of salt

1 tablespoon unsalted butter, melted

Vanilla ice cream, for serving

Here's the thing about apple crisps: you usually need to eat the whole thing right away or else the crispy crumb topping begins to absorb the moisture of the beautifully baked and spiced apples beneath it. And nobody likes a soggy crumble. So if you're a single person (or someone who lives alone, or someone who has a roommate who hates dessert and has other questionable characteristics . . . the list goes on), you now have the recipe for a *single-serve* apple crisp that you can make any night of the week for you, yourself, and you.

1 *First, prepare the apple.* Preheat the oven to 375°F. Generously grease the bottom and sides of a 6-ounce ramekin with nonstick cooking spray.

2 In a medium bowl, combine the chopped apple, brown sugar, cinnamon, ginger, nutmeg, and salt with a silicone spatula, then pour into the prepared ramekin.

3 *Next, make the oat crisp.* In that now-empty mixing bowl (no need to clean it!), use a fork to stir together the flour, oats, brown sugar, cinnamon, and salt. Add the melted butter and use the fork or your fingers to stir everything until it resembles wet sand and clumps together. Use your fingers to squeeze the crumble into crumbs, then break it apart into big and small clusters, sprinkling them all over the apple.

4 Place the ramekin on a sheet pan (to catch any drips as the crisp cooks). Bake until the crumb topping is golden brown and the apples are bubbling around the edges, 25 to 30 minutes. Place the ramekin on a cooling rack and allow the crumble to cool slightly before serving with a big scoop of vanilla ice cream on top.

FULL SIZE
For the full-size version of this recipe, scan the QR code above.

Chocolate Cupcakes for Two

MAKES 2 CUPCAKES

PREP TIME 20 MINUTES
(PLUS 20 MINUTES COOL TIME)
COOK TIME 25 MINUTES
TOTAL TIME 1 HOUR 5 MINUTES

FOR THE CUPCAKES

¼ cup all-purpose flour

3 tablespoons granulated sugar

2 tablespoons Dutch-processed cocoa powder

¼ teaspoon baking powder

⅛ teaspoon baking soda

⅛ teaspoon salt

1 large egg white, at room temperature

2 tablespoons vegetable oil

2 tablespoons milk (any dairy or nondairy milk works)

½ teaspoon vanilla extract

1 tablespoon brewed coffee, hot (hot water also works)

FOR THE CHOCOLATE BUTTERCREAM

2 tablespoons (¼ stick) unsalted butter, at room temperature

2 tablespoons Dutch-processed cocoa powder

6 tablespoons confectioners' sugar

2 teaspoons milk (any dairy or nondairy milk works)

½ teaspoon vanilla extract

Pinch of salt

Chocolate sprinkles, for topping (optional)

There are certain things that make sense only at birthday parties: animatronic mice, clowns named Larry, and cupcakes. Only one of those things deserves to be seen more, and it's not Larry. Obviously, it's cupcakes. They're the easiest way to cheer up your week. Here, the fluffy chocolate cake batter is made in one bowl (*woohoo!*) and is conveniently portioned into two cupcakes (because halving an egg white is a nightmare, and who's going to be mad about two cupcakes?). While the cupcakes are baking, whisk together the chocolate buttercream and try not to eat it before the cupcakes cool.

1 *First, make the cupcakes.* Preheat the oven to 350°F. Line two muffin cups of a standard muffin tin with muffin liners, then spray the muffin liners and the top of the tin with nonstick cooking spray.

2 In a small bowl, whisk the flour, granulated sugar, cocoa powder, baking powder, baking soda, and salt until combined. Use the whisk to make a well in the center of the bowl and add the egg white, vegetable oil, milk, and vanilla extract. Whisk until no lumps remain—the batter will be thick. Pour in the hot coffee and whisk gently until the batter is smooth.

3 Use a silicone spatula to scrape the batter evenly into the prepared muffin cups. Bake until the cupcakes have domed up, resist light pressure when you press on them, and a butter knife inserted into the center of a cupcake comes out mostly clean (a crumb or two attached is okay), 20 to 25 minutes. Place the muffin tin on a cooling rack and allow the cupcakes to cool slightly in the pan before removing them from the pan and placing them directly on the cooling rack to cool completely, about 20 minutes.

4 *While the cupcakes bake, make the chocolate buttercream.* In a small bowl, whisk the butter and cocoa powder until the mixture is homogeneous and lightens in color slightly, about 1 minute. Add the confectioners' sugar, milk, vanilla extract, and salt and whisk until combined.

5 Transfer the buttercream to a piping bag fitted with a small star tip (you can also spoon the buttercream on top). Pipe the buttercream onto the cupcakes. Top with sprinkles, if you have them, and serve.

FULL SIZE
For the full-size version of this recipe, scan the QR code to the left.

A Single Peanut Butter–Fluff Crispy Treat

MAKES 1 BAR

PREP TIME 15 MINUTES
(PLUS 15 MINUTES CHILL TIME)
COOK TIME 5 MINUTES
TOTAL TIME 35 MINUTES

½ cup Rice Krispies cereal

1 teaspoon unsalted butter

½ cup large marshmallows

Pinch of salt

1 tablespoon creamy peanut butter (such as Jif, Skippy, or Peter Pan—*not* natural peanut butter)

1 tablespoon Marshmallow Fluff

I apologize for this recipe. Why? Because it's so easy (and so delicious) you're going to be making it all the time. Its brilliance lies in its simplicity: Rice Krispies Treats are basically squares of Marshmallow Fluff–bound cereal, and what pairs better with Fluff than *peanut butter*? Adding the peanut butter barely requires extra work; just dollop a bit of your favorite PB (mine's Jif) into your bowl and you're done. Because we're making only one treat, we're getting innovative by using a loaf pan to get that perfect rectangular shape, but know that the mixture won't fill the entire pan.

1 Line a 1-pound loaf pan with parchment paper on all sides (see page 23) and grease the parchment with nonstick cooking spray.

2 In a small bowl, add the Rice Krispies cereal. Set aside.

3 In a small saucepan over medium-low heat, add the butter and cook, stirring occasionally with a silicone spatula, until the butter melts completely. Add the marshmallows and salt and cook, stirring occasionally, until the marshmallows melt completely.

4 Pour the melted marshmallows into the bowl with the Rice Krispies and use the spatula to fold the mixture together until evenly combined. Drop the peanut butter and Marshmallow Fluff into the mixture by the teaspoon and fold once or twice to combine. Do not overmix; you want big ribbons of peanut butter and Fluff.

5 Place the mixture in one side of the prepared loaf pan in an even layer (it'll cover maybe a quarter of the pan, not the whole thing). Rinse off your spatula, then use it (still a little bit wet; this will help) to pat the mixture into a Rice Krispies Treat–size rectangle (you'll basically push the bar into three of the sides of the loaf pan and use the spatula to form the remaining side). Place in the fridge to set for 15 minutes, then remove and enjoy.

FULL SIZE
For the full-size version of this recipe, scan the QR code above.

Just Two Snickerdoodles

MAKES 2 COOKIES

PREP TIME 10 MINUTES
COOK TIME 13 MINUTES
TOTAL TIME 23 MINUTES

FOR THE CINNAMON SUGAR

2 tablespoons granulated sugar

½ teaspoon ground cinnamon

FOR THE COOKIES

2 tablespoons (¼ stick) unsalted butter, at room temperature

2 tablespoons packed light brown sugar

1 tablespoon granulated sugar

1 large egg yolk, at room temperature

1 teaspoon full-fat sour cream (plain Greek yogurt also works)

¼ teaspoon vanilla extract

6 tablespoons all-purpose flour

¼ teaspoon cream of tartar

⅛ teaspoon baking soda

⅛ teaspoon salt

Life can't always be about chocolate chips. Sometimes it needs soft vanilla cookies rolled in cinnamon sugar. In this small-batch snickerdoodle, I use an egg yolk instead of a whole egg to create the same chewy consistency of a full-batch cookie (save the egg white for a cocktail or tomorrow's breakfast scramble), while the sour cream creates a tangy, moist crumb. And like the other single-serve cookies in this chapter, this recipe makes two large cookies. You're welcome.

1 *First, make the cinnamon sugar.* Preheat the oven to 350°F. Line a sheet pan with parchment paper.

2 In a small bowl, combine the granulated sugar and cinnamon with a fork. Set aside.

3 *Next, make the cookies.* In a medium bowl, add the butter, brown sugar, and granulated sugar and use a silicone spatula to mix until combined (if it's not fully coming together, microwave the mixture for 3 seconds—and make sure your bowl is microwave safe!).

4 Add the egg yolk, sour cream (or yogurt), and vanilla extract and mix well. Add the flour, cream of tartar, baking soda, and salt and mix until combined and no streaks of flour remain.

5 Divide the dough in half and roll each half into a ball between your palms. Place each ball of dough in the cinnamon sugar and roll it around until it's evenly coated. Place the cookies at least 3 inches apart on the prepared sheet pan.

6 Bake until the cookies have started to crackle on the top and are set and firm around the edges but still somewhat soft in the middle, 12 to 13 minutes. Remove the sheet pan from the oven and allow the cookies to cool slightly on the sheet pan before serving.

FULL SIZE
For the full-size version of this recipe, scan the QR code above.

A Handful of Chocolate-Covered-Pretzel Muddy Buddies

MAKES 1 SCANT CUP MUDDY BUDDIES

PREP TIME 10 MINUTES
TOTAL TIME 10 MINUTES

¼ cup confectioners' sugar

2 tablespoons creamy peanut butter (such as Jif, Skippy, or Peter Pan—*not* natural peanut butter)

2 tablespoons semisweet or bittersweet chocolate chips

½ cup Rice Chex cereal

¼ cup pretzels, lightly crushed (any kind of pretzel works)

Recipes for Muddy Buddies (also called Puppy Chow) use nearly an entire box of cereal to make enough for a flock of kindergartners. Flash forward to five days later and you've got more than a half gallon of soft and stale Buddies. I just want one sandwich bag of that confectioners' sugar–coated crunchy stuff for my adult self. And let's make it a sweet *and* salty situation with an addition of crushed pretzels. It's a whimsical little treat for traveling, office snacking, and unsuspecting friends you're meeting for lunch.

1 Pour the confectioners' sugar into a pint- or quart-size resealable plastic bag. Set aside.

2 In a medium microwave-safe bowl, combine the peanut butter and chocolate chips. Microwave in 15-second increments, using a silicone spatula to stir between each, until the mixture is fully melted.

3 Remove the bowl from the microwave and gently fold in the Rice Chex and pretzels until evenly combined.

4 Use the silicone spatula to transfer the mixture into the resealable plastic bag. Seal the bag tightly, then shake it vigorously to coat the mixture in the confectioners' sugar. If the mixture isn't getting well coated, try blowing some air into the bag and sealing it in (this creates more space for the mixture to be shaken around). Serve on a plate (or eat straight from the bag).

FULL SIZE
For the full-size version of this recipe, scan the QR code above.

Cinnamon Swirl–Banana Bread Mug Cake

MAKES 1 MUG CAKE

PREP TIME 8 MINUTES
COOK TIME 2 MINUTES
TOTAL TIME 10 MINUTES

FOR THE CAKE

1 tablespoon packed light brown sugar

1 teaspoon ground cinnamon

⅓ cup mashed overripe banana (about 1 medium)

1 tablespoon unsalted butter, melted

3 tablespoons granulated sugar

3 tablespoons full-fat sour cream (plain Greek yogurt also works)

½ teaspoon vanilla extract

5 tablespoons all-purpose flour

⅛ teaspoon baking powder

⅛ teaspoon baking soda

Pinch of salt

FOR THE ICING

2 tablespoons confectioners' sugar

1 teaspoon milk (any dairy or nondairy milk works)

Respect the mug cake! Some food snobs (hey, love ya) look down on mug cakes, but I'm here to show you how gourmet they can be, while saving energy and time by *not* using the oven. This recipe makes a fluffy banana cake swirled with cinnamon sugar layers (yes, layers!) that will fill your kitchen with the scent of baking cake in less than ten minutes.

1 *First, make the cake.* Grease a standard-size mug with nonstick cooking spray.

2 In a small bowl, combine the brown sugar and cinnamon and mix with a fork. Set aside.

3 In a separate small bowl, use a fork to whisk together the mashed banana, melted butter, and granulated sugar. Add the sour cream (or yogurt) and vanilla extract and whisk to combine. Add the flour, baking powder, baking soda, and salt and mix until combined and no streaks of flour remain.

4 Transfer half of the batter into the mug. Top with half of the cinnamon sugar mixture. Repeat with the second half of the batter, then the second half of the cinnamon sugar. Use a butter knife to drag and swirl the cinnamon sugar mixture through the batter.

5 Microwave on high for 90 seconds. The cake should rise and a butter knife inserted into the center will come out mostly clean (a crumb or two attached is okay). Place on the counter and allow to cool slightly while you make your icing.

6 *Make the icing.* In a small bowl, combine the confectioners' sugar and milk and use a fork to whisk until smooth. Use a spoon to drizzle the icing over the mug cake, then eat!

FULL SIZE
For the full-size version of this recipe, scan the QR code above.

Molten Lava Cakes for Two

MAKES 2 LAVA CAKES

PREP TIME 15 MINUTES
COOK TIME 11 MINUTES
TOTAL TIME 26 MINUTES

¼ cup (½ stick) unsalted butter, plus more for the ramekins

1 tablespoon Dutch-processed cocoa powder, plus more for the ramekins

½ cup semisweet or bittersweet chocolate chips

¼ cup packed light brown sugar

1 large egg plus 1 large egg yolk, at room temperature

1 teaspoon vanilla extract

2 teaspoons all-purpose flour

⅛ teaspoon salt

Vanilla ice cream or confectioners' sugar, for serving

Sometimes a regular night calls for a volcanic dessert. It's unabashedly sexy, definitely impressive, and so much less intimidating when baked in small batches. Make this after you *Lady and the Tramp* a platter of spaghetti, and don't forget the taper candles. Romantic!

1 Preheat the oven to 425°F. Generously grease the bottom and sides of two 6-ounce ramekins with butter. Lightly dust the inside of the ramekins with cocoa powder. Set aside.

2 In a medium microwave-safe bowl, combine the butter and chocolate chips. Microwave in 15-second increments, using a silicone spatula to stir between each, until the mixture is fully melted. Set aside.

3 In a medium bowl, whisk the brown sugar, egg, extra egg yolk, and vanilla extract until frothy and pale in color, about 2 minutes.

4 Pour the melted chocolate mixture into the egg mixture, whisking to combine. Add the flour, cocoa powder, and salt. Use a silicone spatula to gently fold everything together until fully combined and no streaks of flour remain. The batter will be thick.

5 Divide the batter evenly between the prepared ramekins. Bake until the cakes have puffed up and the edges are fully set but the middles are still wobbly, about 11 minutes.

6 Transfer the lava cakes to a cooling rack to cool just long enough that they can set, 2 to 3 minutes. Run a butter knife along the sides of the ramekins, then invert each cake onto a small plate. Serve right away with vanilla ice cream or a dusting of confectioners' sugar.

FULL SIZE
For the full-size version of this recipe, scan the QR code above.

Individual Chocolate Chip Cookies

MAKES 2 COOKIES

PREP TIME 10 MINUTES
COOK TIME 13 MINUTES
TOTAL TIME 23 MINUTES

3 tablespoons unsalted butter, melted

¼ cup packed light brown sugar

1 tablespoon granulated sugar

1 large egg yolk, at room temperature

¼ teaspoon vanilla extract

7 tablespoons all-purpose flour

⅛ teaspoon baking soda

⅛ teaspoon salt

3 tablespoons semisweet or bittersweet chocolate chips

Sometimes when you're alone, it doesn't matter that you *could* make a whole batch of cookies . . . you just don't *want* to. But that shouldn't stop you from having a cookie. This is a scaled-down version of The Best Chocolate Chip Cookies in the World (page 77) sans the browned butter. As with all the single-serve recipes in this chapter, precision is everything. So make sure you're spooning and leveling each tablespoon of flour, packing in each tablespoon of brown sugar, and being as accurate as possible at every step (except for the final step, which is eating them with Cookie Monster abandon).

1 Preheat the oven to 350°F. Line a sheet pan with parchment paper.

2 In a medium bowl, add the melted butter, brown sugar, and granulated sugar and use a small silicone spatula to mix until combined.

3 Add the egg yolk and vanilla extract and mix well. Add the flour, baking soda, and salt and mix until combined and no streaks of flour remain. Use the silicone spatula to fold in the chocolate chips until just combined.

4 Divide the dough in half and roll each half into a ball between your palms. Place at least 3 inches apart on the prepared sheet pan.

5 Bake until the cookies have puffed up and are set and firm around the edges but still somewhat soft in the middle, 12 to 13 minutes. Remove the sheet pan from the oven and allow the cookies to cool slightly on the sheet pan before serving.

FULL SIZE *For the full-size version of these cookies, see The Best Chocolate Chip Cookies in the World on page 77.*

Une Crème Brûlée

MAKES 1 CRÈME BRÛLÉE

PREP TIME 10 MINUTES (PLUS 1 HOUR CHILL TIME)
COOK TIME 40 MINUTES
TOTAL TIME 1 HOUR 50 MINUTES

1 large egg yolk
1 tablespoon plus 1 teaspoon granulated sugar, divided
½ cup heavy cream
½ teaspoon vanilla extract

Were you hoping this would be here? Me too. This single-serve crème brûlée requires only four staples: egg yolks, sugar, heavy cream, and vanilla extract. I like to make it in the morning, then pop it into the fridge and go about my day. Once nightfall hits, I remember I have a homemade crème brûlée in the fridge, do a little Happy Food Dance (remember that from page 212?), and torch that baby up. It's planning ahead at its finest.

1 Preheat the oven to 325°F. Place a 6-ounce ramekin in a baking pan (any pan size works as long as it's bigger and taller than your ramekin). Create a water bath for your crème brûlée by placing boiling water in the pan until it comes halfway up the sides of the ramekin.

2 In a small bowl, whisk the egg yolk and 1 tablespoon of the granulated sugar until the mixture becomes pale in color, about 1 minute. Set aside.

3 In a small microwave-safe bowl, add the cream. Microwave in 15-second increments, using a silicone spatula to stir between each, until the cream is hot but not boiling. Remove the cream from the microwave and stir in the vanilla extract.

4 While whisking the egg yolk mixture constantly, slowly stream in the hot cream. Whisk until completely combined.

5 Pour the mixture into the prepared ramekin. Bake the creme brûlée until the center is just set and the custard jiggles slightly but does not feel soupy, 30 to 40 minutes.

6 Remove the ramekin from the water bath and place on a cooling rack to cool completely. Transfer the ramekin to the fridge for at least 1 hour and up to 3 days (if chilling for more than a few hours, cover the top of your ramekin tightly with plastic wrap).

7 When ready to serve, evenly sprinkle the top of the custard with the remaining 1 teaspoon granulated sugar. Use a kitchen torch to melt the sugar by zig-zagging back and forth until the sugar bubbles and becomes golden brown in some parts. Dive in.

FULL SIZE
For the full-size version of this recipe, scan the QR code above.

Personal Edible Chocolate Chip Cookie Dough

MAKES 1 CUP COOKIE DOUGH

PREP TIME 15 MINUTES (PLUS 15 MINUTES COOL TIME)
COOK TIME 17 MINUTES
TOTAL TIME 47 MINUTES

½ cup all-purpose flour

1 teaspoon flaxseed meal

1 tablespoon water

3 tablespoons unsalted butter

¼ cup packed light brown sugar

1 tablespoon granulated sugar

1 teaspoon milk (any dairy or nondairy milk works)

½ teaspoon vanilla extract

¼ teaspoon baking soda

⅛ teaspoon salt

⅓ cup semisweet or bittersweet mini chocolate chips

FULL SIZE
For the full-size version of this recipe, scan the QR code above.

I have yet to meet a human being on this planet who can resist the pull of raw cookie dough. It's even more tempting when someone tells you not to eat it because there's raw eggs in there and yada yada yada. Solution: This raw cookie dough that takes care of all the ingredients that might betray you. We'll make a flaxseed "egg" to bind things together, and we're "baking" our flour to cook off potential bacteria (because *technically* you shouldn't eat raw flour). Plot twist: You can also bake this dough into cookies (at 350°F until lightly golden and soft) after you get tired of eating it raw, if that's even a possibility???

1 Preheat the oven to 350°F. Line a sheet pan with parchment paper.

2 Spread the flour evenly over the parchment paper. Once the oven has preheated, bake the flour for 10 minutes, stirring the mixture with a silicone spatula halfway through. This step "pasteurizes" the flour, removing any harmful bacteria and making it safe to eat raw. Place the sheet pan on a cooling rack and allow the flour to cool to room temperature.

3 Next, make a flaxseed "egg." In a small bowl, combine the flaxseed meal and water. Allow to sit until thickened and congealed, about 5 minutes.

4 While the flaxseed egg sits, brown the butter. In a small saucepan, add the butter and cook over medium-low heat. Use a silicone spatula to stir and scrape the butter from the bottom and sides of the pan every 10 to 15 seconds. At first, the butter will melt and foam, then over time the foam bubbles will get smaller and the butter will begin to emit a warm, nutty aroma. Continue to cook, occasionally stirring and scraping with the spatula, until the butter begins to take on color and you see small, floating brown bits (these are the milk solids in your butter separating and toasting), 5 to 7 minutes. Once the butter is golden brown, remove it from the heat and allow it to cool to room temperature in the saucepan, about 15 minutes.

5 Add the cooled brown butter to a medium bowl. Use a silicone spatula to stir in the brown sugar and granulated sugar. Add the flaxseed egg, milk, and vanilla extract and mix well.

6 Add the cooled flour, baking soda, and salt and mix until combined and no streaks of flour remain. Fold in the chocolate chips until just combined. Dig in with a spoon.

Small-Batch Blueberry Muffins

MAKES 2 MUFFINS

PREP TIME 10 MINUTES
COOK TIME 23 MINUTES
TOTAL TIME 33 MINUTES

2 tablespoons (¼ stick) unsalted
butter, melted

¼ cup granulated sugar

1 large egg white

2 tablespoons full-fat sour cream
(plain Greek yogurt also works)

1 teaspoon vanilla extract

½ cup all-purpose flour

¾ teaspoon baking powder

⅛ teaspoon salt

⅓ cup fresh or frozen blueberries

Demerara sugar, for topping
(optional)

Someone commented on one of my social media posts about muffins, "My home ec. teacher always used to say, 'A little muff to keep the hands warm,'" and now I say that to myself every time I make muffins. These blueberry muffins are fluffy and moist, with a full teaspoon of vanilla extract for an extra flavor boost. Not a fan of blueberries? Swap them out for your favorite muffin mix-ins: chocolate chips, bananas and walnuts, chopped apples . . .

1 Preheat the oven to 425°F. Line two muffin cups of a standard muffin tin with muffin liners, then spray the muffin liners and the top of the tin with nonstick cooking spray.

2 In a medium bowl, add the melted butter and granulated sugar and use a silicone spatula to mix until combined. Add the egg white, sour cream (or yogurt), and vanilla extract and mix well.

3 Add the flour, baking powder, and salt and mix until combined and no streaks of flour remain. Use the silicone spatula to gently fold in the blueberries.

4 Divide the batter evenly between the two prepared muffin cups. Top with Demerara sugar (if using).

5 Bake the muffins for 5 minutes at 425°F, then reduce the oven temperature to 375°F. Continue baking until the tops of the muffins are golden brown and spring back to the touch, about 18 minutes more.

6 Place the muffin tin on a cooling rack and allow the muffins to cool slightly in the pan before removing and serving.

FULL SIZE
*For the full-size version
of this recipe, scan the
QR code above.*

Small-Batch Blondies

MAKES 2 BLONDIES

PREP TIME 10 MINUTES
COOK TIME 12 MINUTES
TOTAL TIME 22 MINUTES

2 tablespoons (¼ stick) unsalted butter, melted

¼ cup packed light brown sugar

1 large egg yolk

⅛ teaspoon vanilla extract

¼ cup all-purpose flour

⅛ teaspoon salt

3 tablespoons semisweet or bittersweet chocolate chips

Blondies are basically deep-dish cookies, and who doesn't like the sound of that? (You'll like the taste even more.) This recipe makes enough for you and a friend, but the usual baking pan is too big, so we're dropping this brown sugar batter into a muffin tin instead to create thick, chewy, golden nuggets of chocolate chip blondie goodness. I'm all about underbaking these babies so that they're extra gooey on the inside, so as always, set your timer to the low end of the baking time to test for doneness and ensure you don't end up overcooking them.

1 Preheat the oven to 350°F. Grease two muffin cups of a standard muffin tin with nonstick cooking spray or line the cups with muffin liners.

2 In a small bowl, combine the melted butter and brown sugar and use a small silicone spatula or a fork to mix well. Add the egg yolk and vanilla extract and use the fork to whisk until the mixture lightens in color, about 1 minute.

3 Add the flour and salt and mix until combined and no streaks of flour remain. Fold in the chocolate chips until just combined. Use the silicone spatula to scrape the batter evenly into the prepared muffin cups.

4 Bake until the blondies are golden brown and are set and firm around the edges but still somewhat soft in the middle, 10 to 12 minutes. Place the muffin tin on a cooling rack and allow the blondies to cool slightly in the pan before removing and serving.

FULL SIZE
For the full-size version of this recipe, scan the QR code above.

A Scoop of Double-Chocolate Cookies and Cream Ice Cream

MAKES ½ CUP ICE CREAM

PREP TIME 15 MINUTES
(PLUS 3 HOURS CHILL TIME)
TOTAL TIME 3 HOURS 15 MINUTES

1 tablespoon Dutch-processed cocoa powder

2 tablespoons warm water

2 tablespoons sweetened condensed milk

1 teaspoon vanilla extract

3 tablespoons heavy cream

3 Oreo cookies, coarsely chopped

2 tablespoons chopped semisweet or bittersweet chocolate

I've talked before in this book about my time working at an ice cream store (ahem, page 106), but I haven't talked about my favorite flavor there: a dark chocolate ice cream with crushed-up Oreos *and* chocolate chunks. We're re-creating it here with a single-serve, no-churn recipe that's ready to eat after a three-hour chill, where a full batch would need eight, so make this in the afternoon to have after dinner. Since you're using only a smidge of that condensed milk, save the rest in the fridge (for up to three weeks) to make the No-Churn Peach Crumble Ice Cream (page 132).

1 In a small bowl, combine the cocoa powder and warm water and use a fork to stir until smooth. Add the sweetened condensed milk and vanilla extract and mix well. Set aside.

2 In a medium bowl, add the cream and whisk by hand until soft peaks form (you can also use a hand mixer, if you'd prefer).

3 Use a silicone spatula to scrape the cocoa mixture into the whipped cream. Gently fold everything together until just combined. Fold in most of the cookies (you want a few crumbs to crumble on top) and the chopped chocolate.

4 Transfer the ice cream to a small freezer-safe container and top with the reserved cookie crumbs. Freeze for at least 3 hours and up to 2 weeks before serving (if freezing longer than 3 hours, cover the ice cream tightly in plastic wrap to prevent freezer burn).

FULL SIZE
For the full-size version of this recipe, scan the QR code above.

THANK YOU

While my name is on the cover of this cookbook, it really should have about twenty-five names on it, because I couldn't have done it alone. To have been able to work alongside some of the most talented people in the food and publishing industry was a dream come true, and I'm so thankful to each and every person for putting their heart and soul into this book.

To Sofi Llanso, my official co-recipe developer and unofficial other half. You are a force of nature whose talent knows no bounds. From brainstorming to recipe development to copywriting and editing (so much editing), I am so appreciative of the hours you've put into this book. I don't know what I did in life to have you on my team, but I couldn't have made up a better person to work alongside. *Sweet Tooth* and Broma Bakery do not exist without you. I'm endlessly proud of you, and I love you so much.

To my agent, Kitty Cowles. From our first conversation, I knew that working with you meant I'd be in the best hands. Your guidance has been invaluable, and your level of expectation encouraged me to push myself to create the best version of this book I could. You are a titan, and I am astonished that I get to have you in my corner. I couldn't imagine going through this process without you, and am so, so grateful that you believed in me.

To my editor, Raquel Petzel. Between our mutual love of chocolate chip cookies and the ease with which we can talk for hours, getting to know (and to work with) you has been a joy. Your willingness to pick up the phone at any time of day and talk me through roadblocks big and small did not go unnoticed, and I can't thank you enough for everything you've done to make this book happen.

To the entire Clarkson Potter team, including but not limited to Darian Keels, Elaine Hennig, Ian Dingman, Patricia Shaw, Jessica Heim, Chloe Aryeh, Lauren Chung, Jana Branson, Allison Renzulli, and Katherine Tyler. Your enthusiasm for and dedication to this project has given me all the confidence an author could ask for. Your hard work, expertise, and commitment were apparent at every step of the way. Thank you.

To my collaborator, Alex Beggs. The spirit this book took on is because of you. You took my half-baked ideas and turned them into sensical sentences, while injecting in my exact humor and voice. I'm in awe of your talent, and proud to be able to call you my friend.

To my designer, Alaina Sullivan. From creating a design concept for this book in a matter of days (a week before Christmas, no less) to polishing the final look and feel of this cookbook, your work is truly art, and it was inspiring to experience. The collaborative nature with which you considered my ideas and the immense thoughtfulness of your design choices brought these recipes to life. I'm thrilled with what you've created.

To my illustrator, Meghan Kreger. From the minute I saw your work, I knew I wanted you on this project. Your art energizes every page and makes baking from this book that much more fun.

To my PR team at Mona Creative, Eva Karagiorgas, Nicole Scharf, and Dani Haskins. You are the best in the business for a reason. Your excitement for this book has radiated in every email, call, and text, and I'm so excited to see what we create together, now and in the future.

To my food stylist, Rebecca Jurkevich, and my prop stylist, Sarah Smart. You two are the most talented people I could've asked for for this project. From finishing each other's ideas to pointing to the exact angle / object / color to change in a scene, working with you both was one of the most creatively inspiring things I've ever been a part of.

To my lifestyle photographer, Bettina Bogar. It's been so meaningful to watch our nearly decade of friendship and work grow stronger and stronger with each project. Thank you for flying across the country to do this. No one could have captured me better.

To my production assistants, Dorean Collins and Alejandra Rodriguez. You both seamlessly flowed between grocery-getter, baker, and styling assistant as if reading my mind. Your work made my job so much easier, and your patience is superhuman.

To my recipe testers, Katharine Canfield, Rebecca Fennel, Roo and Paul Kuklinski, Cathy Llanso, Alejandra Rodriguez, Ashley Wagner, Elena Besser, Blaize Vitas, Jen Aceto, Maura Friedlander, Becca Cross, Samira Saghafi, Kate Henley, and the fifty-six Broma testers, thank you for your time and taste buds. Because of you, the recipes in this book are the best they can be.

To my Broma Bakery team, Kaila McWilliams, Grace Meagher, and Robin Radomski. You are the people behind the curtain who keep Broma going. I've never felt so taken care of. You mean so much to me.

To the Broma fans. Because of you, this book came to be. Thank you for encouraging me to write it, for loving those chocolate chip cookies so much (iykyk), and for all of your support through the years. I hope you fill these pages with flour and butter, and let me know which recipes you love best.

And to my husband, Alex, the first and Number 1 Broma Fan. You push me to think differently, analyze deeply, and to follow my dreams. I wouldn't be who I am today without you. I love you.

Index

Published in the United States by Clarkson Potter/Publishers,
an imprint of the Crown Publishing Group, a division of Penguin
Random House LLC, New York.
ClarksonPotter.com

CLARKSON POTTER is a trademark and POTTER with colophon
is a registered trademark of Penguin Random House LLC.

Library of Congress Cataloging-in-Publication Data
Names: Fennel, Sarah, author, photographer. Title: Sweet tooth
/ Sarah Fennel; photographs by Sarah Fennel. Description:
New York: Clarkson Potter/Publishers, [2024] | Includes index. |
Identifiers: LCCN 2023044220 (print) |
LCCN 2023044221 (ebook) | ISBN 9780593581995 (hardcover) |
ISBN 9780593582008 (ebook) Subjects: LCSH: Baking. |
LCGFT: Cookbooks. Classification: LCC TX763. F46 2024 (print) |
LCC TX763 (ebook) | DDC 641.7/1—dc23/eng/20240314
LC record available at https://lccn.loc.gov/2023044220
LC ebook record available at https://lccn.loc.gov/2023044221

ISBN 978-0-593-58199-5
Ebook ISBN 978-0-593-58200-8

Printed in China

Editor: Raquel Pelzel | Assistant editor: Darian Keels
Designer: Alaina Sullivan
Production editor: Patricia Shaw
Collaborator: Alex Beggs
Production manager: Jessica Heim
Compositors: Merri Ann Morrell and Zoe Tokushige
Production assistants: Alejandra Rodriguez and Dorean Collins
Food stylist: Rebecca Jurkevich
Prop stylist: Sarah Smart
Recipe assistant and tester: Sofi Llanso
Copy editor: Deborah Weiss Geline
Proofreaders: Bridget Sweet, Karen Ninnis, and Sigi Nacson
Indexer: Elizabeth T. Parson
Publicist: Lauren Chung | Marketer: Chloe Aryeh
Illustrations: Meghan Kreger

10 9 8 7 6 5 4 3 2 1

First Edition